IFIP Advances in Information and Communication Technology 582

Editor-in-Chief

Kai Rannenberg, Goethe University Frankfurt, Germany

Editorial Board Members

IFIP – The International Federation for Information Processing

IFIP was founded in 1960 under the auspices of UNESCO, following the first World Computer Congress held in Paris the previous year. A federation for societies working in information processing, IFIP's aim is two-fold: to support information processing in the countries of its members and to encourage technology transfer to developing nations. As its mission statement clearly states:

IFIP is the global non-profit federation of societies of ICT professionals that aims at achieving a worldwide professional and socially responsible development and application of information and communication technologies.

IFIP is a non-profit-making organization, run almost solely by 2500 volunteers. It operates through a number of technical committees and working groups, which organize events and publications. IFIP's events range from large international open conferences to working conferences and local seminars.

The flagship event is the IFIP World Computer Congress, at which both invited and contributed papers are presented. Contributed papers are rigorously refereed and the rejection rate is high.

As with the Congress, participation in the open conferences is open to all and papers may be invited or submitted. Again, submitted papers are stringently refereed.

The working conferences are structured differently. They are usually run by a working group and attendance is generally smaller and occasionally by invitation only. Their purpose is to create an atmosphere conducive to innovation and development. Refereeing is also rigorous and papers are subjected to extensive group discussion.

Publications arising from IFIP events vary. The papers presented at the IFIP World Computer Congress and at open conferences are published as conference proceedings, while the results of the working conferences are often published as collections of selected and edited papers.

IFIP distinguishes three types of institutional membership: Country Representative Members, Members at Large, and Associate Members. The type of organization that can apply for membership is a wide variety and includes national or international societies of individual computer scientists/ICT professionals, associations or federations of such societies, government institutions/government related organizations, national or international research institutes or consortia, universities, academies of sciences, companies, national or international associations or federations of companies.

More information about this series at http://www.springer.com/series/6102

Vladimir Ivanov · Artem Kruglov ·
Sergey Masyagin · Alberto Sillitti ·
Giancarlo Succi (Eds.)

Open Source Systems

16th IFIP WG 2.13 International Conference, OSS 2020
Innopolis, Russia, May 12–14, 2020
Proceedings

 Springer

Editors
Vladimir Ivanov (iD)
Innopolis University
Innopolis, Russia

Sergey Masyagin (iD)
Innopolis University
Innopolis, Russia

Giancarlo Succi (iD)
Innopolis University
Innopolis, Russia

Artem Kruglov (iD)
Innopolis University
Innopolis, Russia

Alberto Sillitti
Innopolis University
Innopolis, Russia

ISSN 1868-4238   ISSN 1868-422X (electronic)
IFIP Advances in Information and Communication Technology
ISBN 978-3-030-47239-9   ISBN 978-3-030-47240-5 (eBook)
https://doi.org/10.1007/978-3-030-47240-5

This Springer imprint is published by the registered company Springer Nature Switzerland AG
The registered company address is: Gewerbestrasse 11, 6330 Cham, Switzerland

Preface

This volume contains the papers presented at the 16th International Conference on Open Source Systems (OSS 2020) held during May 12–14, 2020, in Innopolis, Russia[1].

All of the submitted research papers went through a rigorous peer-review process. Each paper was reviewed by at least two members of the Program Committee. Only 20 were accepted as short papers with a 47% acceptance rate.

Open Source Software (OSS) development has emerged in the last decades as one of the most important phenomenon of computer science and engineering. It has been instrumental for education and research in academia, providing free access to essential tools such as compilers, word processors, spreadsheets, etc.; it has changed the way people perceive the software business and it has often kept the software market away from monopolies. As such, a deep understanding of OSS requires the understanding of a wide spectrum of issues. Therefore, OSS 2020 provided a forum to discuss theories, practices, experiences, and tools on development and applications of OSS systems, with specific focus on two aspects: (a) the development of open source systems and the underlying technical, social, and economical issues, and (b) the adoption of OSS solutions and the implications of such adoption both in the public and in the private sector. OSS 2020 brought together researchers from industry, public administration, and academia to share experiences and ideas, and to provide an archival source for important papers on open source topics. The conference provided information and education to practitioners, identified directions for further research, and will be an ongoing platform for technology transfer.

We hope that you find the OSS 2020 proceedings useful for your professional and academic activities, and that you enjoyed the conference. Finally, we would like to thank all the people who have contributed to OSS 2020 including the authors, the sponsors, the reviewers, the volunteers, and the chairs.

March 2020

Vladimir Ivanov
Artem Kruglov
Sergey Masyagin
Alberto Sillitti
Giancarlo Succi

---

[1] Due to the COVID-19 pandemic, the conference was held virtually.

Organization

Program Committee

Antonios Andreatos	Hellenic Air Force Academy, Greece
Lefteris Angelis	Aristotle University of Thessaloniki, Greece
Matina Bibi	University of Ioannina, Greece
Timofey Bryksin	Saint Petersburg State University, Russia
Javier Luis Canovas Izquierdo	IN3, UOC, Spain
Andrea Capiluppi	Brunel University, UK
Kevin Crowston	Syracuse University, USA
Minas Dasygenis	University of Western Macedonia, Greece
Breno de França	UNICAMP, Brazil
Khalid Elbaamrani	ENSA of Marrakech, Morocco
Alexander Elizarov	Kazan Federal University, Russia
Stefane Fermigier	Nuxeo, France
Jesus M. Gonzalez-Barahona	Universidad Rey Juan Carlos, Spain
Imed Hammouda	Mediterranean Institute of Technology, Tunsia
Akinori Ihara	Wakayama University, Japan
Vladimir Ivanov	Innopolis University, Russia
George Kakarontzas	University of Thessaly, Greece
Daniel S. Katz	University of Illinois Urbana-Champaign, USA
Fabio Kon	University of São Paulo, Brazil
Artem Kruglov	Innopolis University, Russia
Ignasi Labastida	Universitat de Barcelona, Spain
Filippo Lanubile	University of Bari, Italy
Luigi Lavazza	Università degli Studi dell'Insubria, Italy
Valentina Lenarduzzi	LUT University, Finland
Panos Louridas	Athens University of Economics and Business and Greek Research and Technology Network, Greece
Bjorn Lundell	University of Skövde, Sweden
Konstantinos Margaritis	University of Macedonia, Greece
Manuel Mazzara	Innopolis University, Russia
Dimitrios Michail	Harokopio University of Athens, Greece
Sandro Morasca	Università degli Studi dell'Insubria, Italy
Dmitry Mouromtsev	NRU ITMO, Russia
Mohammad Ashraf Ottom	Yarmouk University, Jordan
Nikolaos Papaspyrou	National Technical University of Athens, Greece
Peter Rigby	Concordia University, Canada

Contents

The Ecosystem of openKONSEQUENZ, A User-Led Open Source Foundation

Bettina Schwab, Dirk Riehle, Ann Barcomb, and Nikolay Harutyunyan(✉)

Friedrich-Alexander-Universität Erlangen-Nürnberg, Erlangen, Germany
bettina.schwab@gmx.net, dirk@riehle.org, ann@barcomb.org,
nikolay.harutyunyan@fau.de

Abstract. Companies without expertise in software development can opt to form consortia to develop open source software to meet their needs, as an alternative to the build-or-buy decision. Such user-led foundations are little understood, due to a limited number of published examples. In particular, almost nothing is known about the ecosystems surrounding user-led foundations. Our work seeks to address this gap, through an exploratory qualitative survey of openKONSEQUENZ, from the German energy sector. We find that the technological goals are quite homogeneous, independent of a participant's role in the ecosystem, but that economic conflicts exist between foundation members and supplier companies due to the consortium's efforts to transform the software market structure to limit dependency on specific vendors.

Keywords: Open source foundations · Sponsored open source · Commercial open source · Open source software · User-led open source foundations

1 Introduction

Companies are now using open source software (OSS) not only as infrastructure and to support development, but also as part of their software supply chains [7,13,33]. However, not all enterprise software needs are addressed by classic, community-led, volunteer-driven OSS communities. In particular, community-led projects struggle to address the challenge of providing software for institutions rather than individuals, such as financial or HR systems [23]. In part this is because many community-led projects are founded by IT professionals to meet their own needs, what Raymond famously described as developers scratching their own itches [29]. Mackie [23] identified several other possible reasons why community-led OSS has not met commercial needs: the number of developers with relevant skills might be too few to build a community, the benefits of the

Electronic supplementary material The online version of this chapter (https://doi.org/10.1007/978-3-030-47240-5_1) contains supplementary material, which is available to authorized users.

software may be too diffuse to encourage collaboration, and the software may be too complex to be developed on a voluntary basis.

These limitations suggest that a non-volunteer OSS, created by businesses collaborating to jointly develop the software, could be a valid option for niche enterprise markets. Such an approach could offer an alternative to the build-or-buy decisions companies currently face. In contrast to off-the-shelf proprietary solutions, OSS can help companies avoid the costs of extensive customization and vendor lock-in, which lead to a high total cost of ownership [3,21]. At the same time, it is cheaper than custom software, and has the potential to become the de-facto standard, reducing training costs [22,39]. In the last fifteen years, there has been a significant increase in *vendor-led foundations*. Unlike community-led OSS, vendor-led OSS does not develop organically but is synthetically created by a consortium of companies [28]. Vendor-led OSS should not be confused with *single-vendor* OSS, where development is led by a single company with a business model based on complementary software or services [31].

Vendor-led foundations have proved popular in industries made up of companies developing software, where OSS can be used as a base for the company's commercial offerings [19,28]. Often this is done in order to dilute the power of a market leader, to reduce costs, and to create standards [6,30,37].

Creating a consortium to develop mutually beneficial software using an open source approach is less common when it concerns enterprise software to address internal needs. We refer to this approach as a *user-led foundation*, to highlight the differences between the collaborative creation of software in the supply chain, and enterprise software [39]. In the latter case, the user-led foundation members often lack software development expertise, and must commission vendors to perform the development, with the associated administrative challenges [17,25].

Despite the strong potential of user-led OSS foundations to address enterprise business needs in under-served or monopolistic markets [3], very little research has been conducted on the topic. The majority of examples are drawn from the education sector and are grant-funded [19,40]. Furthermore, existing studies have focused on foundation members, with the ecosystem described primarily in terms of potential (e.g., [36]).

This paper addresses this gap through an exploratory study of a user-led OSS foundation. We examined openKONSEQUENZ (oK), a foundation from the German energy sector representing the interests of distribution system operators (DSOs). The goal of our study was to use oK to develop a preliminary understanding of the ecosystem surrounding the user-led OSS foundation and the conflicts within it. We addressed this goal through a qualitative survey of software vendors, consultants, and DSOs associated with oK. The contribution of this paper is a description of the software ecosystem of oK, which includes the economic objectives of participants, and the conflicts arising from different economic objectives. We see our work as the basis for future investigation into the differences and similarities between user-led consortia.

The rest of this paper is organized as follows. Related literature is covered in Sect. 2. The research approach is explained in Sect. 3. Results are presented in

Sect. 4. Limitations and a discussion of the results are covered in Sect. 5. The paper concludes with a summary in Sect. 6.

2   Related Work

While some government-backed open-source enabled collaboration projects have been studied [5,34], we reviewed the research on vendor-led and user-led foundations that were directly related to our study. Firstly, the vendor-led foundations and their ecosystems were considered, because of the potential similarity to user-led foundations and the greater body of work. Secondly, we covered the existing literature on user-led open source foundations.

2.1   Vendor-Led Open Source Foundations

Vendor-led foundations have been a topic of greater academic interest than user-led foundations. O'Mahoney and West [28] describe them as synthetic communities, as distinct from organic, or community-led communities. Vendor-led foundations are usually initiated by a commercial entity, and governed by the company, or involve two or more organizations jointly founding a project which addresses an industry need. The latter type can be called a multi-vendor OSS project, where the foundation is used for governance. Multi-vendor foundations are also known as sponsored [39], federated [16], or consortia [32].

Vendor-led foundations can foster the necessary ecosystems that enable vendor company innovation. In this context, open source software development can be seen as a successful variation of collective invention by building a pro-social intrinsic motivation of a critical mass of participants [27]. Companies have been recognizing the potential to collaborate on the basis of open source, as a result of which several types of collaboration strategies for research and development (R&D) have emerged [16,38]. In contrast to the non-collaborative proprietary innovation model, vendor-led foundations enable a collaborative innovation model through a consortia of software vendors that leverage pooled resources [30,37].

2.2   User-Led Open Source Foundations

User-led foundations are an emerging way for companies to collaborate on software development projects. Unlike vendor-led foundations, open source user-led foundations bring together companies or institutions that are the users of the foundation-developed open source software, and often not the actual software development companies [39]. This does not necessarily mean that the actual users (end-users operating the software product to perform their work) are represented and directly engaged in the software development process. Furthermore, not only software user firms are members of the consortium, but usually also other participants of the ecosystem, especially software vendors and service providers.

While there is little literature on the topic of user-led governance structures of open source communities, practitioners like Wheeler have studied the phenomenon using the examples of the existing user-led foundations such as Kuali Foundation, calling it *community source* [12,35]. We have opted to refer to it in this paper as *user-led*, due to the risk of confusion with classic, volunteer-driven OSS, which is frequently described as community-led. The Kuali Foundation, founded in 2005 to provide software for higher education institutions, is the most prominently discussed case of community source. Kuali's community source approach, its antecedents, and a framework for investment decisions have been described [18–20,22]. Haganu [12] calls community source "the pub between the cathedral and the bazaar." The hybrid form between commercial software development and open source software development draws on advantages of both worlds, but is complex to handle because diverse and possibly conflicting requirements of the involved members have to be balanced [17].

3 Methodology

To address our research goal, we performed a qualitative survey to investigate the phenomenon of the ecosystem surrounding a user-led consortium [1,15,24]. Our primary reason for opting for this approach is that there is little published information about user-led consortia. An exploratory study is appropriate when the topic being studies is a real-world phenomenon, and little is known about it. The ecosystems surrounding user-led foundations have not previously been studied in depth, and it is unclear if the limited software development expertise of user-led foundation members creates a significantly different environment than the vendor-led foundation [18]. An additional consideration was the fact that all the supplemental material we found concerning the focus of our study—the open source user foundation called openKONSEQUENZ (oK)—was outdated, leading us to reject the alternative of a case study.

The main subject of our qualitative survey was the Germany-based open source user foundation oK, a foundation from the German energy sector representing the interests of distribution system operators (DSOs). While oK and the software ecosystem for DSOs have not been subject of research yet, six companies—potential early members of the foundation—published a preliminary feasibility study [26] in 2013, followed by two publications on software architecture and quality [9,10]. We selected oK due to our insider access to the foundation. oK also exemplifies the case of the user-led foundation members commissioning software rather than developing it themselves, and therefore the situation might display some differences from vendor-led foundations where development is kept in-house.

3.1 Data Sources

We conducted six semi-structured interviews with representatives of the participants of the openKONSEQUENZ ecosystem. Interview data was collected in

Table 1. Interviewees by oK membership type, ecosystem and company roles

Membership	Ecosystem role	Company role
DSO	Customer	User representative
Service provider	Software supplier	Project lead
-	Software supplier	Development lead
Guest	Consultant	Domain expert
DSO	Customer	User representative
Service provider	Software supplier	Business development

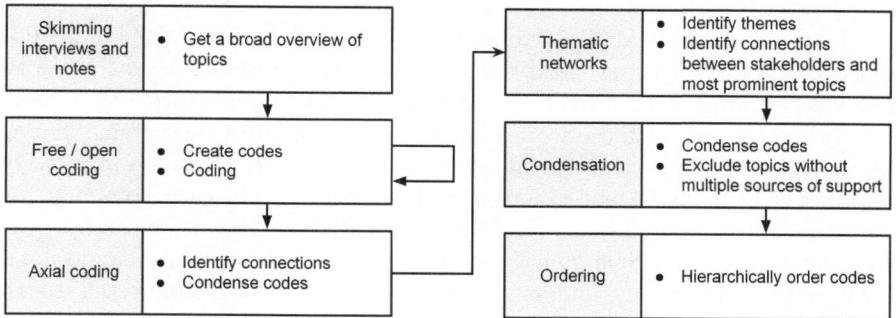

Fig. 1. Coding steps and activities

advance of analysis due to constraints of access to the informants. The interviews were collected between December 2017 and March 2018 and were conducted in German. The quotations used in this paper are our translations.

In our selection of interviews we sought to interview a representative of each type of participant in the oK foundation: DSOs, service provider members, and guest members. We also included a non-member. All interviewees wished to remain anonymous. Table 1 summarizes the study participants in terms of oK foundation membership type, role in the ecosystem, and role in their company.

3.2 Analysis

We made use of a data analysis process inspired by Eisenhardt [4], with the addition of thematic networks [2]. Eisenhardt [4] offers guidance specifically for building organizational theories. Figure 1 depicts all six steps of the process: skimming, open coding, axial coding, condensation, and ordering. Open coding was an iterative process, which resulted in a gradually evolving set of codes. Each step, however, was performed sequentially. The coding was done using MaxQDA.

4 Results

Below we first describe the oK software ecosystem, before examining the goals of individual participants, and conflicts in economic objectives.

4.1 The oK Software Ecosystem

Changes in the regulations for German energy companies provided the initial impetus for DSOs to look for a more open approach. The core control unit, also known as the supervisory control and data acquisition (SCADA) system, was at the forefront of these changes. DSO employees using SCADA systems began participating in a user group organized by a software vendor.

A law calling for the digitalization of the energy transition issued in 2016 [8] pushed DSOs further toward additional collaboration and innovation. With the employees working with SCADA system already engaging in a form of collaboration, oK was created with the scope of collaborating on software systems that are used in grid operation management and which are closely connected to SCADA. Grid operation management is largely independent within each company, and grid operations are similar for all DSOs, even if requirements and scope vary somewhat (i.e., some DSOs manage gas and water grids, while others do not).

At present, software vendors offering products closely connected to the SCADA system can be considered part of the oK ecosystem, along with the DSOs which are the driver members of oK. We define the scope as the companies which are currently affected by oK. The consortium has not yet had a significant impact on other systems and vendors.

Investments in oK are done collaboratively. A DSO who wants to develop a module takes a leading role in the resulting project and usually covers 70% of the necessary financial investment and human resources. The rest of the DSO members in oK will cover the remaining 30% of the cost. This principle ensures that development costs are distributed among the DSOs, which is economically beneficial compared to in-house development financed by a single DSO.

4.2 Economic Goals

In describing the economic goals we summarized the perspectives of each (potential) participant in the ecosystem based on the role in the ecosystem.

DSOs are regulated by the German Federal Network Agency (Bundesnetzagentur), but are nonetheless for-profit enterprizes. DSOs do not compete with one another because their activities are regionally exclusive. The Federal Network Agency set up an incentive regulation to encourge DSOs to lower operational costs. Due to regulated pricing, DSOs can increase their profits by decreasing their operational costs. There are three approaches to lowering software costs that DSOs intend to use: lowering costs of development through collaborative investment, lowering costs in software procurement, and lowering costs in grid operations through better software tools.

Despite the desire to lower costs, DSOs were not primarily driven by cost to create the oK consortium. Insufficient software quality and long delivery times for new functionality made vendor lock-in particularly painful. This was especially pronounced during the maintenance and support phase of the software life cycle. Sometimes software vendors dictated prices which DSOs could not agree to for support and maintenance. Therefore the main goal of DSOs was to break vendor lock-in to provide themselves with more flexibility in software procurement and maintenance contracts. The pricing of the software played a role, but quality and functionality were even more important factors. One participant explained: *"It was not primarily an economic goal. It was primarily a goal to increase the quality of software."*

DSO representatives reported that they wanted to choose the most appropriate software tools to operate their grid more efficiently and thereby lower operational costs. Choosing the most appropriate software is only possible when the software has a modular design based on standardized interfaces. If the consortium can reach its goal of offering a vendor-independent open source platform, DSOs will be able to engage in flexible software selection by combining modules to reach optimal operational efficiency.

Having modular grid management software might also reduce procurement prices, although this is not the key anticipated benefit as prices are already low compared to other types of software. Another possible outcome is that more service providers will enter the market, offering DSOs even more flexibility and negotiating power.

DSOs do not necessarily have to participate in the oK consortium. Because the platform software is open source, it is possible for DSOs to become free riders. For the free rider, the benefit is getting software and access to an ecosystem without investing resources, but the drawback is having no power to influence the direction of software development.

Widespread free riding would be problematic for the strength of the consortium. However, some free riding could be positive in that it would help to make the platform a standard, increasing the impact of the consortium. One respondent explained: *"The big network operators won't cause problems for small municipal utilities if they just use the modules. They expressly wish for this."*

Software Suppliers constitute the most diverse group in the ecosystem. Software vendors vary by their product and service portfolio: some vendors sell SCADA systems and other modules and services, while others are IT service providers which develop modules on demand.

All software suppliers stated that their current investment of time, expertise, and membership fees to oK exceeds the short-term profits that are made via the consortium. One supplier of on-demand development expressed that the short-term goal is to win future tendering processes. The software suppliers we interviewed engage in oK because they strive for long-term goals. One respondent explained: *"The pre-sale expenses are already very high. We also spend more being in committees than we get through our margins in the short term. We are there because we believe in the idea."* Software suppliers who participate in oK want to have their technical perspective considered in reshaping the structure of grid management software. This helps ensure that their own products will be compatible and competitive in the future. By promoting a modular approach with standardized interfaces, they also shift the market from favoring general contractors to more specialized service providers, making it more difficult for competitors to acquire the necessary expertise. Being part of the consortium is also a way of signaling to buyers that the supplier is a trusted vendor [14].

Part of this strategy is accomplished by donating modules to the consortium. Such donations need to be adapted and fitted to consortium quality standards and guidelines. A donation is attractive for oK software provider members because they can spread their technologies and strengthen their future market position. Developers are motivated when their work is open sourced and when they know it will be put to a good use. According to one respondent: *"Our developers are of course interested in modern platforms and modern tools."*

Software suppliers that are not part of oK can be motivated to maintain their position in the new market, to grow market share, to maintain the existing market structure to ensure predictable revenues, or to change the market in other ways (for example, by promoting development toward cloud technology). The last two motivations can be seen as a reason for not joining the consortium. Suppliers who are interested in growing or maintaining their position may find the costs, which currently exceed the benefits, too high to justify membership.

Consultants are motivated to sell consulting projects, but are otherwise as diverse as software suppliers. For those who are oK members, the most important objective is not economic. Some participants in this category are research groups, and primarily benefit through the data and experience acquired from close industry collaboration: *"We are also active in other research projects where we are pushing for something to be developed based on the oK technology stack and components. It would be nonsense to develop everything again."* As with software suppliers, service providers who decide not to join oK have likely decided that the costs of joining the consortium outweigh the expected benefits.

4.3   Conflicting Economic Goals

Homogeneity of goals within the oK consortium is high. Even though the different member classes have different economic goals, these play a secondary role and the common goal is emphasized by all members. The service provider members collaborate in the consortium, but they are aware that they are still competing companies. The economic conflict within the consortium is therefore to be located between participants in the same category, with the exception of DSOs, which are natural monopolies. As one interviewee stated: *"One should not forget that these are all different companies."* Another explained *"Of course, if there are modules for the tender, everybody (competing service provider members) would like to do it."*

The main economic conflict occurs between oK members and non-members, or more specifically, those who want to change the technological approach from monolithic to modular, and therefore the business model of software vendors and the market structure of the ecosystem, and those who would like to stick with the current business model. According to the interviewees, the attitude towards the consortium is mainly dependent on the perspective of decision-makers on the software ecosystem. An interviewee elaborated: *"For them, this is a business model where they can only lose. At least that's what the boardroom thinks."*

The old business model delivered operational security to the software vendor, but also to the DSOs. The pricing and maintenance were fixed for a certain period of time (in most cases for five years or more). Established software vendors prefer this model because it provides them with influence and authority. One participant stated: *"The software vendors could sit back, because they knew their existing customers could not run away."*

Enabling a different business model could lead to a profound change of the market structure. Vendor lock-in was and is possible because software vendors and consultants could not be substituted. The consortium aims to change the business model by altering the technical situation that led to vendor lock-in. Instead of monolithic systems owned by vendors, oK is based on a vendor-independent platform that enables software modularity.

Market leaders see the change as a threat. Speaking of a market leader, one respondent said, *"They are afraid that open source will sell less software."* Vendors have not taken any actions against the consortium. One interview partner described the current attitude of these vendors towards oK as one of curiosity.

5   Limitations and Discussion

5.1   Limitations

This study followed a methodology suggested by Eisenhardt [4]. And while building theory from interviews comes with the strength of close ties with empirical data and a high likelihood of generating novel theory, there are also some downsides concerning choice of methods. The results are often rather modest and no grand theory emerges. This is one of the reasons we consider this an exploratory study. Qualitative research can, according to Guba [11], be assessed as follows.

Credibility concerns identifying and eliminating obfuscating factors. We use two approaches to improve credibility: prolonged engagement and member checking. Our research group is a guest member of the consortium, and one of the authors has been involved in oK since its inception. Furthermore, each person we interviewed received a preliminary copy of this study. *Transferability* involves identifying situational variations to ensure the result applies to a broader context. As our study concerns a single consortium, we do not make this claim. Instead, we present this as an exploratory study. *Confirmability* refers to researcher neutrality. This study was provided as part of a larger report to oK, thus making it available to a professional audience that was familiar with oK but not a direct data source. We triangulated on each category of participant by asking interview partners about not only their own experiences, but also about other members of the ecosystem. *Dependeability* is about ensuring the consistency of results. We created an audit trail by preserving three phases of the code system (see Fig. 1), namely open coding, thematic networks, and the final code system. The code system can be found in the Appendix.

5.2 Discussion

The findings of this research concerning economic conflicts in the software ecosystem are general. The main conflict that was identified is evolving around business model change to break vendor lock-in. This is not a new insight because this conflict was essentially willingly established by the user consortium oK in the first place. However, this source of conflict is not commonplace in vendor-led foundations [37], suggesting that user-led foundations are somewhat different. The main reason for persistence of conflict is the low maturity of the user foundation: most interview partners mentioned that oK is still in an early phase of its development and will need more time to impact the ecosystem.

The empirical evidence collected here points towards something else: the slow advancement of the consortium might allow it to open doors that seemed to be shut. Technologically, many goals are congruent even with non-member institutions. One incumbent suggested that even though they are not in favor of business model change, the technological advancements of the consortium towards the standardization of interfaces is very interesting.

Consortium members expect that it will take another 5–10 years for oK to have a real effect on the ecosystem around DSOs. We see a chance of maintaining the consortium goal to develop a vendor-independent platform that allows a flexible and modular use of technology to control smart grids, but at the same time to unite the whole software ecosystem and lead a standardization effort in the industry. Future research could take a longitudinal look at oK, from inception to possible success, potentially creating a road-map for other user-led consortia.

Our findings add to the research field by describing a user-led consortium which is different from the previous descriptions from the educational sector. As user-led consortia become more widespread, there will be the opportunity for research which goes beyond exploring the single foundation, in order to draw more generalizable conclusions about user-led consortia and their ecosystems.

6 Conclusion

This paper presented an exploratory qualitative survey of a software ecosystem surrounding a user-led consortia in the German energy sector. We described three main categories of participants: distribution system operators (DSOs), or software users; software suppliers; and consultants. We explained the situation of openKONSEQUENZ (oK) members and non-members in each category.

The data analysis provided an overview of the different participants in the ecosystem and their goals. The primary economic conflict comes from the change of business model. The consortium was founded to change the balance of power in the ecosystem by offering an alternative platform and standardized interfaces. This has the potential to break vendor lock-in by allowing more competition. However, it also provides small software vendors the opportunity to specialize. Software vendors who are established do not like the idea of losing bargaining power. Interestingly, despite the disagreement over the economic impact of the

modular and flexible design, all companies in the ecosystem support the technological aspects of the change.

Our study provides a look at a user-led consortia which is neither drawn
from the education sector nor grant-sponsored. There is significant promise for
industry in the user-led consortium approach, but our work shows that, at least
in the case of oK, it may take significant time to realize the benefits. Additionally, companies seeking to establish software consortia should be aware of the
possibilities for conflict, even when there is technological consensus.

References

1. Andersson, C., Runeson, P.: Verification and validation in industry–a qualitative
   survey on the state of practice. In: 2002 Proceedings of International Symposium
   on Empirical Software Engineering, pp. 37–47. IEEE (2002)
2. Attride-Stirling, J.: Thematic networks: an analytic tool for qualitative research.
   Qual. Res. **1**(3), 385–405 (2001)
3. Courant, P.N., Griffiths, R.J.: Software and collaboration in higher education: a
   study of open source software, Ithaca, New York (2006)
4. Eisenhardt, K.M.: Building theories from case study research. Acad. Manag. Rev.
   14(4), 532–550 (1989)
5. Feller, J., Finnegan, P., Nilsson, O.: Open innovation and public administration:
   transformational typologies and business model impacts. Eur. J. Inf. Syst. **20**(3),
   358–374 (2011)
6. Germonprez, M., Allen, J.P., Warner, B., Hill, J., McClements, G.: Open source
   communities of competitors. Interactions **20**(6), 54–59 (2013)
7. Germonprez, M., Link, G.J., Lumbard, K., Goggins, S.: Eight observations and
   24 research questions about open source projects: illuminating new realities. Proc.
   ACM Hum.-Comput. Inter. **2**(CSCW), 57 (2018)
8. Gesetz zur digitalisierung der energiewendebundesgesetzblatt jahrgang 2016 teil i
   nr. 43 2034, August 2016
9. Goering, A., Meister, J., Lehnhoff, S., Herdt, P., Jung, M., Rohr, M.: Reference
   architecture for open, maintainable and secure software for the operation of energy
   networks. CIRED-Open Access Proc. J. **2017**(1), 1410–1413 (2017)
10. Goering, A., Meister, J., Lehnhoff, S., Jung, M., Rohr, M., Herdt, P.: Architecture
    and quality standards for the joint development of modular open source software for
    power grid distribution management systems. In: 5th DA-CH+ Energy Informatics
    Conference in Conjunction with 7th Symposium on Communications for Energy
    Systems (ComForEn), vol. 36 (2016)
11. Guba, E.G.: Criteria for assessing the trustworthiness of naturalistic inquiries.
    Educ. Technol. Res. Dev. **29**(2), 75–91 (1981)
12. Hanganu, G.: The community source development model (2008). http://oss-watch.
    ac.uk/resources/communitysource
13. Harutyunyan, N.: Corporate open source governance of software supply chains.
    Doctoral thesis, Friedrich-Alexander-Universität Erlangen-Nürnberg (FAU) (2019)
14. Heiskanen, A., Newman, M., Eklin, M.: Control, trust, power, and the dynamics
    of information system outsourcing relationships: a process study of contractual
    software development. J. Strateg. Inf. Syst. **17**(4), 268–286 (2008)

15. Jansen, H.: The logic of qualitative survey research and its position in the field of social research methods. In: Forum Qualitative Sozialforschung/Forum: Qualitative Social Research, vol. 11, no. 2 (2010)
16. Levy, M., Germonprez, M.: Is it egalitarianism or enterprise strategy? Exploring a new method of innovation in open source. In: 21st Americas Conference on Information Systems, AMCIS 2015. Americas Conference on Information Systems (2015)
17. Liu, M., Hansen, S., Tu, Q.: The community source approach to software development and the Kuali experience. Commun. ACM **57**(5), 88–96 (2014)
18. Liu, M., Hull, C.E., Hung, Y.T.C.: Antecedents of community source network formation: the case of Kuali. In: 2013 46th Hawaii International Conference on System Sciences (HICSS), pp. 4267–4276. IEEE, Piscataway (2013)
19. Liu, M., Wang, H., Zhao, L.: Achieving flexibility via service-centric community source: the case of Kuali. In: AMCIS 2007 Proceedings, p. 103. Americas Conference on Information Systems (2007)
20. Liu, M., Wang, H.J., Zhao, J.L.: Technology flexibility as enabler of robust application development in community source: the case of Kuali and Sakai. J. Syst. Softw. **85**(12), 2921–2928 (2012)
21. Liu, M., Wheeler, B.C., Zhao, J.L.: On assessment of project success in community source development. In: ICIS 2008 Proceedings, p. 121. IEEE/ACM, Piscataway (2008)
22. Liu, M., Zeng, D.D., Zhao, J.L.: A cooporative analysis framework for investment decisions in community source partnerships. In: AMCIS 2008 Proceedings, p. 278 (2008)
23. Mackie, C.J.: Open source in open education: promises and challenges. Opening up education: the collective advancement of education through open technology, open content and open knowledge, pp. 119–131 (2008)
24. Myers, M.D.: Qualitative research in information systems. Manag. Inf. Syst. Q. **21**(2), 241–242 (1997)
25. Niazi, M., et al.: Challenges of project management in global software development: a client-vendor analysis. Inf. Softw. Technol. **80**, 1–19 (2016)
26. OpenKonsequenz: Machbarkeit konsortiale softwareentwicklung auf basis von open source softwarevon (2013)
27. Osterloh, M., Rota, S.: Open source software development–just another case of collective invention? Res. Policy **36**(2), 157–171 (2007)
28. O'Mahony, S., West, J.: What makes a project open source? Migrating from organic to synthetic communities. In: Academy of Management Annual Meeting. Citeseer (2005)
29. Raymond, E.: The cathedral and the bazaar. Knowl. Technol. Policy **12**(3), 23–49 (1999)
30. Riehle, D.: The economic case for open source foundations. Computer **43**(1), 86–90 (2010)
31. Riehle, D.: The single-vendor commercial open course business model. Inf. Syst. e-Bus. Manag. **10**(1), 5–17 (2012)
32. Riehle, D., Berschneider, S.: A model of open source developer foundations. In: Hammouda, I., Lundell, B., Mikkonen, T., Scacchi, W. (eds.) OSS 2012. IAICT, vol. 378, pp. 15–28. Springer, Heidelberg (2012). https://doi.org/10.1007/978-3-642-33442-9_2
33. Riehle, D., Harutyunyan, N.: License Clearance in Software Product Governance, chap. 5, pp. 83–96. NII Shonan, Tokyo, Japan (2017)

34. Robles, G., Gamalielsson, J., Lundell, B.: Setting up government 3.0 solutions based on open source software: the case of X-road. In: Lindgren, I., et al. (eds.) EGOV 2019. LNCS, vol. 11685, pp. 69–81. Springer, Cham (2019). https://doi.org/10.1007/978-3-030-27325-5_6
35. Taft, D.K.: Community-source development appeals in tough times: a combination of traditional and open-source development models, community source can save companies money and reduce vendor lock-in (2009). http://www.eweek.com/development/community-source-development-appeals-in-tough-times
36. Wang, H., Blue, J., Plourde, M.: Community source software in higher education. IT Prof. **12**(6), 31–37 (2010)
37. Weikert, F., Riehle, D., Barcomb, A.: Managing commercial conflicts of interest in open source foundations. In: Hyrynsalmi, S., Suoranta, M., Nguyen-Duc, A., Tyrväinen, P., Abrahamsson, P. (eds.) ICSOB 2019. LNBIP, vol. 370, pp. 130–144. Springer, Cham (2019). https://doi.org/10.1007/978-3-030-33742-1_11. https://dirkriehle.com/wp-content/uploads/2019/09/weikert-etal-2019-managing.pdf
38. West, J., Gallagher, S.: Challenges of open innovation: the paradox of firm investment in open-source software. R&D Manag. **36**(3), 319–331 (2006)
39. West, J., O'Mahony, S.: Contrasting community building in sponsored and community founded open source projects. In: 2005 Proceedings of the 38th Annual Hawaii International Conference on System Sciences. HICSS 2005, p. 196c. IEEE, Piscataway (2005)
40. Wheeler, B.: Open source 2010: reflections on 2007. Educause Rev. **42**(1), 49–52 (2007)

The Development of Data Collectors in Open-Source System for Energy Efficiency Assessment

Daniel Atonge[✉], Vladimir Ivanov, Artem Kruglov, Ilya Khomyakov,
Andrey Sadovykh, Dragos Strugar, Giancarlo Succi, Xavier Zelada Vasquez,
and Evgeny Zouev

Innopolis University, Innopolis, Russia
d.atonge@innopolis.university

Abstract. The paper is devoted to the development of the data collectors for Windows OS and MacOS. The purpose of these plugins is to collect the process metrics from the user's device and send it to the backend for further processing. The overall open source framework is aimed at energy efficiency analysis of the developing software products. The development presented here as a sequence of the life cycle stages, including requirements analysis, design, implementation and testing. Specifics of the implementation for each targeted operating system are given.

Keywords: Process metrics · Energy metrics · Collector · Windows · MacOS · Open source software

1 Introduction

Modelling the energy consumption of applications, gathering valid data from active and passive application processes (i.e., applications in focus and idle applications) is a crucial activity which can be used to find correlations and trends in various areas of research such as developer's productivity, applications with the highest energy consumption profiles and more. To this aim, researchers have proposed hardware-based tools as well as model-based [13] and software-based [14] techniques to approximate the actual energy profile of applications. However, all these solutions present their own advantages and disadvantages. Hardware-based tools are highly precise, but at the same time their use is bound to the acquisition of costly hardware components. Model-based tools require the calibration of parameters needed to correctly create a model on a specific hardware device. Software-based approaches are cheaper and easier to use than hardware-based tools, but they are believed to be less precise. We present the collectors (Windows, MacOs), a software-based approach whose duty is to gather all valuable

Supported by the Russian Science Foundation grant No 19-19-00623.

V. Ivanov et al. (Eds.): OSS 2020, IFIP AICT 582, pp. 14–24, 2020.
https://doi.org/10.1007/978-3-030-47240-5_2

data about active and passively running applications together with energy based metrics. This data when collected can later be processed on the server and result in precise trends and predictions which could enormously benefit software development teams. Making it Open Source exhibits several advantages, as evidenced in several scientific venues [7, 9, 15, 21].

2   Collector Development

The development life-cycle of the collector applications were broken down into the various parts.

2.1   Analysis

Before analysis of the application and design methods, we had a series of requirements both functional and non-functional that lead to the implementation of the current application [6, 22, 23, 26]. These requirements established the services that the client requires from our system and the constraints under which our system operates and is developed.

The functional requirements are the following:

- The list of collected metrics should be easily modifiable
- The metrics should be collected and send to DB automatically after authorization
- The time interval to send the data to server should be specifiable
- The collector should support automatic updates
- Clients should be able to send error reports
- Energy related metrics should be collected
- Product metrics should be collected
- Collectors should implement search functionality

Similarly, the non-functional requirements for the collector are the following:

- Modifiability
- Maintainability
- Adaptability
- Security
- Reusability
- Reliability

With these requirements in place, analysis of the developed application and documentation of the design decisions were made.

Analysis is that iterative process that continues until a preferred and acceptable solution or product emerges. During the analysis of our system, factual data was collected (i.e. what is lacking, what was done, what is needed, etc.). Understanding the processes involved, identifying problems and recommending feasible suggestions for improving the systems' functioning was done. This involved studying logical processes, gathering operational data, understanding the information flow, finding out bottlenecks and evolving solutions for overcoming the weaknesses of the system so as to achieve the organizational goals for the collector. Furthermore, subdividing of complex processes involving the entire system and the identification of data store and manual processes where made (Fig. 1).

During the early stages of development, we felt the need of a simple but purposeful representation of our entire system. This representation was needed in order to:

- Specify the context of our system
- Capture system requirements
- Validate systems architecture
- Drive implementation and generate test cases

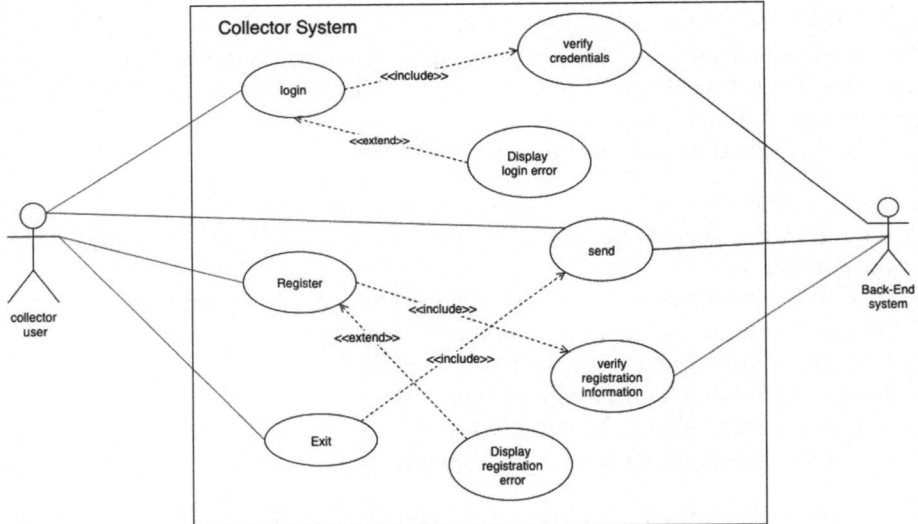

Fig. 1. Use case diagram for the collector

This was more of a thinking process and involved the creative skills. We attempted to give ideas to an efficient system that satisfies the current needs of our clients and has scope for future growth within the organizational constraints.

Overall we followed an agile development process [5,12,18,24,25], also employing techniques for Internet-based working [16], and organizing our development using a component-based approach [25].

2.2 Design

The system was designed to satisfy the requirements stated in the specifying stage. The requirements identified during Requirements Analysis were then transformed into a System Design Document [10] that accurately describes the design of the system and that can be used as an input to system development (see Fig. 2).

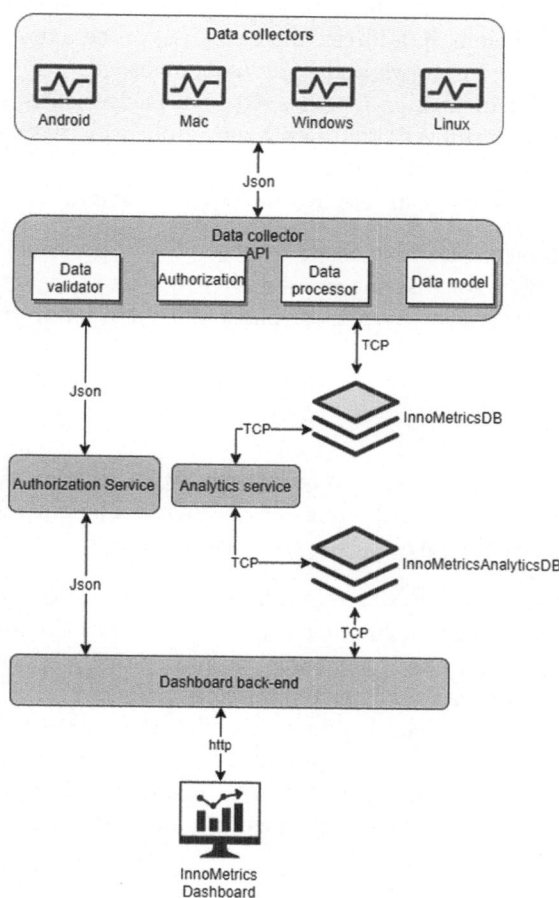

Fig. 2. Logical system design

2.3   Implementation

The logical design was then implemented to build a workable system. This demands the coding of design into computer understandable language, i.e., programming language (in our case native and specific to the targeted platform). Here, program specifications were converted into computer instructions (programs). The programs written coordinate the data movements and control the entire process in our system. Having maintainability as one of our non-functional requirements, code was well written to reduces the testing and maintenance effort. This helps in fast development, maintenance and future changes, if required. We used Visual Studio Code 2019 and the C# programming language (for Windows OS), Xcode and Swift 4.0 (for MacOs) and lastly, QtCreator and C++ (for Linux).

We aim at gathering valuable data related to each running application process. We choose the following; process name, process id, status (app focus or idle), start time, end time, ip address, mac address, process description, processor, hard disk, memory, network and input/output usage.

The internal implementation includes external packages installed via NuGet like RestSharp, A powerful API that assist our application with sending request and reading responses from the server (in windows).

The collector is presently an application with the following interfaces:

- Registration interface for new users
- The Login interface for existing users and
- The Collector Interface: Which displays data collected from the host's machine

2.4   Testing

Before deciding to install our system and put it into operation, a test run of the system was done removing all the bugs as necessary. The output of all our test matched expected results. We ran the two categories of test:

- Program test: Referring to our requirements for expected results of our system, coding, compiling and running our executable was the routine. After our locally based collector application was up and running, each use-case of our system was tested to match expected outcome. We carried out various verification and noted unforeseen happenings which were eventually corrected.
- System test: After carrying out program test and errors removed, running the overall system with the back-end and making sure it meets the specified requirements was done. Our system was fully developed and ready for usage by clients.

3   Integration with the Back-End System

In order to be able to perform authenticated requests, such as sending the collected metrics, collectors should first authenticate with the back-end. That is performed using the POST HTTP request to the back-end system. Then, back-end API requests the Auth Token from the Authentication Service, which is also a part of the back-end system. Then, the Auth Service gets the user information from the database, and if everything turns out to be alright, responds with the token to the collectors.

Then, collectors perform the needed actions described in the sections above, i.e. primarily store the activities along with energy efficiency metrics locally. When the time comes to send the report to the back-end, the collector sends a

POST HTTP request with the Auth Token to the back-end containing all the information about processes that were in use.

Back-end services, upon receiving the request from the collectors, validate the authenticity of the user and receives, and stores in the database the data sent by the collector.

The sequence diagram (see Fig. 3) showcases the above mentioned scenario, adding to the picture the Innometrics Dashboard, a go-to tool for managers to have an overview of the entire reporting process [11].

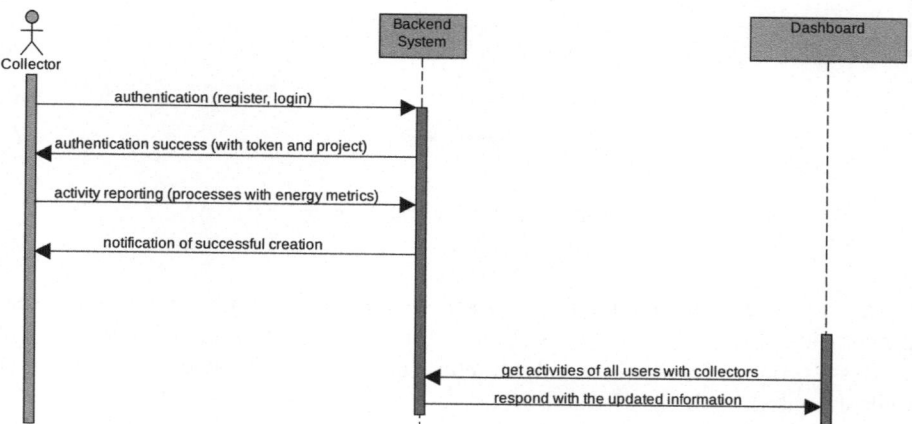

Fig. 3. Logical system design

4 Implementation for the Different OS

This section provides with the peculiarities of developing the collectors for different types of OS. For now the collectors for Windows OS and MacOS are developed. Further, the collectors for X11 and Android OS are planned to be developed.

4.1 Specific of Windows OS Collector

The collector is compose of 3 forms which will come up occasionally (i.e. Account verification (at login) form, Registration form, Collector form). These are the only means of communication with the system from a user perspective.

In Code, best programming practices where used such as those specified by the object-oriented, service-oriented paradigm. Furthermore, good code related practices where enforced such as the DRY (Do Not Repeat Yourself) principle, Naming conventions and more [8].

The main interface (Fig. 4), consists of table view, which is automatically updated by a running service to make sure our application does not block at any time and that, the user can always interact with the collector.

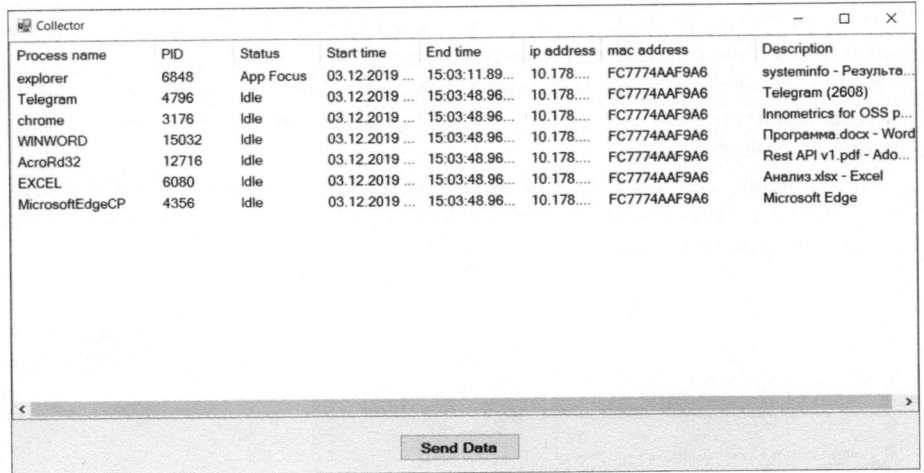

Process name	PID	Status	Start time	End time	ip address	mac address	Description
explorer	6848	App Focus	03.12.2019 ...	15:03:11.89...	10.178....	FC7774AAF9A6	systeminfo - Результа...
Telegram	4796	Idle	03.12.2019 ...	15:03:48.96...	10.178....	FC7774AAF9A6	Telegram (2608)
chrome	3176	Idle	03.12.2019 ...	15:03:48.96...	10.178....	FC7774AAF9A6	Innometrics for OSS p...
WINWORD	15032	Idle	03.12.2019 ...	15:03:48.96...	10.178....	FC7774AAF9A6	Программа.docx - Word
AcroRd32	12716	Idle	03.12.2019 ...	15:03:48.96...	10.178....	FC7774AAF9A6	Rest API v1.pdf - Ado...
EXCEL	6080	Idle	03.12.2019 ...	15:03:48.96...	10.178....	FC7774AAF9A6	Анализ.xlsx - Excel
MicrosoftEdgeCP	4356	Idle	03.12.2019 ...	15:03:48.96...	10.178....	FC7774AAF9A6	Microsoft Edge

Send Data

Fig. 4. Logical system design

Data being collected by running services are the following; process name, process id, status (app focus or idle), start time, end time, ip address, mac address, process description, battery consumption. All other details have been well presented in the sections above.

Battery draining applications result in bad user experience and dissatisfied users. Optimal battery usage (energy usage) is an important aspect that every client must consider.

Application energy consumption is dependent on a wide variety of system resources and conditions. Energy consumption depends on, but is not limited to, the processor the device uses, memory architecture, the storage technologies used, the display technology used, the size of the display, the network interface that you are connected to, active sensors, and various conditions like the signal strength used for data transfer, user settings like screen brightness levels, and many more user and system settings.

For precise energy consumption measurements one needs specialized hardware. While they provide the best method to accurately measure energy consumption on a particular device, such a methodology is not scalable in practice, especially if such measurements have to be made on multiple devices. Even then, the measurements by themselves will not provide much insight into how your application contributed to the battery drain, making it hard to focus on any application optimization efforts [4].

The collector aims at enabling users to estimate their application's energy consumption without the need for specialized hardware. Such estimation is made possible using a software power model that has been trained on a reference device representative of the low powered devices applications might run on.

Using the PerformanceCounter, PerformanceCounterCategory and many more related classes (made available by the .NET Framework [3]), the energy usage can be computed. Performance counter(s) provided information such as CPU time, Total Processor Time per process, CPU usage, Memory usage, network usage and more. The MSDN documentation [2] was used to better understand how we could utilise the available components in attaining our goal (collecting energy consumption metrics).

It is difficult to match up constantly changing application process IDs and names. Imperfection in designed power model as energy consumption depends on a variety of factors not limited to those we can collect using these available performance classes.

4.2   Specific of MacOS Collector

The developed MacOS application is a status menu bar application, as shown in Fig. 5.

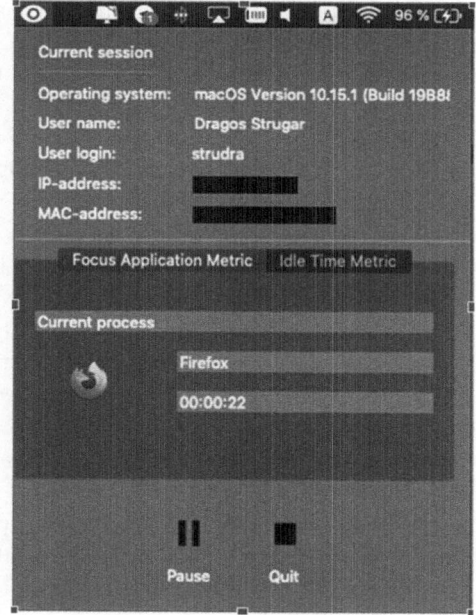

Fig. 5. Logical system design

The application shows the most important information about the user that is collecting the activities. It shows the currently running process, along with the time it is active. In background, it stores this data locally and prepares to send it to the back-end service, as described above.

A collection of information about the currently running process can be obtained using the NSProcessInfo class in the Task Management subsection of Foundation API. This includes thermal state, app performance as well as other specifics. It allows developers to track the information about an activity in the currently running application. However, the problem here arises when we want to access such information for other processes; MacOS has security built-in that does not allow our application to monitor such information.

MetricKit [1] came as a stable solution, that allowed us to aggregate and analyze per-device reports on power and performance metrics, particularly important for prediction [17, 19, 20]. However, what it does it collects metrics and sends them once every 24 h, and is thus not fully suitable to our case.

Thus, we have decided to exclude the CPU utilization, while other metrics, like battery power, memory, GPU and others are already in development and testing stage.

5   Conclusion

Our profiling method and the tools we have available are only able to attribute energy consumption at process level. Any finer granularity, although desirable, is not possible.

Hardware resource usage could fill the gap when it comes to accurately relating EC to individual software elements hence enabling us to compute the UEC.

Profiling the performance requires basic understanding of the hardware components that has to be monitored through "performance counters" in windows and when interpreting performance data for further analysis, context information has to be taken into account (e.g. hardware-specific details).

To evaluate Unit Energy Consumption we can monitor the following hardware resources [14]: Hard disk: disk bytes/sec, disk read bytes/sec, disk write bytes/sec Processor: % processor usage Memory: private bytes, working set, private working set Network: bytes total/sec, bytes sent/sec, bytes received/sec IO: IO data (bytes/sec), IO read (bytes/sec), IO write (bytes/sec)

Attributing some weights to elements of the UEC or by some reliable assumption such as considering the power model to be linear in nature for each individual component, We can compute the SEC Metric.

Reporting these metrics is also useful in identifying potential trade-offs between energy efficiency and other aspects of software quality (e.g. maintainability)

Acknowledgments. The work presented in this paper has been performed thanks to the support by the Russian Science Foundation grant No 19-19-00623.

References

1. Metrickit documentation. https://developer.apple.com/documentation/metrickit. Accessed 12 Apr 2019
2. Microsoft, performance counters. https://docs.microsoft.com/en-us/windows/win32/perfctrs/performance-counters-portal. Accessed 12 May 2019

3. Performance counters in the .net framework. https://docs.microsoft.com/en-us/dotnet/framework/debug-trace-profile/performance-counters. Accessed 12 May 2019
4. Acar, H., Alptekin, G.I., Gelas, J., Ghodous, P.: The impact of source code in software on power consumption. IJEBM **14**, 42–52 (2016)
5. Coman, I.D., Robillard, P.N., Sillitti, A., Succi, G.: Cooperation, collaboration and pair-programming: Field studies on backup behavior. J. Syst. Softw. **91**, 124–134 (2014)
6. Corral, L., Sillitti, A., Succi, G.: Software assurance practices for mobile applications. Computing **97**(10), 1001–1022 (2015). https://doi.org/10.1007/s00607-014-0395-8
7. Di Bella, E., Sillitti, A., Succi, G.: A multivariate classification of open source developers. Inf. Sci. **221**, 72–83 (2013)
8. Dooley, J.: Software Development and Professional Practice. Apress, Berkeley (2011)
9. Fitzgerald, B., Kesan, J.P., Russo, B., Shaikh, M., Succi, G.: Adopting open source software: A practical guide. The MIT Press, Cambridge (2011)
10. Hao-yu, W., Hai-li, Z.: Basic design principles in software engineering. In: 2012 Fourth International Conference on Computational and Information Sciences, pp. 1251–1254 (2012)
11. Ivanov, V., Larionova, D., Strugar, D., Succi, G.: Design of a dashboard of software metrics for adaptable, energy efficient applications. J. Vis. Lang. Comput. **2019**(2), 145–153 (2019)
12. Janes, A., Succi, G.: Lean software development in action. Lean Software Development in Action, pp. 249–354. Springer, Heidelberg (2014). https://doi.org/10.1007/978-3-642-00503-9_11
13. Kalaitzoglou, G., Bruntink, M., Visser, J.: A practical model for evaluating the energy efficiency of software applications. In: ICT4S (2014)
14. Kor, A.L., Pattinson, C., Imam, I., AlSaleemi, I., Omotosho, O.: Applications, energy consumption, and measurement. In: 2015 International Conference on Information and Digital Technologies. IEEE (2015)
15. Kovács, G.L., Drozdik, S., Zuliani, P., Succi, G.: Open source software for the public administration. In: Proceedings of the 6th International Workshop on Computer Science and Information Technologies (2004)
16. Maurer, F., Succi, G., Holz, H., Kötting, B., Goldmann, S., Dellen, B.: Software process support over the Internet. In: Proceedings of the 21st International Conference on Software Engineering. ICSE 1999, pp. 642–645. ACM (1999)
17. Musílek, P., Pedrycz, W., Sun, N., Succi, G.: On the sensitivity of COCOMO II software cost estimation model. In: Proceedings of the 8th International Symposium on Software Metrics. METRICS 2002, pp. 13–20. IEEE Computer Society (2002)
18. Pedrycz, W., Russo, B., Succi, G.: A model of job satisfaction for collaborative development processes. J. Syst. Softw. **84**(5), 739–752 (2011)
19. Pedrycz, W., Russo, B., Succi, G.: Knowledge transfer in system modeling and its realization through an optimal allocation of information granularity. Appl. Soft Comput. **12**(8), 1985–1995 (2012)
20. Ronchetti, M., Succi, G., Pedrycz, W., Russo, B.: Early estimation of software size in object-oriented environments a case study in a CMM level 3 software firm. Inf. Sci. **176**(5), 475–489 (2006)

21. Rossi, B., Russo, B., Succi, G.: Modelling failures occurrences of open source software with reliability growth. In: Ågerfalk, P., Boldyreff, C., González-Barahona, J.M., Madey, G.R., Noll, J. (eds.) OSS 2010. IAICT, vol. 319, pp. 268–280. Springer, Heidelberg (2010). https://doi.org/10.1007/978-3-642-13244-5_21
22. Scotto, M., Sillitti, A., Succi, G., Vernazza, T.: A relational approach to software metrics. In: Proceedings of the 2004 ACM Symposium on Applied Computing. SAC 2004, pp. 1536–1540. ACM (2004)
23. Sillitti, A., Janes, A., Succi, G., Vernazza, T.: Measures for mobile users: an architecture. J. Syst. Architect. **50**(7), 393–405 (2004)
24. Sillitti, A., Succi, G., Vlasenko, J.: Understanding the impact of pair programming on developers attention: a case study on a large industrial experimentation. In: Proceedings of the 34th International Conference on Software Engineering. ICSE 2012, pp. 1094–1101. IEEE Press (2012)
25. Sillitti, A., Vernazza, T., Succi, G.: Service oriented programming: a new paradigm of software reuse. In: Gacek, C. (ed.) ICSR 2002. LNCS, vol. 2319, pp. 269–280. Springer, Heidelberg (2002). https://doi.org/10.1007/3-540-46020-9_19
26. Vernazza, T., Granatella, G., Succi, G., Benedicenti, L., Mintchev, M.: Defining metrics for software components. In: Proceedings of the World Multiconference on Systemics, Cybernetics and Informatics. vol. XI, pp. 16–23 (2000)

Challenges of Tracking and Documenting Open Source Dependencies in Products: A Case Study

Andreas Bauer(✉), Nikolay Harutyunyan, Dirk Riehle,
and Georg-Daniel Schwarz

Friedrich-Alexander-Universität Erlangen-Nürnberg, Erlangen, Germany
{andi.bauer,nikolay.harutyunyan,georg.schwarz}@fau.de, dirk@riehle.org

Abstract. Software vendors need to manage the dependencies of the open source components used in their products. Without this management, license compliance would be impossible, export restrictions could not be maintained, and security vulnerabilities would remain unknown to the vendor.

The management of these dependencies has grown in an ad-hoc fashion in most companies. As such, vendors find it hard to learn from each other and improve practices.

To address this problem, we performed exploratory single-case study research at one large established software vendor. We gathered and analyzed the key challenges of tracking and documenting open source dependencies in products. We wanted to understand whether these ad-hoc solutions could be based on a single unified conceptual model for managing dependencies.

Our study suggests that underlying the various point solutions that we found at this vendor lies a conceptual model that we tentatively call the product (architecture) model. In future cross-vendor work, we will investigate whether this conceptual model can be expanded to become a unifying model for all open source dependency management.

Keywords: Open source software · FLOSS · FOSS · Open source governance

1 Introduction

The growth of free/libre, and open source software (FLOSS) leads the software industry to new opportunities but also challenges. FLOSS promise significant shortcuts by reusing existing software components in commercial products [1, 4, 7, 13, 15, 16]. However, to avoid legal and other risks of using FLOSS in commercial products, such as license noncompliance, software vendors need to manage their FLOSS dependencies. Furthermore, this allows to track known security vulnerabilities introduced by such dependencies, as well as export restrictions and other important metadata.

© IFIP International Federation for Information Processing 2020
Published by Springer Nature Switzerland AG 2020
V. Ivanov et al. (Eds.): OSS 2020, IFIP AICT 582, pp. 25–35, 2020.
https://doi.org/10.1007/978-3-030-47240-5_3

The management of FLOSS dependencies has grown in an ad-hoc fashion in most companies. The architectural models used for this are often designed to satisfy a managerial perspective and neglect more fine-grained issues such as compliance information of bill of materials (BOM) details. As a consequence, there is a mismatch between an architectural model that supports the management of FLOSS dependencies and the models we found in industry. This leads to costly integration operations to ensure license compliance. Many companies develop own tooling to merge documented license information and generate more comprehensive reports about the use of FLOSS in their products. The lack of consistent concepts in the underlining models also causes manual intervention in the dependency management and license compliance processes, which slows down production. The vast, and still increasing, amount of the commercially used open source components additionally complicates the process of license compliance.

To address this industry-relevant yet underresearched issue, we performed exploratory single-case study research at one large established software vendor. We wanted to identify the challenges companies face regarding software dependency documentation in the context of FLOSS license compliance and tracking. We also studied the ad-hoc solutions to these challenges in the context of the studied company. The main contribution of our paper is a systematic analysis of the challenges related to the tracking and documentation of open source components and dependencies in companies. As a result of our study, the following categories of challenges coupled with their point solutions emerged:

- Data Gathering for the Compliance Process
- Usage of FLOSS in Products
- Custom Reports
- SPDX Support
- A Central System to Manage Products

For each category, we report the current issues discovered in the course of the case study, as well as the solutions found at the studied company supported by the analyzed qualitative data through interview quotes and observatory descriptions. We suggest that the identified challenges and solutions can fit together into a conceptual model that we tentatively call the product (architecture) model, which we will investigate and evaluate in further research aiming for broader generalizability beyond this single-case case study.

2   Related Work

In previous work, we reported our findings on industry requirements for FLOSS governance tools [10]. We found a hierarchical list of requirements that indicated the following four key categories: Tracking and reuse of FLOSS components, License compliance of FLOSS components, Search and selection of FLOSS components, and Other requirements (security, education, etc.). We then extended our findings in a subsequent journal article [11] with a new round of qualitative data analysis using five additional interviews, which added the fifth category to the proposed theory focusing on the architecture model for software products.

Among other requirements for tooling, it showed that companies develop their own tools to incorporate FLOSS governance relevant information with architectural information to manage software products. In this paper, we follow up on the topic of software dependency documentation in the context of FLOSS compliance, and focus on the challenges companies face in doing this. We did not identify any literature focusing on this specific topic, but found literature on FLOSS governance and compliance more broadly.

Hammouda et al. [8] introduced open source legality patterns, which help with architectural design decisions motivated by legal concerns associated with FLOSS licenses. They focus on how the interaction between different components can be managed so that the overall product contains no license violations. The patterns are grouped in the following categories: Interaction legality patterns, Isolation legality patterns, and Licensing legality patterns. An example of an Interaction legality pattern is to switch from static to dynamic linking if a proprietary component depends on a strong copyleft licensed component.

Fendt et al. [2,3] conducted practitioner-driven research on FLOSS governance, compliance, and policy. In 2016 [3], the authors suggested processes for the successful management of FLOSS use in companies that want to avoid the related legal risks. The proposed processes were designed to serve as best practices and a basis for corporate governance, strategy, policy, and process implementation. In 2019 [2], Fendt and Jaeger followed up with an experience report on their use of open source tools and services for open source license compliance. They used several well-known tools such as SW360[1] and Fossology[2], integrated in a complete compliance toolchain.

From a model perspective, the Software Package Data Exchange (SPDX™) specification is the de-facto standard to exchange the bill-of-materials of a product. The goal of the SPDX specification is to enable companies and other organizations to share license and component metadata for a software package. This specification was the result of a shared effort from different organizations to address the needs of various participants in software supply chains [17]. The SPDX License List is a key factor for the adoption of the SPDX standard in companies [5]. This curated list contains the commonly used open source licenses and enables open source license identification through a unique identifier.

German et al. [6] described a method to model dependencies that are required to build and execute a program. The classification criteria for dependencies in this model contain information about a dependency's type (explicit or abstract), if it is optional, in which stage it is required (build-time, run-time, etc.), and the usage method (stand alone, library, and more). The packages in this model are also aware of licenses. Additionally, they suggested a method to visualize the dependency graph of a software package based on their model. It also allowed showing inconsistencies, such as license conflicts between packages. For their analysis, they used packages of a FLOSS distribution (Debian 4.0) and demonstrated how the model could help provide insights into the FLOSS ecosystem.

---

[1] https://projects.eclipse.org/proposals/sw360.
[2] https://www.fossology.org.

3   Research Methods

Given the unexplored nature and the practical relevance of the research topic, we conducted a single-case case study informed by Yin [18] to study the software dependency documentation in terms of FLOSS license compliance and tracking. We chose the case study methodology over alternatives (e.g. grounded theory, experiments) because of its suitability for the emerging and complex phenomena that can be best studied in their practical contexts [18]. Given the complexities of the corporate FLOSS use, governance, and compliance in general [9] and of the software dependency documentation issues in particular [11], we chose a case study company that actively uses open source components in products, while encountering issues in tracking and documenting this use as part of the complete product architecture.

We chose a large multinational enterprise software company with mature FLOSS awareness and use. The company provides services to retail and enterprise customers, and distribute open source and closed source software to them as well. In our search for the appropriate case study company, we leveraged our professional network and a German industry-academia collaboration project that two of the co-authors were part of Software Campus[3]. This enabled us to find a company that is a heavy open source software user at a certain FLOSS governance maturity level where the basics are covered but more advanced aspects of such governance are in flux. The latter included our focal research topic – software dependency documentation in terms of FLOSS license compliance and tracking. The company and the interview data are anonymized as per the company's request.

We outlined in the case study protocol [18] that our case study was both descriptive and explanatory. It was descriptive in detailing reports of what the current state of open source governance at the studied company was when it came to the software dependency documentation focused on FLOSS license compliance and tracking. It was explanatory in presenting some reasons why certain issues in product architecture and open source software dependency documentation arise. When addressing the descriptive side of our study the main co-author visited the case study company for direct observation of the current practices in their real-life context. As for the explanatory aspect, we conducted interviews with five employees at the case study company to cover the breadth of issues faced by the people in different roles responsible for product architecture and FLOSS tracking and documentation. We interviewed employees with different views on the usage of FLOSS within the company. The first two were FLOSS compliance managers. The third person was a product owner and covered the role of a user of open source. The next person was a product manager. The last person was a developer and in his role responsible for the company's architecture model which was used for FLOSS compliance.

To analyze the conducted interviews, we employed computer-assisted qualitative data analysis (QDA) software (CAQDAS) to ensure the systematic analysis

---

[3] https://softwarecampus.de/.

of the data and the traceability of our theory to the data. Informed by Jansen's logic of qualitative survey research [12], we conducted an open (inductive) survey, in which the relevant topics of product architecture and FLOSS tracking were identified through the interpretation of raw data – employee interview transcripts. This approach was in contrast to the other type of qualitative surveys – the pre-structured survey, in which some main topics, dimensions, and categories would be defined before the study, which was not suitable for our exploratory study on this emerging domain.

4   Results

In this section, we present our results on the challenges of tracking and documenting open source dependencies in products.

As Fendt and Jaeger [2] show, the required process to be compliant is more complex than just running a license scanner tool on the codebase. Instead, it should be embedded into a bigger process of FLOSS management. Even a company with mature FLOSS awareness and use does not always have a good solution in place to overcome all the challenges of FLOSS dependency management. This leads to workarounds which often force a manual treatment.

In the following, we describe our findings and discuss their implications on the whole FLOSS license compliance process. The main challenges we found are:

– Data Gathering for the Compliance Process
– Usage of FLOSS in Products
– Custom Reports
– SPDX Support
– A Central System to Manage Products

Data Gathering for the Compliance Process. If a developer wants to use a FLOSS component it needs to be approved by the company's open source software office. FLOSS compliance processes are in place to manage the approval of a FLOSS component use. Fendt et al. [3] describe that a FLOSS management process inside their company consists of several phases. The first phase is the Request Phase, in which development teams initiate an approval request for a new FLOSS component they would like to use. The FLOSS compliance process of our case study company matches this first phase by requesting the use of a FLOSS component. The usage of only approved FLOSS components helps to avoid legal compliance risks introduced by unknown components. In our previous studies about industry requirements on FLOSS governance and compliance tools, we found that companies want to have an automated process of adding new FLOSS components and their metadata into a common architectural model [11], captured in the following requirement:

> *"The tool should allow automated adding of FLOSS components and their metadata into the repository using the product architecture model"*
> – Requirement 5.b. [11]

But in reality, users of FLOSS components often have to provide information about a component by hand. This manual step of collecting information is time-consuming and can slow down the whole approval process. The typical required information for an approval decision includes:

- Licenses and copyright information
- Project references, like the homepage URL
- Uploaded source code and binaries, or provide location to download them
- Clarification if component include cryptographic functionalities
- Export Control Classification Number (ECCN)[4]
- Does the component require a specific runtime, like Java Runtime Environment (JRE)

As a key challenge at the studied company, we find that if a developer is uncertain whether the component in a specific version is already approved, he has to use a similar process by entering all the information about the component into the system used for the approval process. This is time-consuming, according to an interviewee from the case study company:

"It's very time-consuming to collect all the necessary information to provide the [FLOSS approval] request" – Product owner (user of open source)

Usage of FLOSS in Products Whether a FLOSS component and its license are suitable for a company's product also depends on how the product is to be used. At our studied company they distinguish between the following four usage types: 1) on-premise installation on a client's machine; 2) providing services as a cloud solution, aka. software-as-a-service (SaaS); 3) used as a library to be integrated into other products; 4) internal use only. These usage types are not exclusive and can be combined, e.g. the product is provided as a cloud service and is only available for internal use, which increases the complexity of the underlining architectural model.

One interviewee explained that, once a FLOSS component is listed in the catalog of approved components, every developer can use these components in the limits of the usage type. For example, the Microsoft SQL Server (with an on-premises license purchased without software assurance and mobility right)[5] can be bundled and shipped with a product, but you're not allowed to use it in a product that is a cloud service (SaaS).

For a different usage type, FLOSS components used in a product that is only for internal use do not have to go through a costly clarification process. This comes with the fact that internally used software is not distributed and as such, there is no need to ensure license compliance.

---

[4] https://www.bis.doc.gov/index.php/licensing/commerce-control-list-classification/export-control-classification-number-eccn.

[5] https://www.microsoft.com/en-us/licensing/news/updated-licensing-rights-for-dedicated-cloud.

"You can download everything, but once it goes into the product that's delivered to customer, you have to ask: Can you use it?" – FLOSS compliance manager

Custom Reports. We found that at our case study company the management demanded reports for their products which included information about the incorporated FLOSS components. This helped track FLOSS assets and assisted in FLOSS risk management.

To provide reports of FLOSS usage in products, license information has to be combined with the architectural documentation of a product. For that, companies develop their own tools which combine all the necessary information from different sources.

One particular challenge here is to keep reliable references between a FLOSS component, their artifacts, and related data. Inconsistencies in these references lead to manual data clean up work. For example, a scan for FLOSS components would identify multiple already known components but couldn't match them with data from a central FLOSS management system.

"This [specific] report tries to figure out where in our vault is the third part component and it matches with my product. Quite often it happens that it doesn't match even if I have provided the very similar and identical source and binaries." – Product owner (user of open source)

A combined model could help simplify the creation of reports and avoid mismatches of components by inconsistent references.

SPDX Support. SPDX is the defacto standard to exchange license compliance information. This is especially useful within software supply chains, where suppliers are often expected to provide SPDX documents [9] alongside the delivered software. Many license compliance tools support SPDX as an exchange format for license compliance information and other metadata. Therefore, companies develop custom tools to be able to consume and produce SPDX documents.

At the case study company, we see the benefits of SPDX and integrated support in their toolchain for it. While SPDX standardizes the exchange of license information, a valid SPDX document can lack information and thus not ensure a complete BOM representation. When the studied company required the BOM from a supplier both parties had to agree on how certain information would be stored in the SPDX document.

"But we learnt that SPDX has no clear prescription, what is required, and what's not, to give you, you can do this and that, and we ended up adding a few own fields for those information we think we need." – FLOSS compliance manager

A Central System to Manage Products. One interview partner reported that they used a central system to manage their products in which they could incorporate all the information needed for reports and license compliance artifacts. While our interview partner saw high value in having a central system, it did not circumvent all the challenges of license compliance. For example, they reported that relationships between components of a product were represented only as simple dependencies. This simplification produced a high-level view on the composition of a product, which was not enough to generate precise reports on the full product architecture.

"[A central system] is for me not enough [...] we have all the data but the relations between things [are insufficient]" – Product manager

As described before, data gathering from different tools and systems to feed the central system tends to be error-prone. A central system to manage products often grew over time from a system that was not designed to ensure license compliance in the first place. Therefore, some aspects of license compliance result in costly operations, which constitutes another major challenge we discovered during our case study.

5   Discussion

The previous section presents five major challenges the analyzed company has regarding their FLOSS component management processes. In the following paragraphs we present the implications of our findings.

Coping with Amount of FLOSS Dependencies. One factor that makes the described challenges even more difficult is the sheer quantity of FLOSS dependencies. FLOSS itself is often built on top of other FLOSS, which results in a snowball effect of dependencies. According to a report [14] from 2016, the average commercial product 80% of the code comes from FLOSS. Our interview partners also described that the sheer amount of FLOSS in their products leads to a time-consuming FLOSS license compliance process. To cope with the increasing amount of FLOSS dependencies, the aim is to automate the license compliance process as much as possible.

Considering Product Shipping Information. Because the architecture documentation was initially not designed with compliance information in mind, it is difficult to deal with FLOSS in products. As described, costly operations are required to collect and maintain license compliance information. Another effect is that **the documentation of a product does not represent the actual shipped product**. An example of such a divergence is when a product's feature depends on the purchased product key, like a home vs a professional version of a product. While the product is still the same, the shipped version of the product differs in accessible components. More detailed documentation on how a product is used could allow deriving a BOM which only covers all necessary components of the actual shipped product.

Describing Inter-dependency Relationships. We found that products and their dependencies on FLOSS components and infrastructure are represented in a simplified manner. Besides issues on representing a product in its shipped version, FLOSS licenses may have different obligations dependent on how the component is incorporated in a product. For example, the LGPL license family distinguishes between static and dynamic linking for applying the viral copyleft effect. Information about required runtime environments, which also may introduce additional dependencies, are hard to represent next to architectural and license relevant information. Nevertheless, the studied company relies on this information and has to put additional effort into developing and maintaining custom tools to generate accurate reports and artifacts like the BOM.

Existence of an Underlying Conceptual Model. Regarding an architectural model, FLOSS license information must be incorporated in an unambiguous fashion. For example, using unique SPDX license identifier instead of unstructured text to describe the declared license. Our previous studies cover the requirements for automation of the FLOSS compliance process, but those requirements are not fulfilled by tools to the extent which is required [10, 11]. An elaborate representation of inter-dependency relationships should be an inherent part of the architectural model. Also, information for shipping the product as mentioned above should be included in this model. The need for automation and the resulting interoperability of tools suggests there is a need for a general underlying conceptual model representing the product. The consensus on such a conceptual model may also help to avoid the development of company-specific tooling solutions.

6   Limitations

Since we investigated the challenges of FLOSS dependency documentation and tracking in the context of only one company, we do not claim generalizability for the findings. Acknowledging this common limitation of single-case case studies, we were nonetheless able to deeply investigate this emerging research topic identifying five advanced subtopics that went beyond the previous research on FLOSS license compliance and dependencies. Moreover, to mitigate the anticipated limitation, we were careful to choose a representative company with some familiarity of using open source components in products, but limited awareness when it came specifically to FLOSS component tracking and documentation.

7   Conclusion

To study the emerging issue of tracking FLOSS components and dependencies in software product architectures, we performed a case study in a multinational enterprise software company as part of an industry-academia collaboration project. In this exploratory study, we conducted and analyzed five interviews with key stakeholders of FLOSS component tracking and documentation in the studied company.

We identified the core challenges of managing FLOSS dependencies and their integration with existing product architecture infrastructures within a company context. We discussed in detail the challenges related to the data gathering for the compliance process, FLOSS usage in products, custom reports, SPDX support, and to the centralized system for managing products.

Our study suggests that underlying the various point solutions that we found at this vendor lies a conceptual model that we tentatively call the product (architecture) model. In future cross-vendor work, we will investigate whether this conceptual model can be expanded to become a unifying model for all open source dependency management.

Acknowledgements. We thank Sebastian Schmid for his generous feedback that helped us improve the paper significantly. We also thank our industry partners that provided their valuable time and expertise for this research project. This research was funded by BMBFs (Federal Ministry of Education and Research) Software Campus 2.0 project (OSGOV, 01IS17045).

References

1. Deshpande, A., Riehle, D.: The total growth of open source. In: Russo, B., Damiani, E., Hissam, S., Lundell, B., Succi, G. (eds.) OSS 2008. ITIFIP, vol. 275, pp. 197–209. Springer, Boston, MA (2008). https://doi.org/10.1007/978-0-387-09684-1_16
2. Fendt, O., Jaeger, M.: Open source for open source license compliance. In: Bordeleau, F., Sillitti, A., Meirelles, P., Lenarduzzi, V. (eds.) Open Source Systems, OSS 2019, IFIP Advances in Information and Communication Technology, vol. 556, pp. 133–138. Springer, Cham (2019). https://doi.org/10.1007/978-3-030-20883-7_12
3. Fendt, O., Jaeger, M., Serrano, R.J.: Industrial experience with open source software process management. In: Proceedings - International Computer Software and Applications Conference, vol. 2, pp. 180–185 (2016). https://doi.org/10.1109/COMPSAC.2016.138
4. Fitzgerald, B.: The transformation of open source software. MIS Q. **30**(3), 587 (2006). https://doi.org/10.2307/25148740
5. Gandhi, R., Germonprez, M., Link, G.J.: Open data standards for open source software risk management routines: an examination of SPDX. In: Proceedings of the International ACM SIGGROUP Conference on Supporting Group Work, pp. 219–229 (2018). https://doi.org/10.1145/3148330.3148333
6. German, D.M., González-Barahona, J.M., Robles, G.: A model to understand the building and running inter-dependencies of software. In: Proceedings - Working Conference on Reverse Engineering, WCRE, pp. 140–149 (2007). https://doi.org/10.1109/WCRE.2007.5
7. Hammond, J., Santinelli, P., Billings, J.J., Ledingham, B.: The tenth annual future of open source survey. Black Duck Softw. (2016)
8. Hammouda, I., Mikkonen, T., Oksanen, V., Jaaksi, A.: Open source legality patterns: architectural design decisions motivated by legal concerns. In: Proceedings of the 14th International Academic MindTrek Conference: Envisioning Future Media Environments, MindTrek 2010, pp. 207–214 (2010). https://doi.org/10.1145/1930488.1930533
9. Harutyunyan, N.: Corporate Open Source Governance of Software Supply Chains, Doctoral thesis, Friedrich-Alexander-Universität Erlangen-Nürnberg (FAU) (2019)

10. Harutyunyan, N., Bauer, A., Riehle, D.: Understanding industry requirements for FLOSS governance tools. In: Stamelos, I., Gonzalez-Barahoña, J.M., Varlamis, I., Anagnostopoulos, D. (eds.) OSS 2018. IAICT, vol. 525, pp. 151–167. Springer, Cham (2018). https://doi.org/10.1007/978-3-319-92375-8_13
11. Harutyunyan, N., Bauer, A., Riehle, D.: Industry requirements for FLOSS governance tools to facilitate the use of open source software in commercial products. J. Syst. Softw. **158**, 110390 (2019). https://doi.org/10.1016/j.jss.2019.08.001
12. Jansen, H.: The logic of qualitative survey research and its position in the field of social research methods. In: Forum Qualitative Sozialforschung/Forum: Qualitative Social Research, vol. 11 (2010)
13. von Krogh, G., von Hippel, E.: The promise of research on open source software. Manag. Sci. **52**(7), 975–983 (2006). https://doi.org/10.1287/mnsc.1060.0560
14. Pittenger, M.: Open source security analysis: the state of open source security in commercial applications. Technical report, Black Duck Software (2016)
15. Riehle, D.: The economic motivation of open source software: stakeholder perspectives. Computer **40**(4), 25–32 (2007). https://doi.org/10.1109/MC.2007.147
16. Riehle, D.: The commercial open source business model. In: Nelson, M.L., Shaw, M.J., Strader, T.J. (eds.) AMCIS 2009. LNBIP, vol. 36, pp. 18–30. Springer, Heidelberg (2009). https://doi.org/10.1007/978-3-642-03132-8_2
17. Stewart, K., Odence, P., Rockett, E.: Software package data exchange (SPDX^{TM}) specification. Int. Free Open Sour. Softw. Law Rev. **2**(2), 191–196 (2012). https://doi.org/10.5033/ifosslr.v4i1.45, https://spdx.org/
18. Yin, R.K.: Case Study Research and Applications: Design and Methods. Sage publications, Thousand Oaks (2017)

An Empirical Investigation of Sentiment Analysis of the Bug Tracking Process in Libre Office Open Source Software

Apostolos Kritikos(✉), Theodoros Venetis, and Ioannis Stamelos

School of Informatics, Aristotle University of Thessaloniki, University Campus,
54124 Thessaloniki, Greece
{akritiko,venetheo,stamelos}@csd.auth.gr
http://www.csd.auth.gr/en/

Abstract. In this work we are studying the sentiment in Open Source Software projects and more specifically in the process of bug reporting, to investigate the human factor, namely, the feedback from the community (end-users, developers, testers, etc.). One of the characteristics for which Open Source Software has gained attention, over the years, is the fact that it is continuously being tested and maintained by its community of volunteers. Sentiment analysis, a rapidly growing field, can enrich software evaluation with a social aspect. Results suggest that FLOSS projects' bug reports can potentially constitute a rich emotionally - imbued information source.

1 Introduction

Since the beginning of Open Source Software, the community around a FLOSS project is one of the greatest strengths of open source software development over closed source development. Eric S. Raymond [1] highlights this strength; *"Given a large enough beta-tester and co-developer base, almost every problem will be characterized quickly and the fix obvious to someone"*. In the community of an Open Source Software project we find developers who usually contribute both in the development and test process. In addition, community members can also be people who do not possess development skills but use the project as end users and contribute to testing. Cerone et al. [2] stress the importance of defining qualitative metrics for indicators of collaboration effectiveness within Open Source Software communities.

In this paper we will be analyzing the sentiment from bug reports posted to Bugzilla. The proposed methodology is being applied to various major versions of the Open Source Software project Libre Office.

The rest of the paper is organized as follows: Sect. 2 provides background information for the basic terms discussed in this work. Section 3 presents scientific work done by other researchers relevant with the aim of this paper. Section 4 analyzes our case study plan. Section 5 provides the statistical analysis conducted to the data we collected. In Sect. 6 we discuss the findings on our statistical analysis, while Sect. 7 speculates on threats to

© IFIP International Federation for Information Processing 2020
Published by Springer Nature Switzerland AG 2020
V. Ivanov et al. (Eds.): OSS 2020, IFIP AICT 582, pp. 36–46, 2020.
https://doi.org/10.1007/978-3-030-47240-5_4

validity. Finally, in Sect. 8 we conclude our work by summarizing our findings and we refer to possible future work. Please note that all the original data for this scientific work are available at http://users.auth.gr/akritiko/datasets/kritikosOSS2020_dataset.zip.

2 Background

This section presents an overview of the research state of the art on sentiment analysis (also known as opinion mining).

Sentiment analysis (often referred to as *opinion mining*) is the process of determining the polarity of an input text. It can be performed mainly at three different levels of granularity [3]: *document-level analysis*, classifying the sentiment expressed in a whole document as positive, negative or neutral; *sentence-level analysis*, which determines the sentiment per sentence in a document; *aspect-level analysis*, which delivers more fine-grained results and is based on the idea that an opinion consists of a sentiment and a respective target, which typically refers to an entity or a specific aspect of it.

The approaches mainly used for deducing the sentiment expressed in a document is the lexicon-based [4] and the machine learning-based [5] approach. Besides these two, there is a third one that involves the deployment of ontology-based methodologies for performing aspect-level sentiment analysis [6].

3 Related Work

In the software engineering domain, there have been the following relevant approaches for studying emotions and related factors in Open Source Software projects. Guzman et al. [7] study emotions expressed in commit comments of several open source projects and analyze their relationship with different factors. Rousinopoulos et al. [8] attempt to analyse the evolution of the sentiment of developers of a Open Source Software project (openSUSE Factory) by applying sentiment analysis techniques on the e-mails sent to the mailing list of the project. Similarly, Garcia et al. [9] perform sentiment analysis on the e-mail archives of another FLOSS project (Gentoo) and attempt to investigate the relation between the emotions in the mailing list and the respective activity of contributors in the project. Finally, the authors of [10] and [11] analyse comments in an issue tracking system, in order to investigate whether a relationship exists between human affectiveness (emotion, sentiment and politeness) and developer productivity (i.e. time needed for fixing an issue).

4 Case Study Plan

We have chosen Libre Office as a candidate to conduct our analysis for a variety of reasons: (1) It is an Open Source Software project with a rich code base (until the time of writing it has had 486,472 commits made by 1,880 contributors representing 9,517,407 lines of code [12]), (2) it has an active community that shows no sign of long-term decline and has attracted the long-term and most active committers in OpenOffice.org (from which Libre Office was originated as a fork).

In this work we will be studying sixteen (16) major versions of the Libre Office productivity suite, namely: 3.3, 3.4, 3.5, 3.6, 4.0, 4.1, 4.2, 4.3, 4.4, 5.0, 5.1, 5.2, 5.3, 5.4, 6.0, 6.1.

4.1 Data Collection – Bugs

We collected our data from the official Libre Office bug tracking tool which is implemented with Bugzilla [13]. We gathered a total of 740 bugs that are related to the versions. Each bug is a threaded discussion with comments related to the bug reported. These 740 bugs are consisted of 6960 comments in total. Apart from the text of the comments to which we have applied the sentiment analysis process we also gather the following information for each bug [14]:

- ASSIGNED_TO: The person to which the bug was assigned to be fixed.
- CREATED: The date of the creation of the bug.
- CREATOR: The creator of the bug.
- LAST_CHANGED: When was the last time that this bug was updated.
- OPEN: If the bug is open or closed.
- COMPONENT_ID: Which component does the bug refer to (i.e. Writer).
- VERSION_ID: Which version does the bug refer to (i.e. 3.3).

As far as the comments of a bug are concerned (threaded discussion) we have gathered the following information:

- CREATED: Date and time that the comment was created.
- CREATOR: The creator of the comment (can be different than the creator of the bug)
- COMMENT_TEXT: The text of the comment.
- COUNT_ORDER: The order of the comment in the discussion (needed to be able to follow the flow of the threaded discussion).
- BUG_CREATOR: Used to identify when a comment is an answer to the thread by the creator of the bug.
- BY_SYSTEM: Used to identify system automated responses (which show zero sentiment by default).

4.2 Data Collection – Sentiment Analysis

As far as the sentiment analysis part is concerned, we used two (2) different tools, namely VADER [15] and MeaningCloud [16].

We consider both tools valuable for our investigation. VADER (Valence Aware Dictionary and sEntiment Reasoner) is an academic product [17] that serves "as a lexicon and rule-based sentiment analysis tool". MeaningCloud, on the other hand is a commercial solution for sentiment analysis that provides a free plan for 20.000 requests per month. Since we are interested in investigating if and how sentiment affects the bug tracking process in open source software, by using both tools we, without loss of generality, get safer results concerning the existence of sentiment in the bug tracking process of open source software whereas, at the same time, we are utilizing the different kinds of information that each tool provides with the aim of succeeding a wider scope in our investigation.

VADER sentiment analyzer provided us with the following data per comment:

- COMPOUND_SCORE: As the authors of the tool describe it, a "normalized, weighted composite score. This score is the sum of the valence scores of each word in the lexicon, adjusted according to the rules, and then normalized to be between −1 (most extreme negative) and +1 (most extreme positive).".
- NEGATIVE, NEUTRAL, POSITIVE: These scores are ratios that show the percentage of the comment that is positive, negative and/or neutral.

MeaningCloud analyzer provided us with the following data per comment:

- SCORE: The sentiment score that can be one of the following values: none (no sentiment), N+ (very negative), N (negative), neutral, P (positive), P+ (very positive).
- CONFIDENCE: Percentage to which the analysis is accurate [0–100].
- IRONY: If the comment is ironic (IRONIC, NONIRONIC).
- SUBJECTIVITY: If the opinion on the comment is considered subjective or objective (SUBJECTIVE, OBJECTIVE).
- AGREEMENT: If the sentences of the comment are in agreement with each other or there are ambiguous meanings (AGREEMENT, DISAGREEMENT).

5 Statistical Analysis

This section presents the statistical analysis of the data collected. As a first step we tried to identify possible outliers that might be misleading for our results to consider possible data reduction [18]. In the following image you can see a visualization of the number of comments distribution per version of Libre Office and the box plots regarding our variables (Fig. 1).

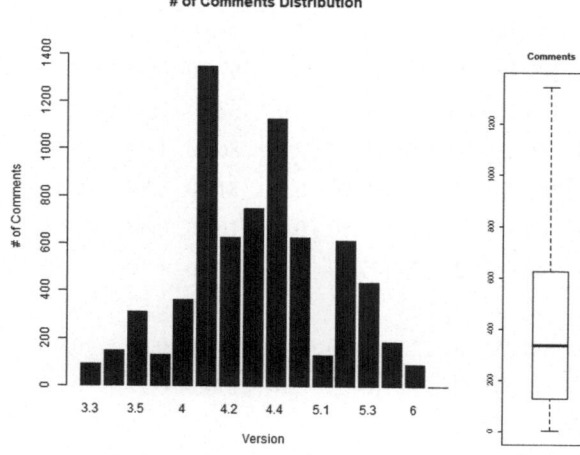

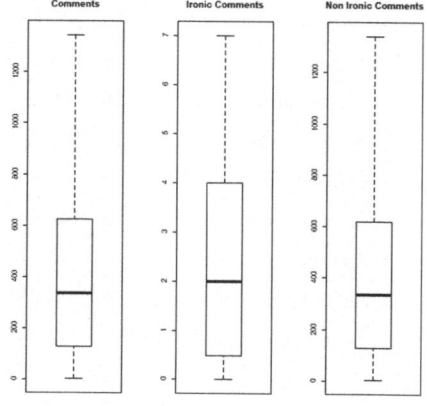

Fig. 1. NOF comments distribution   **Fig. 2.** Box plots for comments, ironic, non ironic

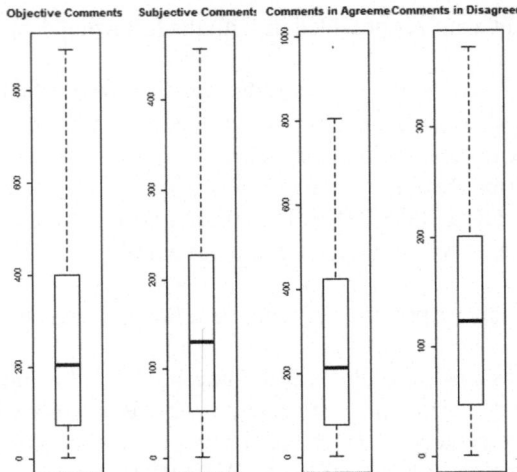

Fig. 3. Box plots for objective, subjective, agreement and disagreement comments

From Fig. 2 and Fig. 3 we can see that our means are being affected by low values of our population. This also becomes obvious by the descriptive statistics provided to Table 1 following.

Table 1. Discriptive analysis for variables.

Variable	n	mean	sd	median	min	max	skew	kyrtosis
Comments	16	435.00	390.32	336.50	2.0	1345.0	0.91	−0.26
Ironic	16	2.44	2.06	2.00	0.0	7.0	0.47	−0.78
NonIronic	16	432.56	389.11	334.50	2.0	1341.0	0.92	−0.24
Subjective	16	279.56	259.58	205.50	1.0	889.0	0.95	−0.20
Objective	16	155.44	131.34	131.00	1.0	456.0	0.83	−0.40
Agreement	16	299.94	282.60	212.50	1.0	973.0	0.99	−0.10
Disagreement	16	135.06	108.60	124.00	1.0	372.0	0.69	−0.67
Vader (Positive)	16	269.88	248.98	200.00	2.0	869.0	1.03	0.00
Vader (Neutral)	16	101.75	92.38	81.00	0.0	311.0	0.84	−0.45
Vader (Negative)	16	63.38	50.76	55.50	0.0	165.0	0.46	−1.13
MeaningCloud (Positive)	16	241.38	229.88	177.50	1.0	808.0	1.10	0.20
MeaningCloud (Neutral)	16	40.94	31.86	35.50	0.0	107.0	0.55	−0.87
MeaningCloud (Negative)	16	60.75	47.12	54.50	0.0	156.0	0.56	−0.93
MeaningCloud (No Sent.)	16	91.94	84.51	67.00	1.0	274.0	0.72	−0.80

Since this work studies the bugs reported to Libre Office per version, we decided not to proceed to data reduction since the versions that seem to act like outliers are provide valuable information. For example, the increased activity of comments in some of the 4.x versions is since 3.6 version was the version that followed the fork from Open Office after which redesign and refactor processes took place. We also chose to let versions with low concentration of comments, i.e. 6.1, to further investigate if this behavior is due to successful bug fixing or it was just a version with low bug tracking activity. In Table 1 you can see the descriptive analysis of the variables we gathered for the sentiment analysis using the tools described in Sect. 4 (Figs. 4 and 5).

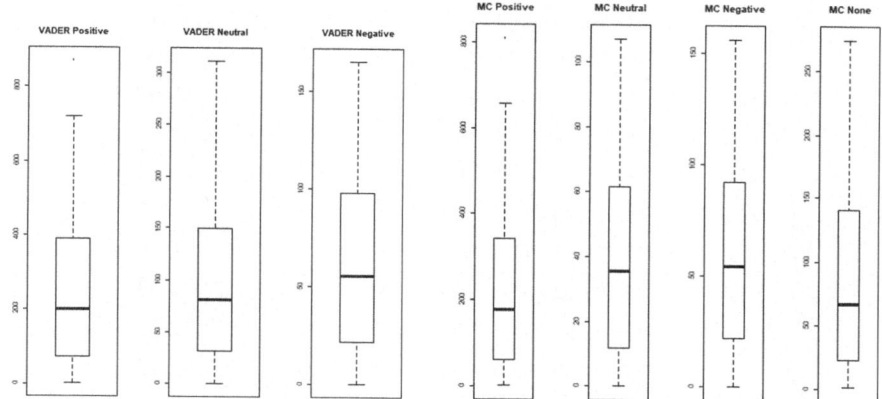

Fig. 4. Box plots for VADER sentiment analyzer

Fig. 5. Box plots for MeaningCloud sentiment analyzer

Finally, we conducted a descriptive analysis separately for the confidence variable per version of the Libre Office project.

Having concluded with the descriptive analysis of the chosen variables we then proceeded in studying our selected variables regarding their normality. Since the descriptive analysis is showing (Table 1) skewness with values around or bigger than 1 we have the indication that some of our variables might not follow the normal distribution. Therefore, we proceeded in applying the Shapiro-Wilk normality test in order to identify which variables follow the normal distribution and which do not from the results we are seeing that there are variables with p-value > 0.05 therefore parametric statistical analysis cannot be carried for them in this study since their data might not follow the normal distribution. Therefore, we will be conducting our statistical tests with the use of nonparametric tests and more specifically using the Spearman's Rank Correlation Coefficient (Table 3).

In Table 4 we have applied the Spearman's Rank Correlation to investigate possible statistical similarities in the distributions of VADER (Positive, Neutral, Negative) and Meaning Cloud (Positive, Neutral, Negative). Our results indicate that all three correlations are statistically significant (p-value < 0.05) and very strong correlated ($\rho > 0,9$).

Table 2. Descriptive analysis for confidence.

Version	n	mean	sd	median	min	max	skew	kyrtosis
v3.3	89	94.83	6.32	100	76	100	−0.75	−0.83
v3.4	145	95.03	6.26	100	76	100	−0.85	−0.52
v3.5	309	95.83	5.24	100	84	100	−0.87	−0.64
v3.6	129	96.05	5.26	100	86	100	−0.94	−0.62
v4.0	364	95.83	5.71	100	74	100	−1.06	−0.06
v4.1	1345	96.98	5.03	100	76	100	−1.41	0.53
v4.2	624	96.78	4.99	100	74	100	−1.48	1.47
v4.3	746	96.79	5.11	100	76	100	−1.42	0.96
v4.4	1126	97.05	4.83	100	83	100	−1.41	0.61
v5.0	624	96.73	4.84	100	73	100	−1.40	1.38
v5.1	128	96.02	4.94	100	76	100	−1.16	1.12
v5.2	615	96.66	5.05	100	73	100	−1.43	1.37
v5.3	435	96.65	5.23	100	84	100	−1.23	−0.06
v5.4	186	97.72	3.86	100	86	100	−1.57	1.63
v6.0	93	96.82	5.09	100	76	100	−1.67	2.52
v6.1	2	93.00	9.90	93	86	100	0.00	−2.75

Table 3. Shapiro-Wilk normality tests.

Variable	W	p-value
Comments	0.87727	0.0352
Ironic	0.90422	0.09393
NonIronic	0.87637	0.03408
Subjective	0.89079	0.05734
Obective	0.87399	0.03131
Agreement	0.86491	0.02275
Disagreement	0.90727	0.1051
VADER (Positive)	0.85854	0.01824
VADER (Neutral)	0.88603	0.04822
VADER (Negative)	0.92277	0.1869
MeaningCloud (Positive)	0.85216	0.01466
MeaningCloud (Neutral)	0.93041	0.2238
MeaningCloud (Negative)	0.92766	0.2238
MeaningCloud (No Sent.)	0.89165	0.05915

Table 4. Spearman's rank correlation for VADER versus MeaningCloud

	Vader POS	Vader NEU	Vader NEG
MC POS	p-value = 2.2e−16 ρ = 0.9617647		
MC NEU		p-value = 2.2e−16 ρ = 0.9588235	
MC NEG			p-value = 1.252e−10 ρ = 0.9757177

6 Discussion

In this work we are studying the sentiment in Open Source Software projects and more specifically in the process of bug reporting in the Libre Office project via its bug tracking platform, Bugzilla. We conducted our experiment in 16 major versions of the software and gathered the respective data (as analyzed in Sect. 4) for 740 bugs consisted of threaded discussions with 6960 comments in total. We proceeded in sentiment analysis of these comments using two different tools (Vader & Meaning Cloud) and statistically analyzed the results.

Our first goal in this investigation was to get a result on whether the sentiment analysis of comments in bug report is meaningful. Given that bug reporting is a technical process, usually made by technical oriented people (developers, and so forth) one might argue that the text of the reports could be standardized with technical language and therefore, possible lack of sentiment. In Table 2, showing the descriptive analysis of the confidence metric of the sentiment analysis across the versions of Libre Office, we can see that the mean is > 90% for all the versions. This gives us a first indicator that the confidence of the sentiment analysis (which is done with the MeaningCloud tool) is strong across all our data. In Table 4 we performed a nonparametric test to get results regarding the similarities for the positive, neutral and negative groups of comments between the two tools we have used. We see that the tests show significant similarities in the distributions of Positive, Neutral and Negative groups of comments for both Vader and Meaning Cloud.

From Table 1 we see that the number of ironic comments (variable Irony) are significantly fewer (min: 0, max: 7, mean: 2.44) than the non-ironic comments (min: 2, max: 1341, mean: 432,56). This seems to be intuitively logical if we consider that Bugzilla is a tool to which a community of Libre Office users (many of them voluntarily) report bugs. Having a closer look to random comments tagged as ironic from MeaningCloud we observed that such comments usually contain capitalized words and although the message does not seem to be ironic, however the tool scores them as such (i.e. *[...] however, it's happened on EVERY release since it started happening 2 years ago (I always move to the n+ 1.0.0 release when it comes out))*.

Looking at the subjectivity related variables we are observing similarly interesting comments as with the irony variable. Starting a bug report with a reference to ourselves is common in bug reporting (i.e. *I have experienced this think while I was doing that*).

However, in some cases if we strip this first-person reference in the beginning of the sentence, we are left with the bug itself (i.e. in the previous example: this is happening when someone does that). In the comments collected there are similar "misunderstandings" by the MeaningCloud which could be considered objective comments otherwise (i.e. *In order to limit the confusion between ProposedEasyHack and EasyHack and to make queries much easier **we are changing** ProposedEasyHack to NeedsDevEval. Thank you and apologies for the noise*).

7   Threats to Validity

We are conducting our experiment to Libre Office. This may be a threat to validity since including all of the components of the project would results in a much bigger dataset with a bigger variety of functionality and thus, variety in bugs.

A significant difficulty we came across during our work involves the domain-specific vocabulary used in the input text (i.e. bug reports) we analysed. This often may result to inaccurate ratings by the sentiment analyser, since most popular sentiment analysis tools have been trained on more generic texts (i.e. Social Media). However, this problem is not new; it constitutes a commonly recognized threat to the validity of sentiment analysis results, not only in the domain we are working on, but in any other specialized field.

Another difficulty lies in the fact that, besides specialized terminology, content like bug reports may often contain extensive use of "every-day" (i.e. Jargon) expressions, abbreviations and even emoticons (sequences of symbols representing an emotion). These expressions are typically very dynamic, changing constantly and are being frequently replaced by other expressions, following each time the popular trends. Thus, even training the sentiment analyser accordingly would unfortunately generate dubious results.

Moreover, attempting to perform sentiment analysis in informal text generated by numerous human users may often involve subjectivity and sarcasm, both of which lead to inaccurate sentiment measurements. A solution to the former problem may involve integrating a subjectivity classifier [19, 20]. The latter problem, on the other hand, is even more challenging and typically appears in online discussions (like e.g. bug reports), although it is not that frequent in reviews of products and services. There have been some initial investigations (e.g. [21] and [22]), although the topic has not been extensively studied yet.

Finally due to space limitation we decided to make this first attempt to run our experiment per version of the Libre Office. This means that our original dataset was "compressed" in groups and, inevitably some of the fields that would otherwise be part of the experiment were omitted. It is however our intention to extend the version in this direction as well, as mentioned in the future work section.

8   Conclusion and Future Work

In this work we investigated the semantic analysis of bugs reported to the Libre Office Open Source Software, a tool written in C++ programming language.

As future work, we plan to replicate our case study on projects written in various programming languages for both desktop and web development (i.e. java, php, and so forth). We also intent to include metrics related with both the structural properties of the source code of the Open Source project alongside with its quality and resilience characteristics.

Additionally, we would like to attempt to enrich the human based dataset (for the sentiment analysis part) by using, additionally to the text originated from the bug reports (which mainly tend to be technical reports), the user ratings (both score and the text of the review) that various FLOSS projects provide. This way we believe we will be capturing the sentiment of both the developers and the end users of the software.

Finally, it is our intention to study other sentiment analyzers found in literature and possibly compare and contrast their application to our dataset.

References

1. Raymond, E.S.: The Cathedral and the Bazaar, 1st edn. Tim O'Reilly (Ed.). O'Reilly & Associates, Inc., Sebastopol (1999)
2. Cerone, A., Fong, S., Shaikh, S.A.: Analysis of collaboration effectiveness and individuals' contribution in FLOSS communities (2012)
3. Liu, B.: Sentiment analysis and opinion mining. Synth. Lect. Hum. Lang. Technol. **5**(1), 1–167 (2012)
4. Taboada, M., Brooke, J., Tofiloski, M., Voll, K., Stede, M.: Lexicon-based methods for sentiment analysis. Comput. Linguist. **37**(2), 267–307 (2011)
5. Pang, B., Lee, L.: Opinion mining and sentiment analysis. Found. Trends Inf. Retriev. **2**(1–2), 1–135 (2008)
6. Kontopoulos, E., Berberidis, C., Dergiades, T., Bassiliades, N.: Ontology-based sentiment analysis of Twitter posts. Expert Syst. Appl. **40**(10), 4065–4074 (2013)
7. Guzman, E., Azócar, D., Li, Y.: Sentiment analysis of commit comments in GitHub: an empirical study. In: Proceedings of the 11th Working Conference on Mining Software Repositories, pp. 352–355. ACM, May 2014
8. Rousinopoulos, A.I., Robles, G., González-Barahona, J.M.: Sentiment analysis of free/open source developers: preliminary findings from a case study. Rev. Eletrôn. Sist. Inf. **13**(2) (2014). https://doi.org/10.5329/resi. ISSN 1677-3071
9. Garcia, D., Zanetti, M.S., Schweitzer, F.: The role of emotions in contributors activity: a case study on the GENTOO community. In: 2013 Third International Conference on Cloud and Green Computing (CGC), pp. 410–417. IEEE, September 2013
10. Ortu, M., Adams, B., Destefanis, G., Tourani, P., Marchesi, M., Tonelli, R.: Are bullies more productive? Empirical study of affectiveness vs. issue fixing time (2015)
11. Murgia, A., Tourani, P., Adams, B., Ortu, M.: Do developers feel emotions? An exploratory analysis of emotions in software artifacts. In: Proceedings of the 11th Working Conference on Mining Software Repositories, pp. 262–271. ACM, May 2014
12. Libre Office Project on Open Hub. https://www.openhub.net/p/libreoffice
13. Libre Office Bugzilla. https://bugs.documentfoundation.org/
14. Libre Office Bugzilla Fields Documentation. https://wiki.documentfoundation.org/QA/Bugzilla/Fields
15. VADER, Github Repository. https://github.com/cjhutto/vaderSentiment
16. MeaningCloud Tool. https://www.meaningcloud.com/

17. Hutto, C.J., Gilbert, E.E.: VADER: a parsimonious rule-based model for sentiment analysis of social media text. In: Eighth International Conference on Weblogs and Social Media (ICWSM 2014), Ann Arbor, MI, June 2014
18. Wohlin, C., Runeson, P., Host, M., Ohlsson, M.C., Regnell, B., Wesslen, A.: Experimentation in Software Engineering, 1st edn. Kluwer Academic Publishers, Boston/Dordrecht/London (2000)
19. Wiebe, J., Riloff, E.: Creating subjective and objective sentence classifiers from unannotated texts. In: Gelbukh, A. (ed.) CICLing 2005. LNCS, vol. 3406, pp. 486–497. Springer, Heidelberg (2005). https://doi.org/10.1007/978-3-540-30586-6_53
20. Barbosa, L., Feng, J.: Robust sentiment detection on Twitter from biased and noisy data. In: Proceedings of the 23rd International Conference on Computational Linguistics: Posters (COLING 2010) (2010)
21. González-Ibánez, R., Muresan, S., Wacholder, N.: Identifying sarcasm in Twitter: a closer look. In: Proceedings of the 49th Annual Meeting of the Association for Computational Linguistics: Human Language Technologies: short papers-vol. 2, pp. 581–586. Association for Computational Linguistics, June 2011
22. Riloff, E., Qadir, A., Surve, P., De Silva, L., Gilbert, N., Huang, R.: Sarcasm as contrast between a positive sentiment and negative situation. In: EMNLP, pp. 704–714 (2013)

Emotional Contagion in Open Software Collaborations

Luigi Benedicenti[(✉)] [iD]

University of New Brunswick, Fredericton, NB E3B 5A3, Canada
luigi.benedicenti@unb.ca

Abstract. Emotional contagion is a mechanism by which affect experienced by one person in a group is transmitted to others in the same group. When this happens, the group dynamic is influenced. This paper provides a method to analyze an Open Software project to determine the connection between emotional contagion and software production in such an environment, if any. The project change management database is mined to extract change comments in chronological order and by user id. Sentiment analysis is employed to determine affect in the change originating from each userid. File changes are tracked to link them together in the same areas, using a temporal and file locality principle. The correlation between affect and area is then used to prove or disprove whether or not emotional contagion influences open software production. Although in this paper the proposed method is applied to only one project, the method is general and can be reused for experimental validation.

Keywords: Emotional contagion · Software Engineering · Open software · Affect Theory

1 Introduction

The application of Affect Theory to Software Engineering is becoming relevant in modern software development that involves collaboration [1–3]. This is particularly relevant in environments in which collaboration occurs remotely, because it is a very well-known fact that online comments allow and sometimes encourage a less respectful engagement. Open Source Systems (OSS) are a particularly apt instance of this trend.

One particularly relevant aspect of Affect Theory in the case of OSS is Emotional Contagion. Emotional Contagion occurs when the affect inherent in a behavior, or in the case of online collaboration a message, is shared with others. The emotional content of the message can alter the affect associated with people who read the message, enacting a propagation of affect that resembles the spread of a contagion [4].

This paper describes a systematic method to analyze an OSS project to determine whether emotional contagion occurs. This method is relevant to validate the hypothesis that emotional contagion occurs in OSS projects, and to determine the point in time when this happens, to create the opportunity to assess how the emotional contagion may be affecting the development process and the quality of its output. The method presented

© IFIP International Federation for Information Processing 2020
Published by Springer Nature Switzerland AG 2020
V. Ivanov et al. (Eds.): OSS 2020, IFIP AICT 582, pp. 47–54, 2020.
https://doi.org/10.1007/978-3-030-47240-5_5

in this paper is sufficiently general to be repeatable, allowing for comparisons and meta-analyses that can quantify the degree of emotional contagion occurrence in OSS and support future analyses and the creation of new development processes.

2   Previous Work

There is a growing body of work on Affect Theory applied to Software Engineering [1–3]. The research in this area is an attempt to characterize the influence of affect on software production from different points of view. Although initially the work has concentrated on the correlation between affect and productivity or quality, gradually this focus has been expanded to a more holistic approach that involves attributes of the development process, qualities of the artifacts produced, and well-being of the participant in the process [4].

Some of the more recent focus of such research is in the agile requirements field [5]. Part of the author's own research has focused on optimization of requirements prioritization methods using decision methods to reduce the occurrence of emotional contagion [6]. In such a knowledge-intensive activity, cognitive trust plays an important role, but so does affective trust, which encompasses the social perspective of trust [3].

In distributed OSS development, interactions are more severely limited, as in most cases opportunities for face-to-face meetings and teleconferences are non-existent. All that remains is, at best, a combination of social networks, email lists, and comments in software repositories. In most cases, in fact, software repositories are all that links together each developer.

The constraints imposed by repository-based online interactions in turn limit the opportunities for cognitive trust, as the information on contributors only comes from a single source. However, given that the source contains a number of artifacts and documented interventions, cognitive trust is not severely impaired. On the other hand, affective trust can only be based on the tone of comments in the repository. This limited amount of information can lead to misunderstandings, creating an environment that is ripe for emotional contagion.

3   Method Workflow

The development of a method to analyze the influence of affect on OSS development, and in particular the presence of emotional contagion, is grounded in a series of principles and assumptions. These principles and assumptions help define the scope of the method, which is important in determining its applicability.

The method presented in this paper works under the assumption that face-to-face interactions among developers are severely limited or non-existent. This assumption is paramount to the definition of the data set for the analysis. Therefore, the applicability of this method on teams in, for example, a company, is not considered.

This method also relies on the locality principle, in that the influence of affect in standard working conditions is mitigated by time and by the location of each change. In other words, recent changes to a common artifact have higher impact than changes distributed over several days and artifacts. This is because most emotions and moods change relatively rapidly (over a period of hours) and the sense of ownership for a specific artifact lowers as the developer's focus shifts.

A further assumption is that there exists a repository that contains a documented evolution of the software being produced. An example of such a repository is GitHub [7].

Given these assumptions and principles, it appears reasonable to limit the scope of the method to situations that do not allow direct face-to-face interaction and that involve a relatively large number of developers. OSS development falls within this scope, and is what this paper focuses on.

The method's workflow, therefore, is as follows.

1. Retrieve data from a repository
2. Sort it by locality
3. Evaluate the affective content of the data
4. Determine if episodes of contagion exist

Each of these steps is described below. To illustrate the method, we will use an example that will be further discussed in the next section.

3.1 Retrieve Data from a Repository

Data retrieval from a repository is a relatively straightforward operation. To keep things as simple as possible, the retrieval makes use of generally available tools like a text editor and a spreadsheet, and adopts general file formats like text and comma-separated values. Even with these simplifications, the data retrieval procedure remains delicate and needs to be checked for accuracy.

The requirements for the choice of a repository is that it contain the information needed to perform an analysis of the affect of a contribution, in a chronological order, and with an indication of the artifacts that have been changed. At a minimum, therefore, the data needed for the analysis is the date of the contribution, the file(s) affected by the contribution, and a comment explaining the contributions made.

Our primary choice for a repository is GitHub [7]. This repository contains all the needed information, is free for most open software development, and it is very popular, although it might not be considered the most advanced software repository currently available. Another advantage is that the software program that allows interaction with the repository, Git, is a free and open source software available on most platforms, has been proven extensively, and is supported by a large community of developers [8].

To retrieve the data from the repository, we first clone it on the local machine. After that, we extract the information we need using Git commands. In particular, the log command can be used to obtain all change information with the exception of the files affected. For that, we need to use the diff command. Depending on the next steps, it might be necessary to further process the data into a format that is readable by the analytical tool. In our case, we have processed the data to create a comma-separated value list that is readable by Wolfram Mathematica, our choice of analytical too [9].

3.2 Sort It by Locality

The sorting by locality is accomplished in two ways. The sorting by date is simple, as we can access the change log and sort it accordingly. The sorting by file is a bit more complex, as a change item can encompass multiple files. In this case, we resort to creating an entry for each file, and then sorting them into separate bins, one per file. This results in a set of bins, one per file, each of which is sorted by date.

3.3 Evaluate the Affective Content of the Data

To evaluate the affective content of the data we make use of a sentiment analysis classifier. Because Mathematica provides an existing classifier, we adopted it, keeping in mind that this built-in classifier only works for English words.

Sentiment Analysis is an effective tool for the determination of affective content, but it has its limitations. Firstly, the classifier comes with a customizable level of confidence. Secondly, it is based on a machine learning algorithm that depends on the level of training that the classifier has received. Thirdly, sentiment analysis only provides an indication of the type of affect in a sentence (Positive, Neutral, or Negative); but not the intensity of the affect.

This can be problematic in many ways. The customizable level of confidence needs to be declared in any analysis to make it repeatable. Further, the use of a preset classifier means that it is not possible to control the type of training the classifier has received. Our reliance on a general-purpose sentiment analysis tool is a restriction of the usefulness of the method, because to make this repeatable we need to ensure that the same classifier is used on every data set.

Additionally, the classifier result is discrete. The provision of an intensity value for sentiment analysis is not available in most tools, which limits the level of refinement of the analysis.

3.4 Determine If Episodes of Contagion Exist

Numerous options exist for this determination. The simplest of these options is to generate a series of affect sequences, which are chronological representations of the changes classified by the sentiment analysis tool for a specific file, and then perform a manual inspection of each generated affect sequence.

Other possibilities include more sophisticated analyses, which involve a pattern recognition algorithm to detect a change in affect following a single change comment (i.e., influencing), or even convolutional analysis with kernels designed to highlight emotional contagion.

Our implementation of this stage is to translate the results of the affect sequence into numerical data: -1, 0, and 1 for positive, neutral and negative values respectively, then integrate these numerical sequences over time, and provide a graphical representation that can be further analyzed.

It is important to note, however, that the preceding data collection and processing is fully repeatable, and that should additional algorithms become available, it would be possible to apply the new algorithms to the same data sets without any loss of generality.

4   Example

The simple example we present in this section exemplifies the steps presented in the previous section. The example has been chosen purposely to make it as simple as possible, rather than as comprehensive as possible. Thus, this example has limited external validity.

Github has a large number of OSS projects. A small but representative one is opencv [10]. This open source computer vision library has received contributions from more than 1,000 contributors and has a change log with more than 27,000 entries. Although not the largest contribution by any means, it is sizeable enough to prove interesting for this example.

To acquire the original data set, we cloned the GitHub library in a local directory on the research machine (an iMac Pro with 64 GB of RAM and a 10-core Intel Xeon W processor). We then extracted the information we needed from the repository with a combination of Git commands, an example of which is below (see Fig. 1).

```
git clone https://github.com/opencv/opencv
git log --pretty=format:'"%an","%ad","%s","%b"' > ./GitlogFullDataset.csv
```

Fig. 1. GitHub commands for data set extraction (Sample).

Following the extraction, we prepared the data for ingestion by Mathematica, and then loaded it (see Fig. 2).

```
In[ ]:= dataSet = Import["/Users/lbenedic/Documents/test/opencv/GitlogFullDataset.csv",
        "CSV", "Numeric" → False]

Out[ ]= {{Alexander Alekhin, Fri Feb 7 11:22:23 2020 +0000,
         Merge pull request #16510 from andrey-golubev:unify_g_typed_kernel, },
         «27975», {Vadim Pisarevsky, Tue May 11 17:44:00 2010 +0000,
         'atomic bomb' commit. Reorganized OpenCV directory structure, }}

    large output    show less    show more    show all    set size limit...
```

Fig. 2. Importing the data into Mathematica.

Sentiment analysis and locality can be applied very simply, when the data is already binned; it is then possible to create an affect sequence (see Fig. 3).

The resulting sequence can be integrated and plotted. In Fig. 4, we show the first 500 data points in the affect sequence and highlight a few instances of emotional contagion found in it. The X axis is time, and the Y axis is the emotional accumulation level.

```
]:= sentimentSet = MapAt[classifyNoThreshold, dataSetWithDate, {All, {3, 4}}]
```

]=
{{Alexander Alekhin, 📅 Fri 7 Feb 2020 11:22:23 GMT-4. , Negative, Positive},
{Alexander Alekhin, 📅 Thu 6 Feb 2020 13:38:21 GMT-4. , Neutral, Positive}, ⬭ 27 974 ⬭,
{Vadim Pisarevsky, 📅 Tue 11 May 2010 17:44:00 GMT-4. , Negative, Positive}}

large output   show less   show more   show all   set size limit...

```
In[ ]:= sortedByDateSet = Sort[sentimentSet, #1[[2]] < #2[[2]] &]
```

]=
{{Vadim Pisarevsky, 📅 Tue 11 May 2010 17:44:00 GMT-4. , Negative, Positive},
{Vadim Pisarevsky, 📅 Wed 12 May 2010 07:33:21 GMT-4. , Negative, Positive},
⬭ 27 974 ⬭, {Alexander Alekhin, 📅 Fri 7 Feb 2020 11:22:23 GMT-4. , Negative, Positive}}

large output   show less   show more   show all   set size limit...

```
In[ ]:= emotionToNumber[z_] := z /. {"Negative" → -1, "Neutral" → 0, "Positive" → 1}
```

```
In[ ]:= sortedEmotionNumberSet = MapAt[emotionToNumber, sortedByDateSet, {All, {3, 4}}]
```

]=
{{Vadim Pisarevsky, 📅 Tue 11 May 2010 17:44:00 GMT-4. , -1, 1},
{Vadim Pisarevsky, 📅 Wed 12 May 2010 07:33:21 GMT-4. , -1, 1}, ⬭ 27 973 ⬭,
{Talamanov, Anatoliy, 📅 Thu 6 Feb 2020 18:12:38 GMT-4. , -1, 1},
{Alexander Alekhin, 📅 Fri 7 Feb 2020 11:22:23 GMT-4. , -1, 1}}

large output   show less   show more   show all   set size limit...

Fig. 3. Sentiment analysis, sorting, and affect sequence creation.

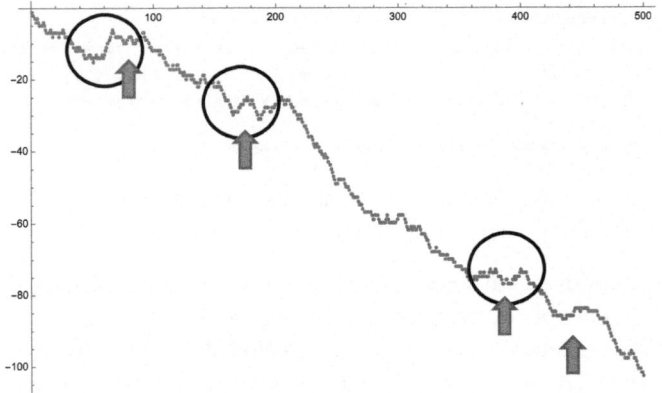

Fig. 4. Affect sequence plot.

5 Discussion

There are a number of restrictions that come from the adoption of principles and assumptions detailed in Sect. 3. These restrictions affect the applicability of the method and its validity.

In terms of applicability, not all repositories are suitable for this kind of analysis. Repositories where work is checked in by a very small group of developers are unsuitable for analysis because the assumption of low cognitive and affective trust is not true. In general, small communities are able to organize much more tightly, which leads to higher levels of cognitive and especially affective trust. This may happen in larger communities too (consider the level of affective trust offered to longstanding community contributors such as Linus Torvalds, for example), but it is much rarer.

As well, repositories where contributors all work in close proximity will not be suitable as the increased level of communication, especially for face-to-face communications, increases the level of affective trust. If this higher level of affective trust is verified, however, these repositories may be used to detect whether a higher level of affective trust changes the occurrences of emotional contagion.

In terms of validity, internal validity greatly depends on the availability of a large number of check-in information, and the ability of the developers to provide clear commentary with some sort of emotional content (either explicit or implied).

The more difficult form of validity, however, is external validity. Results from a single data set have no external validity and can only be representative of the repository they come from. To obtain a degree of external validity, many repetitions will be needed and a common format for the presentation and archival of results will be necessary. If this happens, then a distribution of results will be created that can be representative of a category of software development falling within the scope of this method.

6 Conclusions

This paper presented a method to determine whether emotional contagion occurs in OSS development. The method relies on the locality principle, and assumes that in-person interactions are limited, and that contributors rely on the comments in the repository to coordinate their work. The method works by analyzing the emotional content of developers comments in code check-ins to repositories. The example provided shows that the method is able to detect patterns in emotional content showing emotional contagion in a specific repository.

The method is limited in its scope and validity by the assumptions made in developing it. As well, its external validity cannot be assessed through a single example. Future work includes further streamlining of the data collection, a modified analysis method that relies on interpolated points to perform convolutional analyses in addition to the standard visual inspection, and a better structured manner to integrate the results from each local file bin.

References

1. Graziotin, D.: Towards a theory of affect and software developers' performance. Ph.D. Dissertation as defended on January 12, 2016 at the Faculty of Computer Science of the Free University of Bozen-Bolzano (2016)
2. Graziotin, D., Fagerholm, F., Wang, X., Abrahamsson, P.: On the unhappiness of software developers. In: Proceedings of the 21st International Conference on Evaluation and Assessment in Software Engineering (EASE 2017), pp. 324–333. ACM, New York (2017)
3. Calefato, F., Lanubile, F.: Affective trust as a predictor of successful collaboration in distributed software projects. In: Emotional Awareness in Software Engineering (SEmotion), IEEE/ACM International Workshop, pp. 3–5. IEEE (2016)
4. Graziotin, D., Fagerholm, F., Wang, X., Abrahamsson, P.: What happens when software developers are (un)happy. J. Syst. Softw. **140**, 32–47 (2018)
5. Ochodek, M., Kopczynska, S.: Perceived importance of agile requirements engineering practices–a survey. J. Syst. Softw. **143**, 29–43 (2018)
6. Alhubaishy, A., Benedicenti, L.: Toward a model of emotion influences on agile decision making. In: Proceedings of the 2nd International Workshop on Emotion Awareness in Software Engineering, pp. 48–51. IEEE Press (2017)
7. GitHub homepage. http://www.github.com. Accessed 02 Jan 2020
8. Git homepage. http://git-scm.com. Accessed 02 Jan 2020
9. Wolfram Mathematica homepage. http://www.wolfram.com. Accessed 02 Jan 2020
10. Opencv GitHub page. https://github.com/opencv/opencv. Accessed 02 Jan 2020

An Open Source Solution for Smart Contract-Based Parking Management

Nikolay Buldakov[1]($\boxtimes$), Timur Khalilev[1], Salvatore Distefano[2],
and Manuel Mazzara[1]

[1] Innopolis University, Innopolis, Russian Federation
{n.buldakov,t.khalilev,m.mazzara}@innopolis.ru
[2] University of Messina, Messina, Italy
sdistefano@unime.it

Abstract. This paper discusses an open-source solution for smart-parking in highly urbanized areas. We have conducted interviews with domain experts, defined user stories and proposed a system architecture with a case study. Our solution allows integration of independent owners of parking space into one unified system, that facilitates parking in a smart city. The adoption of such a system raises trust issues among the stakeholders involved in the management of the parking. In order to tackle such issues, we propose a smart contract-based solution encapsulating sensitive information, agreements and processes into transparent and distributed smart contracts.

1 Introduction

It has been estimated that, with the current trend, 60% of people will end up living in urban areas [24]. The increasing pace of the urbanization process made the management of city services more challenging Among such services transportation has strategic importance since the increase of population leads to increased traffic congestion and pollution, which significantly impacts on the citizens' lives.

Several approaches have been adopted to address these issues, and in 1970s some countries decided to widen the roads and create new ones. For example, in Hague, Netherlands, many canals were drained and covered for this purpose [1]. More modern approaches focus on the factors affecting congestion and operate on them. This trend has led to smart management of streetlights [18], and the introduction of payed parking lots and roundabouts.

Several studies have also shown that searching for a free parking stall drastically affects the traffic as vehicles spend some time going around looking for parking [12]. Smart parking solutions can, therefore, significantly improve traffic conditions.

There are several open issues and challenges on the current parking management. First of all, in every district, there are slots of unused land, owned either by

© IFIP International Federation for Information Processing 2020
Published by Springer Nature Switzerland AG 2020
V. Ivanov et al. (Eds.): OSS 2020, IFIP AICT 582, pp. 55–69, 2020.
https://doi.org/10.1007/978-3-030-47240-5_6

private or public entities. Providing easy means of renting out such properties for parking can simplify the process of creating new parking lots. Moreover, collection and aggregation of information about the current occupancy of all parking lots can significantly simplify the process of finding a free stall, thus decreasing traffic congestion.

Another significant issue is the trustworthiness of a potential parking system. With the current solutions on the market, such as [27] sensitive information is stored in a centralised way, which makes it vulnerable and simplifies malicious intrusion.

Finally, various parking providers need aggregation under one universal system, that will guarantee the unbiased treatment of all parking lots. Such strategy will allow potential seekers of parking lots to observe the entire situation in the city instead of seeing only partial information. This work aims at creating an open-source solution in order to tackle the aforementioned problems.

Problem Statement

Every city has governing authorities: city Hall, municipality and it can be divided up into districts with local councils. It can also be organized in terms of smart governance [25]. We will further refer to these authorities as an Administrator. The Administrator is responsible for authorising processes in the city. There are also people and companies possessing pieces of land that are suitable for parking. We refer to them as Landlords. A landlord can be a juridical person or a natural person; it does not matter for the system. A landlord wants to provide their land for parking in order to profit from parking fees. Besides, there are entities called Tenants. A tenant is a company or a person who will to whom a landlord rents out a subset of their parking land-based on some conditions.

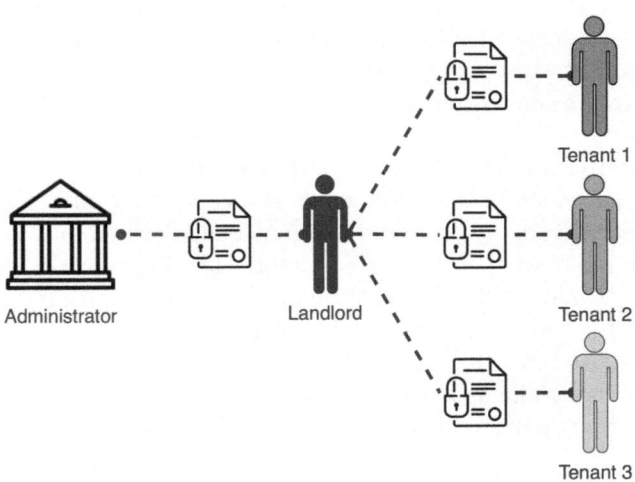

Fig. 1. Contracts' hierarchy

Now that all the roles are defined, one can observe the relations connection different roles in Fig. 1. In order to provide their land for parking, a landlord must first sign a contract with the administrator. There is always only one administrator for each area in the city. The process starting from a request to create such contract (from the landlord's side) up until its signing by both parties will be called *landlord registration*. This process involves checking whether the landlord is eligible for renting out their property, and negotiation on the details of the contract. Eventually, the signed contract contains such details as the tax which the landlord guarantees to pay, information about the registered land, duration of the contract and others. Both parties can further amend the contract, given that they are satisfied with the amendment.

The landlord, in turn, can not only provide their land for parking but also they can rent it out to tenants. In this case, the income from parking will not go directly to the landlord, however, they receive guaranteed rent payments and, possibly, a percentage from each parking transaction. Similarly, another contract preserved the agreement between a tenant and a landlord. This contract describes all the details of the rent. Such details are the duration of the contract, the rent fee, the frequency of payments, the landlord's share in each parking transaction and, most importantly, the exact borders of the area rented to each tenant. Again, all these details can be amended later, given the consensus of both parties.

Assumptions About Parking Lot

There is a set of preconditions, which this study assumes parking lots to hold. First of all, the parking areas have to be divided up into a set of spots. We refer to these spots as *parking stalls*. This partition can be represented by road marking. Moreover, there has to be a tracking device which will make the parking lot fully observable. A particular example can be a camera with an IoT-powered box, produced by Park Smart [2] as described in their patent [26]. This device has to run image processing algorithms in spot in order to tell at each moment which parking stalls are occupied (a particular implementation is provided in [5]) and what the plate numbers of the parked cars are. A visualisation of these assumptions can be found in Fig. 2.

A real example could be a mall with a big parking zone. Stalls can be partitioned among the businesses that are present in the mall. Big companies, like Ikea could rent the closest stalls in order to ease transportation of goods from the store to cars. Restaurants could want to offer reduced fares to their visitors for parking. There can also be stalls that are not rented by any company. In this case, a car parked there pays according to the pricing policy of the landlord, i.e. the mall.

Proposed Solution

The proposed solution presented in this paper aims to tackle the problems described above by using blockchain smart contracts. It assumes a set of roles to be present is the city. One of them is a city hall, that will be responsible for the deployment of the system as well as setting several policies following the local

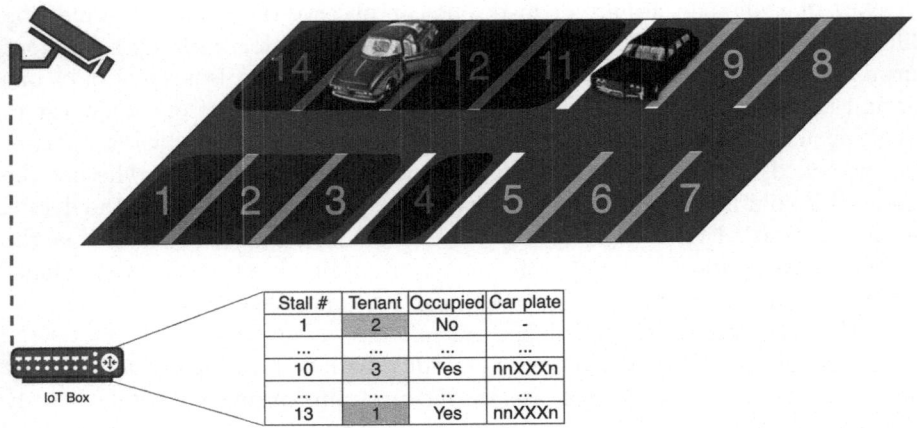

Fig. 2. Example of the assumed parking lot

legislation. Another role is a landlord who possesses a piece of land. A landlord can be a juridical person or a natural person, it does not matter for the system as long as their land satisfies the constraints describer in the Assumptions section. Such situations are common: a landlord does not want to maintain the land fully themselves and rents its parts out, in this case the proposed system allows a landlord to partition their land as they desire and set complex paying policies, that will ensure the agreed-upon conditions at the time of payment for parking. The last role is a driver interested in parking their car. They can observe free spots available at every parking lot and the pricing policy and choose the most suitable one. Payment is also covered conducted through the system, using a micro-payment channel, that makes it possible to enforce and guarantee the distribution of money among the landlords, the city hall and the tenants.

2   Related Work

By the time of writing, various smart parking systems exist in the literature, that focus on various aspects of parking. In principle, we can divide them into two groups: centralized solutions and decentralised solutions.

Centralized Solutions

There is a garden variety of solutions present both in the market and research, which attempt to prove a framework to manage smart parking. However, the major drawback of most of them is their centralised nature. Many of them rely on a particular supreme entity, their "source of truth". In [17] a parking system is proposed that relies on IoT devices and exchanges data by means of TCP/IP protocol. However, the application resides on only one server, that makes it vulnerable to issues with security, trustability and single point of failure.

Decentralized Solutions

Other works propose architectures that utilise the blockchain solutions as their backbone. All centralised solutions share a common set of problems that make them undesirable for practical use. The most important of such issues is trustworthiness. All participants of such systems have to rely on a particular entity, that will possess the power of accessing, chaining and removing their data, with no guarantee at the time of signing an agreement or registering that the owner of the system will obey to the promised rules. Lack of transparency is another significant shortcoming. When the implementation is not exposed to the end-users, they cannot validate that a particular solution is guaranteed to function in accordance with their needs and that it does not have any back- doors. Finally, considering the ongoing competition on any market, including parking, a centralised solution can be unfair to some participants if the owner is biased towards some companies. In [6] a system is proposed for incorporating blockchain into regular parking scenarios. This paper presents a layered architecture that standardizes the typical architecture of an integrated smart parking system. It also describes the major components of the system as well as provides an overview of possible work-flows of the solution. In this system, there are three major

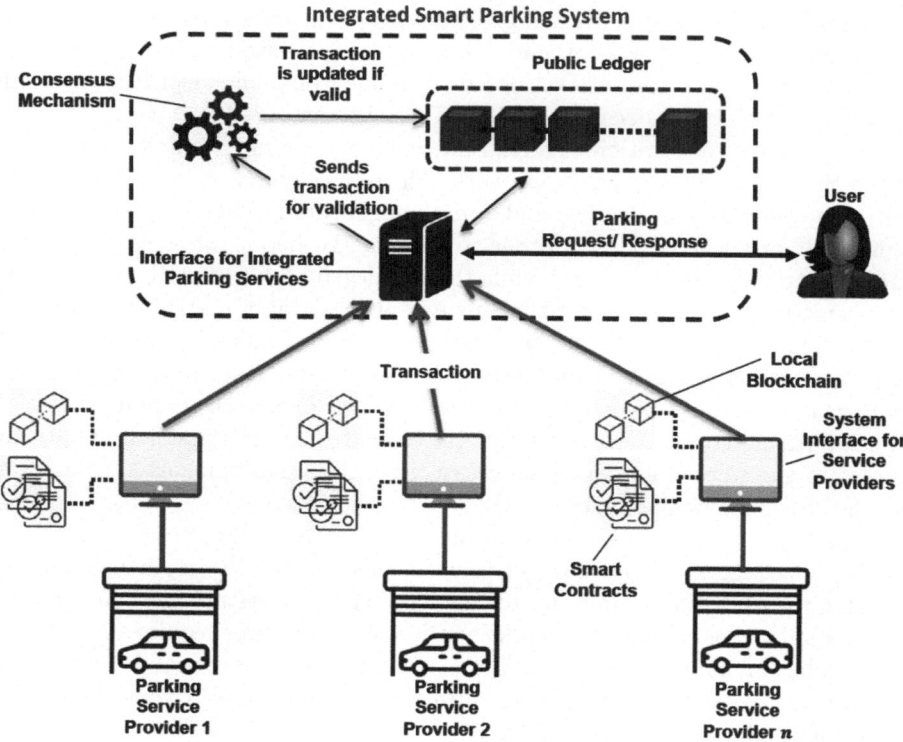

Fig. 3. Overview of integrated smart parking system, taken from [6]

participants: parking service provider, blockchain network, and user. The network enjoys the standard blockchain characteristics: a consensus algorithm, a shared public ledger, running a local copy of the ledger at each parking area. The overview schema of the system can be seen in Fig. 3. The architecture in the described solution consists of four layers: application layer, network layer, transaction layer, and physical layer. This layout of technologies can be considered the current state of the art and is adapted in the solution, proposed in this thesis work. Finally, the authors of the paper describe two main workflows supported by their system: 1. Search and Request of a parking spot and 2. Parking Provider Operations in the system. Even though the paper describes a useful basic concept, it supports a minimal number of scenarios, and thus, one cannot consider it as realistic.

Another blockchain-powered system is presented in [15]. It aims to take into account the process of setting up the parking space for the land-owner. For this they a landlord has to go through government validated process and procedures such as Land Registry and Government mandate external system. The external control is conducted by presenting another entity, named Oracle. In addition to that, they tackle the problem of leasing lands to the so-called contractors by distributing non-fungible tokens among them for a particular period. These tokens are issued to the certified landlords by the government. The critical advantage of this solution is that it describes in great details peculiarities related to how governing authorities and lease of land can be integrated into a blockchain system. However, many processes are supposed to happen off-chain, which is a serious limitation for the true decentralisation of the system.

[16] presents registration, search, rent, payment modules built by the means of the BCOS smart contracts framework. The main novelty of this system is the use of one-time pad mechanism and a group-signature mechanism together with a union of privileged nodes in order to conceal the details of each transaction and thus preserve users' privacy while the privileged nodes can still access users' data. One-time padding means that instead of receiving a real address for each transaction, users, instead, receive a newly generated address each time. This way, the users' addresses are not exposed. A group signature mechanism allows signing a transaction on behalf of a group, which hides the mapping between transactions and users. Other concepts implemented in this system are relatively similar to the works mentioned above, so the privacy mechanisms are the main beneficial feature of the paper.

Finally [11] introduces a gamification approach that simplifies the process of finding a parking lot. It encourages users to take part in the reporting process, by using the data history in order to calculate which places are more likely to be empty and by providing a framework that does not assume or require any particular installation of infrastructure. In this system, the concept of mobile crowdsensing plays a pivotal role. In order to ensure the involvement of drivers, the system assigns individual points to each driver for their collaboration. Examples of such collaborations are the installation of a special beacon or reporting on the number of free parking spaces in the street. Pedestrians can also participate by reporting through a mobile app. These points can be exchanged for free parking minutes. The authors claim their approach to bring a variety of benefits including a faster search for parking (leading to lower CO_2 emissions), easy deployment of the solution as it does not require much an existing infrastructure. Although their reasoning is valid, there is almost no information in the paper how the blockchain technology was incorporated.

Discussion

Although the works mentioned in this literature review present a variety of parking solutions, a significant limitation is in the fact that all of them lack flexibility for the end users. There is a variety of possible configurations of the system present, for example with a governing agency involved [15] or without [6]. However, none of them allows the community to choose what type of configuration they need. The same issue arises with the pricing policy. All papers consider some pricing policy present and even fluctuating depending on some factors as time and demand [6]. However, the details are omitted of how exactly the pricing is organized as well as how shares are distributed among different entities in the system. Finally, the topic of leasing or renting out the land is not thoroughly defined, in particular, how exactly it can be done through the system. In [15] a token system is proposed but the details of how exactly the partitioning of a land will be tackled in the system are not presented.

3   System Design

The objective of this work is to take into account drawbacks of the current centralised parking solutions, as well as limitations of the decentralised parking systems and to design and build a system that would address those issues. The system will utilise smart contracts and take into consideration some realistic requirements gathered by interviewing people from the industry.

Interviewing Industry Representatives

Any proper system-development commences with gathering important requirements of the system. Furthermore, as [13] states "one might use questionnaires or interviews to explore what problems members see as most important, how members place themselves in various classification schemes, etc." Thus, an interview has been conducted with a representative of Park Smart [2]. Park Smart is a smart parking solution company founded in Italy, Messina in 2014 and its main aim is to implement a software-based technology able to analyse, in real-time, the availability of space in in-street parking. The company has already been in the field for a few years. Therefore, was valuable to question them about their experience and to learn what are the main requirements for a parking system.

The interview has shown some essential aspects of the modern smart parking system and it has also revealed some common shortcomings of the existing system. For instance, if a company wants to use this solution for paid parking, they

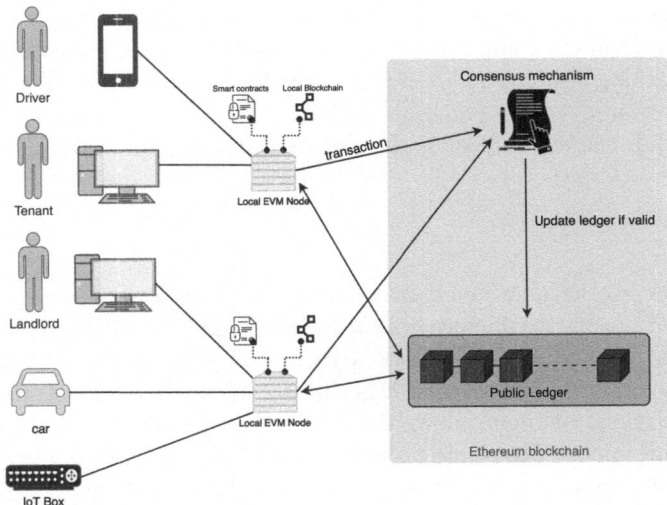

Fig. 4. System overview

can provide their end point to Park Smart in order to receive money through the system. This approach has inspired the idea of service providers in our system. Moreover, the interviewee has confirmed our concern about the centralisation of current systems. Park Smart itself has a patent about blockchain architecture for their system, however, it has not been implemented yet. Besides, the importance of flexible pricing policies has been highlighted. Companies have different rates at a different time of the day, therefore, this part of functionally is to be flexible. Finally, we found out what particular information about users and processes is needed for such a system, and this has affected our decisions of what to store in the proposed solution.

Product Backlog

In order to comprehend the needs of various user roles in the system, user stories have been gathered. The roles that we considered are the following: *Administrator, Landlord, Tenant, Driver,* and *Service Provider.*

The user stories have revealed a particular set of features that every role needed. Here we extract the key functionality from the user stories. First of all, both driver and parking providers (landlords and tenants) require a safe, trustworthy way of conducting payments in such a way that both parties are guaranteed that the amount of funds transferred is equivalent to the provided service. Besides, landlords and tenants want to ensure that both parties respect the renting contracts they make among them and that such contracts can be extended or amended over time. Parking providers also want the system to postulate equal treatment for all parking lots so that there are no privileged ones, promoted by that system. Finally, the administrative authority requires to have privileged over the system (bounded by conditions of contracts made with other parties).

In total, the backlog is constituted by more than 30 user stories, which were considered during the design and implementation phases.

System Design Overview

There are several participants in the system: *landlord, tenant, driver or car, IoT box* installed in each parking system, *administrator* and as a governing authority. The parking system consists of thin clients (such as a mobile or a web app), and each participant can access their part of functionality through the thin client. Every thin client is connected to a local EVM (Etherium Virtual Machine) node, which in turn is connected to the rest of the Etherium network. The local node has an instance of the ledger, shared by all nodes, and also hosts smart contracts.

Whenever a participant wants to perform an action (e.g. initiate parking or update number of free parking sports), the thin client tells the EVM to invoke a corresponding method of some smart contract. This action is performed in the form of a transaction on the blockchain. The blockchain network contains a public ledger and updates the public ledger with the valid transactions only. A consensus mechanism is used to verify the transactions. Once the new transaction is verified, the public ledger is updated, and the local copies of the ledger in each node are synchronised and all participants can observe the new state of the parking system. This overview is visualised in Fig. 4.

Smart Contracts

Smart contracts are the back-end part of the system. The logic is distributed among several contracts, which correspond to logical components of the system. Each contract encapsulates its sensitive data and controls access to its functions. This way, only authorised entities can perform actions in the system, even though the contracts are publicly exposed. Actors of the system deploy some of the contracts, other contracts are deployed automatically in existing contracts. The decision of whether a contract is deployed from the outside of the system or within contracts depends on two questions:

1. Is the nature of the contract static or dynamic?
2. Should the system validate and control the deployment process of a contract?

The nature of a contract matters because some contracts are deployed once and remain active in the system for a long time, whereas others are needed only for a short amount of time, and after their expiration, they cannot be used inside the system anymore. An example of a static contract could be the Parking System contract, which is deployed by the authorities and the life cycle of this contract defines the life cycle of the system itself. On the other hand, an example of a contract of a more dynamic nature could be a Payment Channel. Whenever a new parking process commences, the system automatically generates a payment channel. Such a contract has a short lifetime and cannot be reused. Thus the burden of its creation lies upon the shoulders of a static contract – Parking Provider.

The latter question tackles the problem of validation. Contracts can be inherited, and their behaviour can be changed by other parties. For example, the Parking Lot contract can be modified to surpass the tax obligation. That is why one requests the system to deploy such a contract. The system verifies all information related to the contract and only after that deploys it. For other contracts, on the contrary, extensions are allowed. For instance, Payment Policy defines a set of methods to be implemented to calculate the price of particular parking, however, it is up to a parking provider how exactly the price will be calculated. Thus, a parking provider is entitled to extend and deploy their payment policy and supply the address of this policy to the system.

Parking System

Parking System is the first contract to be deployed to launch the system. It is deployed by an administrative authority (e.g. a city hall) and it implements the main managing functionality of the system. The parking system contract is responsible for the registration of new parking lots and cars as well as for storing addresses of all other entities in the system. Whenever some request cannot be fulfilled automatically by the contract, it saves the request and pends administration's approval. Moreover, this contact provides a means of control and management of the whole system. Thus, the system cannot exists without this contract.

Parking Provider

Parking provider is an abstract contract that cannot be used on its own but should be extended in order to be used. It implements the logic of the parking process and stores information about what parking stalls it possesses and what cars are parked at the stalls. In other words, whenever a car wants to park, the code of this contract is used. In order to park a car sends funds to this contract. It also specifies a stall number and till what time it wants to be parked. The contract calculates the price, checks if the funds sent are sufficient and whether a parking stall is free and after that creates a payment channel. Optionally parking provider can also have a set a service providers, in this case a car can specify which service provider it is using and a fraction of the payments will go to the service provider.

Car

This contract preserves general information about a car. This information includes its plate number, account address of its owner and the rating of the car in the system. In addition to that, it stores information about parking. That includes whether the car is parked now or not, the address of the payment channel, parking history. If one needs some information about a car, this is the contract to address.

Parking Lot
Parking lot extends Parking Provider contract and is deployed by the parking system contracts at a request of a landlord and with approval of the administrator. This contract adds functionality to partition the parking lot among several tenants. In order to do so, a tenant creates a request to this contract. If the landlord approves the request, the contract creates a renting contract between the landlord and the tenant. It also contains general information about the parking lot, such as its rating, address and so on.

Tenant
Tenant also extends Parking Provider contract. Unlike Parking Lot contract, this contract does not need permission from the system to be deployed as it interacts only with a parking lot. A tenant can set its payment policy and it also stores the address of its contract with a parking lot.

Service Provider
Conceptually a service provider is a third-party entity that collaborates with a parking provider in order to place information about the parking provider's stall on their platform. Thus, the contract only facilitates the interaction between a service provider and a parking provider. It contains information about a service provider and about parking provider with whom it collaborates.

Renting Contract
Renting contract implements a relationship between a parking lot and a tenant in such a way that both parties are guaranteed that their agreement will be respected in the system. The contract is deployed when the parking lot contract approves registration of a new tenant. After that, the tenant reviews the contract and if conditions are satisfactory, the renting process begins. The contract also contains logic for penalties in case of delayed payment. Finally, it supports the introduction of amendments from both parties. In the case of mutual agreement, such amendments can modify the behaviour of the contract.

Payment Channel
Payment channel implements the logic for micropayments between two parties, in such a way that both parties are guaranteed to receive the promised funds. One party opens the contract and sends funds to it. After that, the funds are locked in the contract, and neither of the parties can access them. Micropayments are conducted off-chain, therefore, they are not part of this contract. Once the payment process is completed, the receiving party sends the last encrypted message to the contract, and the contract uses encryption algorithms to verify that the party is entitled to receive the funds. If that is the case, funds are sent to the receiver's address. The detailed description of the principles behind this contract can be found in Sect. 3.

Payment Policy
Payment policy is a protocol that defines two methods: get payment rate at a particular time and get a total price for parking given the start and the end time. It is up to parking providers to define their parking policies, depending on

their business goals. A particular implementation of this protocol is provided. It implements a policy that can have a specific rate depending on an hour and a day of the week.

Parking System Front-End

The front-end part of the parking system is a distributed application in the form of web, mobile or embedded software installed on mobile phones and computers of the Administrator, landlords, tenants and drivers as well as in IoT boxes at parking lots. In future they will be referred to as think clients. Every thin client provides a user interface or an API for interaction with the system. User interfaces are used by landlords, administrator, tenants and drivers. The API is used by the IoT box or a smart car. The front-end part is responsible for translating users' actions into requests to the smart contracts.

Communication Between the Smart Contracts and the Parking System

In order for the front-end distributed application to communicate with the EVM, there has to be a specific data-interchange format. This format is called JSON-RPC [14]. It is utilised through a JavaScript library called Web3.js[1], which allows us to interact with a local or remote Ethereum node using a HTTP or IPC connection [4]. As depicted in Fig. 5 Every front-end module of the distributed system communicates mostly with their own smart contract and this contract, in turn, is responsible for the interaction with the Parking System module and other modules.

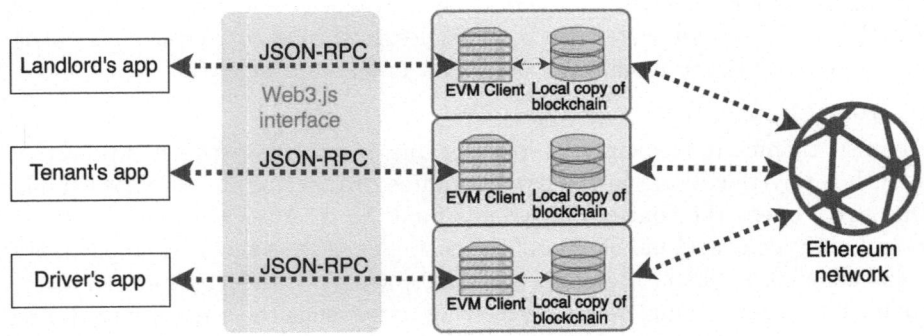

Fig. 5. Communication with the blockchain

Micro-payment Channel

Whenever a car gets parked at a parking lot, there is a mutual agreement between the parking lot and the car: the car receives a service and transfers money for

---

[1] https://github.com/ethereum/web3.js/.

parking. In a traditional system, the payment is conducted in advance for a particular period, [19]. Such system lacks trustworthiness, as a car has to blindly trust the parking provider, that the service will be provided sufficiently and will not be interrupted earlier, the parking provider, in turn, has to ensure that the car is not parked for longer than the paid period, this requires additional control that brings an additional cost. Finally, parking is not a discrete process, unlike the pricing policy in traditional parking systems, which results in drivers oftentimes paying more than they should.

This problem can be solved by implementing a micro-payment channel through a smart contract and direct signed messages. The high-level picture of such payment includes three steps:

1. Driver deploys a contract with locked funds of some amount that exceeds any possible parking period.
2. Driver emits messages directly to the service provider. The messages are the "microtransactions" containing how the amount is transferred. The parking lot can check the validity of the messages as they are signed by car.
3. After the parking process is over, the service provider can use the last message to retrieve the claimed amount of funds from the contract. The remained of the locked funds are sent back to the car.

It is essential to mention that in this scenario only steps 1 and 3 happen on the blockchain and the most intense process of micro-payments is conducted off-chain through a peer-to-peer communication [3]. Thus, the parties do not have to conduct costly blockchain transactions (gas in Etherium terminology [8]) for each

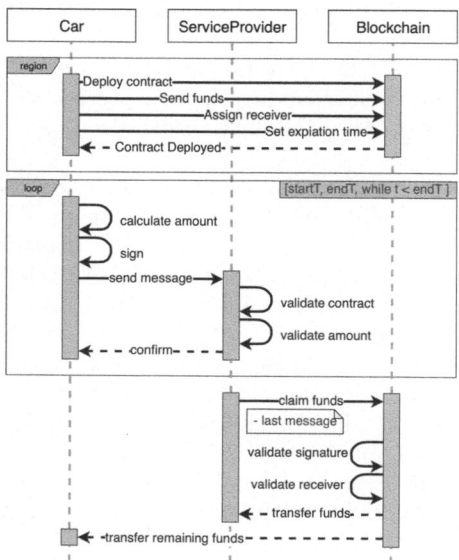

Fig. 6. Sequence diagram of micro-payments over blockchain

payment. Only two transactions are required: to deploy the contract (by the car) and to claim the end of the payment period (by the parking lot). Moreover, the transaction fee will be paid by the service provider, thus removing any additional fees from the car. This process is visualised in Fig. 6.

4 Conclusions

A significant amount of research has been conducted on smart parking. In this paper, we have examined some of the recent work related to this topic and propose a solution. Interviews have been conducted with domain experts, user stories defined and a system architecture has been proposed with a case study. Our solution allows independent owners of parking space to be integrated into one unified system, that facilitates the parking situation in a smart city. The utilization of such a system raises the issues of trust and transparency among several actors of the parking process. In order to tackle those, we propose a smart contract-based solution, that brings in trust by encapsulating sensitive relations and processes into transparent and distributed smart contracts. From the architecture point of view services and, in particular, microservices [7,9,22] and their composition, orchestration [20,23], reconfiguration [21] and recovery [10] have not been discussed. All these are open issues that need to be investigated in future.

References

1. Mvrdv unveils plans to reopen the hague's forgotten canals. https://www.designboom.com/architecture/mvrdv-hague-canals-reopen-09-19-2019/. Accessed 19 Sept 2019
2. Parksmart home page. https://www.parksmart.it. Accessed 30 Sept 2019
3. The peerjs library documentation. https://docs.peerjs.com. Accessed 1 Dec 2019
4. Web3.js documentation. https://web3js.readthedocs.io/en/v1.2.4/. Accessed 30 Sept 2019
5. Acharya, D., Yan, W., Khoshelham, K.: Real-time image-based parking occupancy detection using deep learning. In: Research@ Locate, pp. 33–40 (2018)
6. Ahmed, S., Rahman, M.S., Rahaman, M.S., et al.: A blockchain-based architecture for integrated smart parking systems. In: 2019 IEEE International Conference on Pervasive Computing and Communications Workshops (PerCom Workshops), pp. 177–182. IEEE (2019)
7. Bucchiarone, A., et al. (eds.): Microservices, Science and Engineering. Springer, Cham (2020). https://doi.org/10.1007/978-3-030-31646-4
8. Dannen, C.: Introducing Ethereum and Solidity. Springer, Berkeley (2017). https://doi.org/10.1007/978-1-4842-2535-6
9. Dragoni, N., et al.: Microservices: yesterday, today, and tomorrow. In: Mazzara, M., Meyer, B. (eds.) Present and Ulterior Software Engineering, pp. 195–216. Springer, Cham (2017). https://doi.org/10.1007/978-3-319-67425-4_12
10. Dragoni, N., Mazzara, M.: A formal semantics for the WS-BPEL recovery framework. In: Laneve, C., Su, J. (eds.) WS-FM 2009. LNCS, vol. 6194, pp. 92–109. Springer, Heidelberg (2010). https://doi.org/10.1007/978-3-642-14458-5_6

11. Ferreira, J.C., Martins, A.L., Gonçalves, F., Maia, R.: A blockchain and gamification approach for smart parking. In: Ferreira, J.C., Martins, A.L., Monteiro, V. (eds.) INTSYS 2018. LNICST, vol. 267, pp. 3–14. Springer, Cham (2019). https://doi.org/10.1007/978-3-030-14757-0_1
12. Giuffrè, T., Siniscalchi, S.M., Tesoriere, G.: A novel architecture of parking management for smart cities. Procedia Soc. Behav. Sci. **53**, 16–28 (2012)
13. Goguen, J.A., Linde, C.: Techniques for requirements elicitation. In: Proceedings of the IEEE International Symposium on Requirements Engineering, pp. 152–164. IEEE (1993)
14. JSON-RPC Working Group et al.: JSON-RPC 2.0 specification (2013)
15. Sabeela, J.H., Chandran, N.V., et al.: Parkchain: a blockchain powered parking solution for smart cities. Front. Blockchain **2**, 6 (2019)
16. Hu, J., He, D., Zhao, Q., Choo, K.-K.R.: Parking management: a blockchain-based privacy-preserving system. IEEE Consum. Electron. Mag. **8**(4), 45–49 (2019)
17. Khanna, A., Anand, R.: IoT based smart parking system. In: 2016 International Conference on Internet of Things and Applications (IOTA), pp. 266–270. IEEE (2016)
18. Lau, S.P., Merrett, G.V., Weddell, A.S., White, N.M.: A traffic-aware street lighting scheme for smart cities using autonomous networked sensors. Comput. Electr. Eng. **45**, 192–207 (2015)
19. Litman, T.: Parking pricing implementation guidelines how more efficient parking pricing can help solve parking and traffic problems, increase revenue, and achieve other planning objectives (2018)
20. Mazzara, M.: Towards Abstractions for Web Services Composition. Ph.D. thesis, University of Bologna (2006)
21. Mazzara, M., Abouzaid, F., Dragoni, N., Bhattacharyya, A.: Design, modelling and analysis of a workflow reconfiguration. In: International Workshop on Petri Nets and Software Engineering, pp. 10–24 (2011)
22. Mazzara, M., Bucchiarone, A., Dragoni, N., Rivera, V.: Size matters: microservices research and applications. Microservices, pp. 29–42. Springer, Cham (2020). https://doi.org/10.1007/978-3-030-31646-4_2
23. Mazzara, M., Govoni, S.: A case study of web services orchestration. In: Jacquet, J.-M., Picco, G.P. (eds.) COORDINATION 2005. LNCS, vol. 3454, pp. 1–16. Springer, Heidelberg (2005). https://doi.org/10.1007/11417019_1
24. McGranahan, G., Satterthwaite, D.: Urbanisation Concepts and Trends. IIED, London (2014)
25. Meijer, A., Bolívar, M.P.R.: Governing the smart city: a review of the literature on smart urban governance. Int. Rev. Adm. Sci. **82**(2), 392–408 (2016)
26. Smart, B.J., et al.: Allocating an area to a vehicle, 20 November 2014. US Patent App. 14/344,947
27. Yang, J., Portilla, J., Riesgo, T.: Smart parking service based on wireless sensor networks. In: IECON 2012–38th Annual Conference on IEEE Industrial Electronics Society, pp. 6029–6034. IEEE (2012)

Using Open Source Libraries
in the Development of Control Systems
Based on Machine Vision

Vasiliy N. Kruglov$^{(\boxtimes)}$

Ural Federal University, Yekaterinburg, Russia
v.kruglov@mail.ru

Abstract. The possibility of the boundaries detection in the images of crushed ore particles using a convolutional neural network is analyzed. The structure of the neural network is given. The construction of training and test datasets of ore particle images is described. Various modifications of the underlying neural network have been investigated. Experimental results are presented.

Keywords: Grain-size analysis · Machine vision · Object boundaries detection · Convolutional neural network · Open source libraries · Machine learning

1 Introduction

When processing crushed ore mass at ore mining and processing enterprises, one of the main indicators of the quality of work of both equipment and personnel is the assessment of the size of the crushed material at each stage of the technological process. This is due to the need to reduce material and energy costs for the production of a product unit manufactured by the plant: concentrate, sinter or pellets.

The traditional approach to the problem of evaluating the size of crushed material is manual sampling with subsequent sieving with sieves of various sizes. The determination of the grain-size distribution of the crushed material in this way entails a number of negative factors:

- the complexity of the measurement process;
- the inability to conduct objective measurements with sufficient frequency;
- the human error factor at the stages of both data collection and processing.

These shortcomings do not allow you to quickly adjust the performance of crushing equipment. The need for obtaining data on the coarseness of crushed material in real time necessitated the creation of devices for in situ assessment of parameters such as the grain-size distribution of ore particles, weight-average ore particle and the percentage of the targeted class. The machine vision systems

© IFIP International Federation for Information Processing 2020
Published by Springer Nature Switzerland AG 2020
V. Ivanov et al. (Eds.): OSS 2020, IFIP AICT 582, pp. 70–77, 2020.
https://doi.org/10.1007/978-3-030-47240-5_7

are able to provide such functionality. They have high reliability, performance and accuracy in determining the geometric dimensions of ore particles. At the moment, several vision systems have been developed and implemented for the operational control of the particle size distribution of crushed or granular material. In [9], a brief description and comparative analysis of such systems as: SPLIT, WIPFRAG, FRAGSCAN, CIAS, IPACS, TUCIPS is given.

Common to the algorithmic part of these systems is the stage of dividing the entire image of the crushed ore mass into fragments corresponding to individual particles with the subsequent determination of their geometric sizes. Such a segmentation procedure can be solved by different approaches, one of which is to highlight the boundaries between fragments of images of ore particles. Classical methods for borders highlighting based on the assessment of changes in brightness of neighboring pixels, which implies the use of mathematical algorithms based on differentiation [4,8]. Figure 1 shows typical images of crushed ore moving on a conveyor belt.

Fig. 1. Examples of crushed ore images

Algorithms from the OpenCV library, the Sobel and Canny filters in particular, used to detect borders on the presented images, have identified many false boundaries and cannot be used in practice.

This paper presents the results of recognizing the boundaries of images of stones based on a neural network. This approach has been less studied and described in the literature, however, it has recently acquired great significance in connection with its versatility and continues to actively develop with the increasing of a hardware performance [3,5].

2 Main Part

To build a neural network and apply machine learning methods, a sample of images of crushed ore stones in gray scale was formed. The recognition of the boundaries of the ore particles must be performed for stones of arbitrary size and configuration on a video frame with ratio 768×576 pixels.

To solve this problem with the help of neural networks, it is necessary to determine what type of neural network to use, what will be the input information and what result we want to get as the output of the neural network processing. Analysis of literary sources showed that convolutional neural networks are the most promising when processing images [3, 5–7].

Convolutional neural network is a special architecture of artificial neural networks aimed at efficient pattern recognition. This architecture manages to recognize objects in images much more accurately, since, unlike the multilayer perceptron, two-dimensional image topology is considered. At the same time, convolutional networks are resistant to small displacements, zooming, and rotation of objects in the input images. It is this type of neural network that will be used in constructing a model for recognizing boundary points of fragments of stone images.

Algorithms for extracting the boundaries of regions as source data use image regions having sizes of 3×3 or 5×5. If the algorithm provides for integration operations, then the window size increases. An analysis of the subject area for which this neural network is designed (a cascade of secondary and fine ore crushing) showed: for images of 768×576 pixels and visible images of ore pieces, it is preferable to analyze fragments with dimensions of 50×50 pixels.

Thus, the input data for constructing the boundaries of stones areas will be an array of images consisting of $(768 - 50)*(576 - 50) = 377668$ halftone fragments measuring 50×50 pixels. In each of these fragments, the central point either belongs to the boundary of the regions or not. Based on this assumption, all images can be divided into two classes.

To mark the images into classes on the source images, the borders of the stones were drawn using a red line with a width of 5 pixels. This procedure was performed manually with the Microsoft Paint program. An example of the original and marked image is shown in Fig. 2.

(a) Original image   (b) Marked image

Fig. 2. Image processing (Color figure online)

Then Python script was a projected, which processed the original image to highlight 50×50 pixels fragments and based on the markup image sorted fragments into classes preserving them in different directories To write the scripts, we used the Python 3 programming language and the Jupyter Notebook IDE. Thus, two data samples were obtained: training dataset and test dataset for the assessment of the network accuracy.

As noted above, the architecture of the neural network was built on a convolutional principle. The structure of the basic network architecture is shown in Fig. 3 [7].

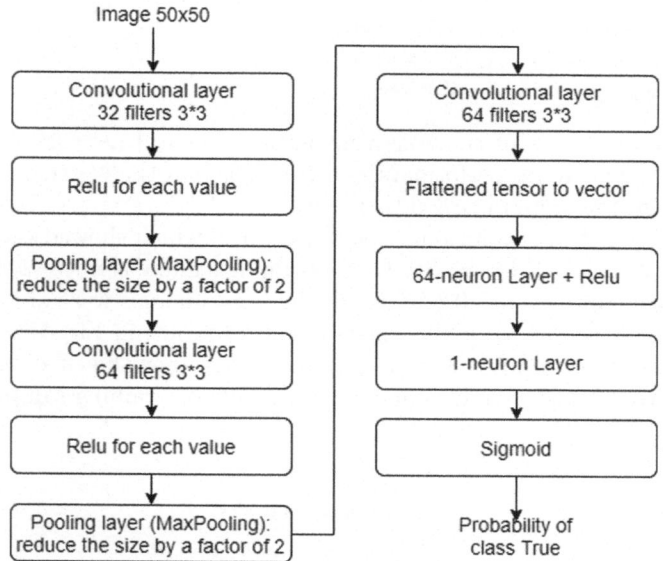

Fig. 3. Basic convolution network architecture

The network includes an input layer in the format of the tensor $50 \times 50 \times 1$. The following are several convolutional and pooling layers. After that, the network unfolds in one fully connected layer, the outputs of which converge into one neuron, to which the activation function, the sigmoid, will be applied. At the output, we obtain the probability that the center point of the input fragment belongs to the "boundary point" class.

The Keras open source library was used to develop and train a convolutional neural network [1, 2, 6, 10].

The basic convolutional neural network was trained with the following parameters:

- 10 epoch;
- error - binary cross-entropy;

– quality metric - accuracy (percentage of correct answers);
– optimization algorithm - RMSprop.

The accuracy on the reference data set provided by the base model is 90.8%. In order to improve the accuracy of predictions, a script was written that trains models on several configurations, and also checks the quality of the model on a test dataset.

To improve the accuracy of the predictions of the convolutional neural network, the following parameters were varied with respect to the base model:

– increasing the number of layers: +1 convolutional +1 pooling;
– increasing of the number of filters: +32 in each layer;
– increasing the size of the filter up to 5*5;
– increasing the number of epochs up to 30;
– decreasing in the number of layers.

These modifications of the base convolutional neural network did not lead to an improvement in its performance - all models had the worst quality on the test sample (in the region of 88–90% accuracy).

The model of the convolutional neural network, which showed the best quality, was the base model. Its quality in the training sample is estimated at 90.8%, and in the test sample - at 83%. None of the other models were able to surpass this figure. Data on accuracy and epoch error are shown in Fig. 4 and 5.

If you continue to study for more than 10 epochs, then the effect of retraining occurs: the error drops, and accuracy increases only on training samples, but not on test ones.

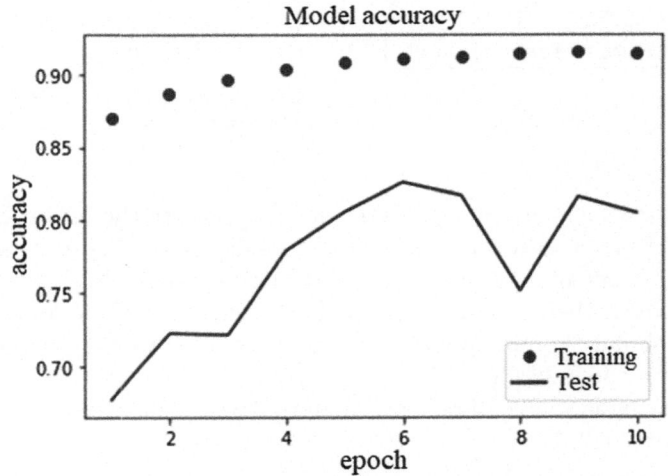

Fig. 4. The dependence of the accuracy on the training and test datasets from the training epochs

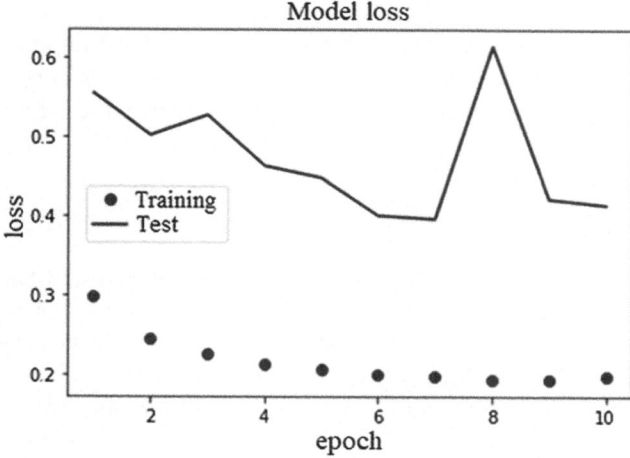

Fig. 5. The dependence of the error on the training and test datasets from the training epochs

Fig. 6. Images of crushed ore particles with boundaries detected by a neural network

Figure 6 shows examples of images with neural network boundaries. As you can see from the images, not all the borders are closed. The boundary discontinuities are too large to be closed using morphological operations on binary masks; however, the use of the "watershed" algorithm [8] will reduce the identification error of the boundary points.

3   Conclusion

In this work, a convolutional neural network was developed and tested to recognize boundaries on images of crushed ore stones. For the task of constructing a convolutional neural network model, two data samples were generated: training and test dataset. When building the model, the basic version of the convolutional neural network structure was implemented. In order to improve the quality of model recognition, a configuration of various models was devised with deviations from the basic architecture. An algorithm for training and searching for the best model by enumerating configurations was implemented.

In the course of the research, it was found that the basic model has the best quality for recognizing boundary points. It shows the accuracy of the predictions for the targeted class at 83%.

Based on the drawn borders on the test images, it can be concluded that the convolutional neural network is able to correctly identify the boundary points with a high probability. It rarely makes mistakes for cases when there is no boundary (false positive), but often makes mistakes when recognizing real boundary points (false negative). The boundary breaks are too large to be closed using morphological operations on binary masks, however, the use of the "watershed" algorithm will reduce the identification error for boundary points.

Funding. The work was performed under state contract 3170ГС1/48564, grant from the FASIE.

References

1. Keras: The python deep learning library. https://keras.io/. Accessed 14 Jan 2020
2. Chollet, F.: Deep Learning with Python, 1st edn. Manning Publications Co., New York (2017)
3. Flach, P.: Machine Learning: The Art and Science of Algorithms that Make Sense of Data. Cambridge University Press, Cambridge (2012)
4. Gonzalez, R.C., Woods, R.E.: Digital Image Processing, 3rd edn. Prentice-Hall Inc., Upper Saddle River (2006)
5. Gron, A.: Hands-On Machine Learning with Scikit-Learn and TensorFlow: Concepts, Tools, and Techniques to Build Intelligent Systems, 1st edn. O'Reilly Media Inc., Newton (2017)
6. Gulli, A., Pal, S.: Deep learning with Keras: Implement Neural Networks with Keras on Theano and TensorFlow. Packt Publishing, Birmingham (2017)
7. Saha, S.: Comprehensive guide to convolutional neural networks - the eli5 way. https://towardsdatascience.com/a-comprehensive-guide-to-convolutional-neural-networks-the-eli5-way-3bd2b1164a53. Accessed 12 Jan 2020

8. Sonka, M., Hlavac, V., Boyle, R.: Image Processing, Analysis and Machine Vision, 2nd edn. CL Engineering, Ludhiana (1998)
9. Thurley, M.J., Ng, K.C.: Identifying, visualizing, and comparing regions in irregularly spaced 3D surface data. Comput. Vis. Image Underst. **98**(2), 239–270 (2005). https://doi.org/10.1016/j.cviu.2003.12.002
10. VanderPlas, J.: Python Data Science Handbook: Essential Tools for Working with Data, 1st edn. O'Reilly Media Inc., Newton (2016)

An Empirical Analysis
of the Maintainability Evolution
# of Open Source Systems

Gerta Kapllani, Ilya Khomyakov, Ruzilya Mirgalimova, and Alberto Sillitti[✉]

Innopolis University, Innopolis, Russian Federation
g.kapllani@innopolis.university,
{i.khomyakov,r.mirgalimova,a.sillitti}@innopolis.ru

Abstract. Maintainability is a key factor for the evolution of an open source system due to the highly distributed development teams that contribute to many projects. In the literature there are a number of different approaches that has been developed to evaluate the maintainability of a product but almost each method has been developed in an independent way without leveraging on the existing work and with almost no independent evaluation of the performance of the models. In most of the cases, the models are only validated through a limited set of projects only by the people that propose the specific approach. This paper is a first step towards a different direction focusing on the independent application of the existing models to popular open source projects.

Keywords: Maintainability · Empirical software engineering · Software evolution

1 Introduction

Maintainability is one of the most important features of software systems [10]. Though, defining maintainability has been a topic of interest for many researchers over decades. A software application might fulfils all the traditional requirements and yet be of little use if the cost of maintaining it is too high. For such reason, maintainability has been considered one of the requirements that must be imposed to software products [3]. Several authors have investigated the models and metrics used for the best estimation of maintainability also known as prediction or software maintainability prediction models. Traditional models based on their accuracy of prediction have been represented by Shafiabady et al. [22]. Moreover, an analysis of the evolution of software maintenance models over the four past decades has been introduced by Lenarduzzi et al. [14]. Defining the right tools on code analysis to perform research studies on software maintenance prediction is also a crucial aspect and has received much attention in the last few years [18]. Recent papers [2,5,11,15,19] have identified tools that are available and can be used to apply maintenance models published in the studies in this area.

© IFIP International Federation for Information Processing 2020
Published by Springer Nature Switzerland AG 2020
V. Ivanov et al. (Eds.): OSS 2020, IFIP AICT 582, pp. 78–86, 2020.
https://doi.org/10.1007/978-3-030-47240-5_8

The paper is organized as follows: Sect. 2 briefly analyzes the state of the art; Sect. 3 introduces our investigation; Sects. 4 and 5 present and discuss the results; finally, Sect. 6 draws the conclusions and introduces future work.

2   Related Research

During the years, several models have been proposed for measuring the maintainability of software. A considerable amount of studies have employed different models and techniques for predicting software maintenance using basic metrics and models: McCall's model in 1976 [20], Barry Boehm's quality model presented in 1978 [1], Sneed-Mercy Model in 1985 [23], Li-Henry Model in 1993 [16], Marcela Genero Model in 2004 [8]. Later, slightly different techniques were used from simple statistical models such as regression [25] to machine learning [7,24], and deep learning [9,13]. To predict maintainability of software, different metrics have been proposed in literature. Among the large variety of metrics, the most used ones are the OO metrics depth of the inheritance tree (DIT), response for a class (RFC), number of children (NOC), coupling between objects (CBO), lack of cohesion of methods (LCOM), and weighted method per class (WMC) [4]. Other metrics are popular, such as: number of methods (NOM), lines of code (LOC), number of semicolons in a class (SIZE1), number of properties (SIZE2), and CHANGE metrics as dependent variable to predict software maintainability by calculating the changed number of lines in the class during maintenance process [16]. Investigating different primary studies and secondary studies from the literature, we have found out that even if there are a number of different methods to predict maintainability, almost all the studies built their models from scratch and do not extend existing ones.

3   Our Investigation

We decided to analyse software maintainability change following the approach proposed in [17] for the jEdit open source project using the JHawk tool to get useful insights. jEdit is an open source project developed in Java available in SourceForge[1] with all existing versions with the related source code. We analyzed the application starting from version 3.2 up to version 5.5, a total of 12 versions. There are in total 41 versions but they have almost no differences compared to the selected ones. A significant difference compared to [17] is that we rely on general information outside the source code to examine and find potential relation between version numbers and changes to maintainability during the evolution of the project.

JHawk is Java-based open source framework which can analyse source code while performing static analysis generating graphical form results. It takes Java code as input and generates code metrics. We are interested in gathering features such as average cyclomatic complexity (CC), number of lines of code (LOC), and maintainability index (MI).

---

[1] https://sourceforge.net/projects/jedit/files/jedit/.

3.1 Collected Metrics

In this study we have focused on the following metrics:

- **Cyclomatic Complexity (CC):** it is used to measure the complexity of a piece of code from the point of view of the possible execution paths. In particular, it measures the independent path through a source code as a proxy of its complexity. The higher the value, the more complex is the system and this fact results in difficulty to maintain the code. We have measured the average of CC which is stated by McCabe to be cyclomatic complexity per function in a file and is calculated as the sum of the CC of all function definitions, divided by the number of function definitions in the file.
- **Lines of code (LOC):** it is used to measure the size of a software by counting the number of lines included in a program. There are multiple ways to count the lines of code but in this work we focus on the simplest definition that consider the physical lines of code of the source files.
- **Maintainability index (MI):** it is based on Halstead Volume (HV) metric, the cyclomatic complexity (CC) metric, and the average number of lines per code per module (LOC) metric. The higher this value, the more maintainable the software results [21]. If MI of software increases it means that the software can be maintained easily, otherwise if it decreases the degree of difficulty to maintain the software is high [12]. Values of MI index as follows:
  - MI < 65: difficult to maintain
  - MI 65–85: maintainable
  - MI > 85: good maintainability

We have to highlight the fact that in JHawk MI is reported in two forms, one that takes into account comments of the program and ones which does not. In our database we have reported both of them, but the final result of the graphs below do contain only the ones with comments. It is stated that the reason that MI formula with comments does exist is because the formula to find comments is not standardized and comments are considered to be subjective from developer to developer and do vary from project to project. In such cases it is recommended to use the MI without comments as reported from official source development of the JHawk tool. However, we think that comments are an important part of the source code, therefore we considered them in our study.

4 Results

In Fig. 1 we present the results achieved from data collection of MI for each version of jEdit, as we have mentioned in the above sections.

We can notice that from version 3.2 to 4.2 there is a constant value of MI of about 130. Upon release of version 4.0, there is a tremendous decrease of MI to about 58. Then, with next releases up to version 5.3.0, there seem to be a slight increase about 68. The last versions have a value of MI up to 144.

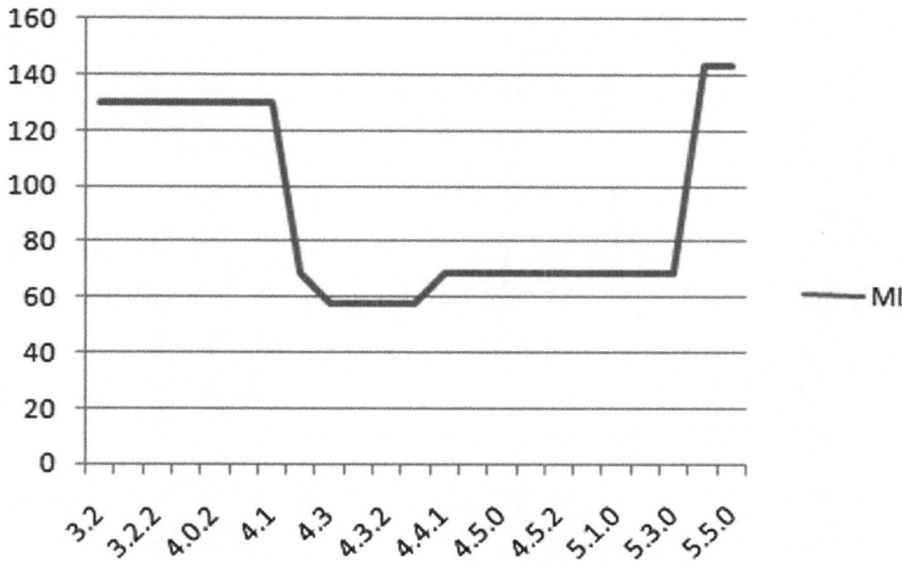

Fig. 1. MI evolution.

We also have to consider the other two features collected (Fig. 2, 3 and 4). It is of high relevance to mention that the value of the average CC has been higher for versions of low MI index in other words for early releases. A slightly different trend follows the LOC metric. For higher values of LOC there is also a higher value for MI and vice versa. We can notice the trend of size metric for each version. For an increase of size from versions 4.3 to 4.4.1, there is a decrease in MI in these versions. For a decrease of size in versions 4.5 to 5.3, there is a slight increase of MI. Surprisingly, for an increase of size in 5.4.0 and 5.5.0, there is also an increase in MI.

From Fig. 3 and 4, we can state that for an increase in CC from version 4.2 to 4.3, there is a decrease in MI. Moreover, for a decrease in CC from versions 4.3.3 to 4.4.1, there is an increase in MI. The same result follows 5.3.0 to 5.4.0 with a decrease in CC and an increase in MI. These outputs clearly highlight the fact that a high value of CC means more complexity added to the system which increases the degree of difficulty for the system to be maintained.

5   Discussion

In this section we are going to investigate further the results obtained from previous section. We are going to test hypothesis of possible correlation of LOC, CC with MI and LOC with CC. Since the MI is defined as a function that include LOC and CC as independent variables, we expect that MI is highly correlated to them but we want to investigate how strong is the effect of such variables on the overall values of the MI.

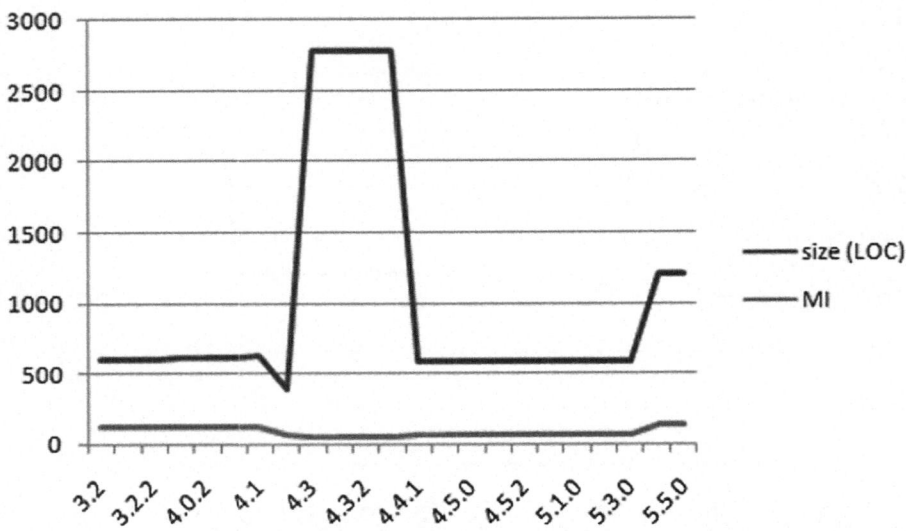

Fig. 2. LOC and MI evolutions.

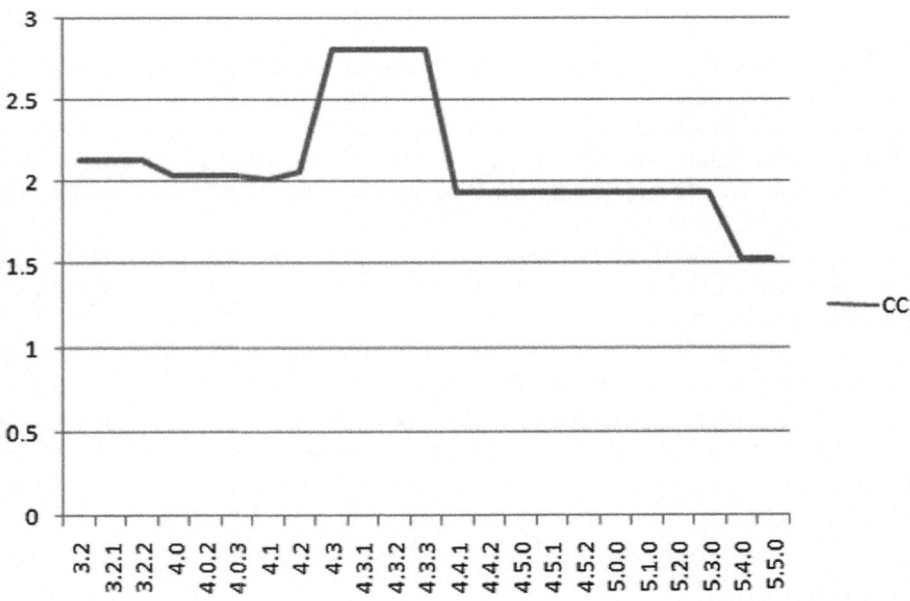

Fig. 3. CC evolution.

We use the same data provided in the initial steps of our work collected with the JHawk tool. To test correlation, we are postulating hypothesis in Table 1. In overall, correlation claims the strength of a relationship. We use the Cohen definition of correlation [6] where he defined a value less than 0.3 as a weak

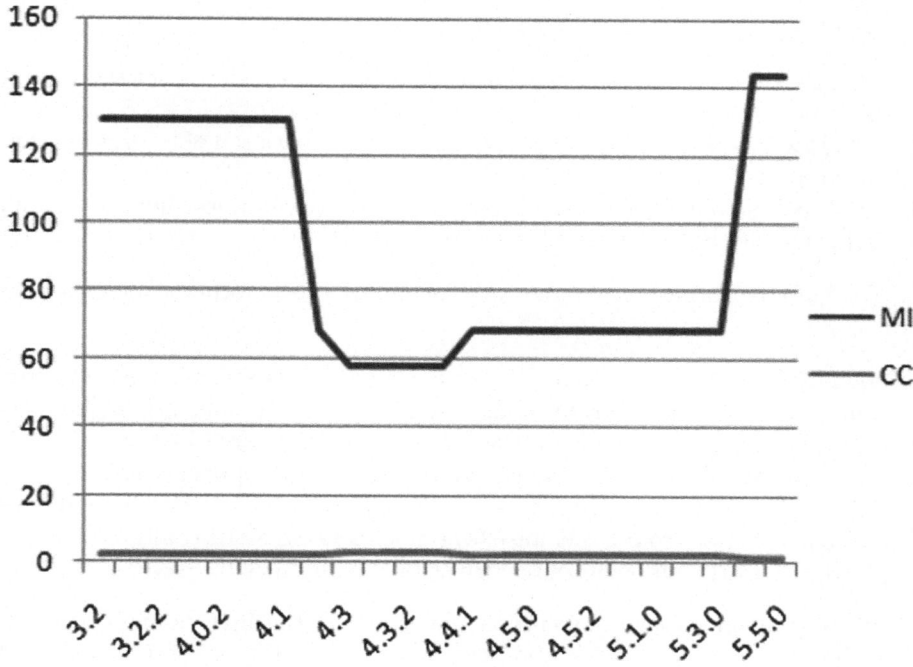

Fig. 4. CC and MI evolutions.

correlation, 0.3 to 0.5 as medium correlation, and greater than 0.5 as strong correlation. We are interested to understand the strength of such correlation. To measure the strength of relationship in our data variables we use Spearman rank correlation for the reason that it does not assume any linear relation between variables and it does not assume any specific distribution of data. We analyze the data in Python, using a Jupyter Notebook with the stats.py statistical package.

Table 1. Hypotheses.

No.	Hypotheses
1	**Null:** LOC and MI are unrelated
	Ha: LOC is positively correlated with MI
2	**Null:** CC and MI are unrelated
	Ha: CC is positively correlated with MI
3	**Null:** LOC and CC are unrelated
	Ha: LOC is positively correlated with CC

For this project, Spearman correlation coefficients are:

1. 0.129 for LOC and MI with p-value 0.522 which aims result is not significant, so we can not reject hypothesis null.
2. −0.098 with a p-value 0.628, again not significant so we can not reject hypothesis null.
3. 0.513 with p-value 0.006 is significant therefore we can reject hypothesis null and conclude that a relationship exists.

We have performed the same kind of analysis over other 4 open source projects:

- SoundHelix (0.6-0.9 versions): a Java framework for algorithmic random music composition. It can generate random songs, play them, and it is highly customizable using XML configuration as described in SourceForge.net.
- jWebUnit (1.0-3.2): a Java framework for testing web applications.
- jXLS (0.7-2.7.1): a Java library for writing Excel files using XLS templates and reading data from Excel into Java objects using XML configuration.
- jTDS (0.1-1.3.1): an open source driver for Microsoft SQL Server

We went again through same process described for the analysis of jEdit to collect LOC, MI, and CC metrics, and perform the correlation analysis as reported in Table 2.

Table 2. Correlations in all the considered projects.

Project	LOC-MI (pval)	CC-MI (pval)	LOC-CC (pval)
jEdit	0.129 (0.522)	−0.098 (0.628)	**0.513 (0.006)**
SoundHelix	−0.816 (0.184)	0.333 (0.667)	−0.816 (0.184)
JTDS	**0.733 (0.000)**	**−0.578 (0.000)**	−0.249 (0.161)
JXLS	**0.695 (0.000)**	**−0.812 (0.000)**	**−0.567 (0.000)**
JWebUnit	−0.320 (0.226)	0.200 (0.457)	**−0.789 (0.00)**

As we can notice in Table 2, the values in red identify significant values. All projects include some significant values except SoundHelix. There is a strong correlation of the LOC metric and MI in JXLS and JTDS and a strong correlation of CC and LOC in jEdit project. Also to be highlighted is the fact that exist strong negative correlations. The not significant results obtained from the SoundHelix project might derive from the fact that it is the project with the least data collected, this could have affected the overall analysis since only 4 versions were analyzed.

6 Conclusions and Future Work

The paper has introduced a preliminary analysis of the maintainability of 5 popular open source projects and how strongly it is correlated with some basic code metrics (lines of code and cyclomatic complexity) that are used in the definition of the Maintainability Index.

A systematic analysis of the maintainability of popular open source projects to understand how the code is managed and how the development team address the evolution of the code is important to increase the level of awareness in the usage of such products and to understand the possible effects in the long term.

References

1. Boehm, B.W., Brown, J.R., Kaspar, H., Lipow, M., McLeod, G., Merritt, M.: Characteristics of Software Quality. North Holland, Amsterdam (1978)
2. Bordeleau, F., Meirelles, P., Sillitti, A.: Fifteen years of open source software evolution. In: 15th International Conference on Open Source Systems (OSS 2019), Montreal, Quebec, Canada, 26–27 May 2019
3. Cheaito, R., Frappier, M., Matwin, S., Mili, A., Crabtree, D.: Defining and measuring maintainability. Technical report, University of Ottawa, Department of Computer Science (1995)
4. Chidamber, S.R., Kemerer, C.F.: Towards a Metrics Suite for Object Oriented Design. Center for Information Systems Research, Slan School of Management, Cambridge (1991)
5. Ciancarini, P., Missiroli, M., Sillitti, A.: Preferred tools for agile development: a sociocultural perspective? In: Technology of Object-Oriented Languages and Systems (TOOLS 50+1), Innopolis, Tatarstan, Russian Federation, 14–19 October 2019
6. Cohen, J.: Statistical Power Analysis for the Behavioral Sciences. Routledge, Abingdon (1988)
7. Elish, M.O.: Application of treenet in predicting object-oriented software maintainability: a comparative study. In: 2009 13th European Conference on Software Maintenance and Reengineering, pp. 69–78. IEEE (2009)
8. Genero, M., Piattini, M., Manso, E., Cantone G.: Building UML Class Diagram Maintainability Prediction Models Based on Early Metrics. IEEE (2004)
9. Jha, S., et al.: Deep learning approach for software maintainability metrics prediction. IEEE Access **7**, 61840–61855 (2019)
10. Kan, S.H.: Metrics and Models in Software Quality Engineering. Addison-Wesley Longman Publishing Co., Inc., Boston (2002)
11. Khomyakov, I., Sillitti, A.: A novel approach for collecting and sharing software metrics data. In: 34th ACM Symposium on Applied Computing (SAC 2019), Limassol, Cyprus, 8–12 April 2019
12. Khondhu, J., Capiluppi, A., Stol, K.-J.: Is it all lost? A study of inactive open source projects. In: Petrinja, E., Succi, G., El Ioini, N., Sillitti, A. (eds.) OSS 2013. IAICT, vol. 404, pp. 61–79. Springer, Heidelberg (2013). https://doi.org/10.1007/978-3-642-38928-3_5
13. Kumar, L., Rath, S.K.: Hybrid functional link artificial neural network approach for predicting maintainability of object-oriented software. J. Syst. Softw. **121**, 170–190 (2016)

14. Lenarduzzi, V., Sillitti, A., Taibi, D.: Analyzing forty years of software maintenance models. In: 39th International Conference on Software Engineering (ICSE 2017), Buenos Aires, Argentina, 20–28 May 2017
15. Lenarduzzi, V., Sillitti, A., Taibi, D.: A survey on code analysis tools for software maintenance prediction. In: Ciancarini, P., Mazzara, M., Messina, A., Sillitti, A., Succi, G. (eds.) SEDA 2018. AISC, vol. 925, pp. 165–175. Springer, Cham (2020). https://doi.org/10.1007/978-3-030-14687-0_15
16. Li, W., Henry, S.: Object-oriented metrics that predict maintainability. J. Syst. Softw. **23**, 111–122 (1993)
17. Molnar, A., Motogna, S.: Discovering maintainability changes in large software systems. In: IWSM Mensura 17: Proceedings of the 27th International Workshop on Software Measurement (2017)
18. Moser, R., Pedrycz, W., Sillitti, A., Succi, G.: A model to identify refactoring effort during maintenance by mining source code repositories. In: Jedlitschka, A., Salo, O. (eds.) PROFES 2008. LNCS, vol. 5089, pp. 360–370. Springer, Heidelberg (2008). https://doi.org/10.1007/978-3-540-69566-0_29
19. Petrinja, E., Sillitti, A., Succi, G.: Comparing OpenBRR, QSOS, and OMM assessment models. In: Ågerfalk, P., Boldyreff, C., González-Barahona, J.M., Madey, G.R., Noll, J. (eds.) OSS 2010. IAICT, vol. 319, pp. 224–238. Springer, Heidelberg (2010). https://doi.org/10.1007/978-3-642-13244-5_18
20. Rawashdeh, A., Matalkah, B.: A new software quality model for evaluating COTS components. J. Comput. Sci. **2**, 373–381 (2006)
21. Scotto, M., Sillitti, A., Succi, G., Vernazza, T.: Dealing with software metrics collection and analysis: a relational approach. Stud. Inform. Univ. Suger **3**(3), 343–366 (2004)
22. Shafiabady, A., Mahrin, M.N., Samadi, M.: Investigation of software maintainability prediction models. In: 18th International Conference on Advanced Communication Technology (ICACT) (2016)
23. Sneed, H.M., Merey, A.: Automated software quality assurance. IEEE Trans. Softw. Eng. **SE–11**(9), 909–916 (1985)
24. Van Koten, C., Gray, A.: An application of Bayesian network for predicting object-oriented software maintainability. Inf. Softw. Technol. **48**, 59–67 (2006)
25. Zhou, Y., Leung, H.: Predicting object-oriented software maintainability using multivariate adaptive regression splines. J. Syst. Softw. **80**, 1349–1361 (2007)

Development of Cloud-Based Microservices
to Decision Support System

Konstantin Aksyonov, Olga Aksyonova, Anna Antonova$^{(\boxtimes)}$, Elena Aksyonova,
and Polina Ziomkovskaya

Ural Federal University, 620000 Yekaterinburg, Russia
antonovaannas@gmail.com

Abstract. Intelligent systems of simulation become a key stage of the scheduling
of companies and industries work. Most of the existing decision support systems
are desktop software. Today there is a need to use durability, flexibility, availability
and crossplatforming information technologies. The paper proposes the idea of
working cloud based decision support system BPsim.Web and this one consists
of some set of services and tools. The model of the multiagent resources conversion process is considered. The process of the simulation model developing via
BPsim.Web is described. An example of the real process model is given.

Keywords: Simulation modeling · Intellectual systems · Artificial intelligence

1 Introduction

Creation of simulation systems (SIM) [1] is one of the promising directions for the
development of decision-making systems for business processes (BP), supply chains
and logistics [2, 3], technological processes (for example metallurgy [4]). Currently, the
presence in SIM of communities of interaction agents that are identified with decision
makers (DM) is significant [5–8].

Currently, commercial simulation solutions based on the market (such as AnyLogic,
ARIS, G2) are desktop applications. ARIS system allows you to create html-pages with
the results of experiments and upload them to the Internet. AnyLogic system is able to
compile java applets with developed models and place them on the network. To start
working with the model, it is necessary to fully download it to the user's electronic
device, playing the simulation experiment of the model applet takes place on the user's
device and requires significant computing resources.

The analysis showed that the greatest functionality of SIM of business processes is
provided by AnyLogic and BPsim products. In the direction of service-oriented architecture, only G2 is developing. Thus, the urgent task is to choose a dynamic model
of a business process and build on its basis a web-service of simulation. Comparative
analysis of SIM is presented in Table 1.

© IFIP International Federation for Information Processing 2020
Published by Springer Nature Switzerland AG 2020
V. Ivanov et al. (Eds.): OSS 2020, IFIP AICT 582, pp. 87–97, 2020.
https://doi.org/10.1007/978-3-030-47240-5_9

Table 1. Comparative analysis of SIM.

№	Parameter	ARIS	G2	AnyLogic
1	Designing a conceptual domain model	No	No	No
2	Description language of BP			
2.1	Description of resources, mechanisms, converters	+	+	+
2.2	Hierarchical model of BP	+	+	+
3	Multi agent model	No	No	+
4	Simulation	+	+	+
5	Expert modeling	No	+	No
6	Web interface	No	No	No
7	Cloud computing	No	+	No
8	Non-programming user orientation	+	No	No
9	Existence of the free version	No	No	No

2 Features of Business Processes

From the point of view of the dynamic component of BP, the following basic requirements for models can be distinguished [2, 3, 5, 6]:

1) accounting for various types of resources [9, 10];
2) accounting for the status of operations and resources at specific times;
3) accounting for the conflicts on common resources and means [11, 12];
4) modeling of discrete processes;
5) accounting for complex resources (resource instances with properties, in the terminology of queuing systems - application (transaction));
6) application of a situational approach (the presence of a language for describing situations (a language for representing knowledge) and mechanisms for diagnosing situations and finding solutions (a logical inference mechanism according to the terminology of expert systems);
7) implementation of intelligent agents (DM models);
8) description of hierarchical processes.

3 Analysis of Existing Models Business Processes

Consider the following approaches and models of multi-agent systems and BP:

1) model of a multi-agent process of resource conversion;
2) SIE-model A.U. Filippovich;
3) models of active and passive converters (APC) B.I. Klebanov, I.M. Moskalev.

3.1 Model of Multi-agent Resource Conversion Processes

The dynamic model of multi-agent resource conversion processes (MARCP) [5, 6] is designed to model organizational and technical, BP and support of management decisions. The MARCP model was developed on the basis of the following mathematical schemes: Petri nets, queuing systems and system dynamics models. The key concept of the MARCP model is a resource converter having the following structure: input, start, conversion, control, and output. "Start-up" determines the moment the converter is started on the basis of: the state of the conversion process, input and output resources, control commands, means. At the time of launch, the conversion execution time is determined based on the parameters of the control command and available resource limitations. The MARCP model has a hierarchical structure. Agents manage the objects of the process based on the content of the knowledge base (KB).

3.2 Analysis of the SIE Model A.U. Filippovich

Integrated situational, simulation, expert model A.U. Filippovich (SIE-model) is presented in [13]. Due to the fact that this model is focused on the problematic area of prepress processes (printing), some of its fragments will be described in terms of the MARCP model. SIE-model is presented in the form of several different levels, corresponding to the imitation, expert and situational presentation of information [13]. The first level of the model is intended to describe the structure of the system. For this, a block is associated with each object (subject). Blocks are interconnected by interaction channels. Each block processes a transaction for a certain time and delays it for a time determined by the intensity. We formulate the following conclusions:

1. The SIE-model can serve as the basis for creating a multi-agent BP model.
2. The SIE-model has the following advantages: apparatus/ mechanism for diagnosing situations; a combination of simulation, expert and situational approaches.
3. The SIE model does not satisfy the requirements of the BP model: the presence of a DM (agent) model; problem orientation to business processes.

3.3 Model I.M. Moskalev, B.I. Klebanov

In the work of I.M. Moskalev, B.I. Klebanov [14–16] presents a mathematical model of resource conversion process, the specificity of which is the allocation of active and passive converters (APC). In this model, the vertices of graph X are formed by passive transducers, active transformers, stock of instruments and resource storages, and many arcs are represented by resource and information flows, flows to funds. The model of active and passive converters is focused on solving production-planning problems and based on scheduling theory. This model has not worked the possibility of implementing intelligent agents (models of DM) with a production knowledge base, as well as the implementation of a language for describing mechanisms and situations for diagnosing situations and finding solutions.

The results of the analysis of the considered approaches and models of dynamic modeling of situations are given in Table 2.

Table 2. Analysis of approaches and dynamic models of situations.

Characteristics	MARCP	SIE-model	Model of APC
1. Different types of resources	+	+	+
2. Time attendance	+	+	+
3. Conflicts on shared resources and tools	+	+	+
4. Discrete operation	+	+	+
5. Complex resource (application), application queue	+	+	+
6. Language for describing situations, diagnosing situations and finding solutions	+	+	No
7. Decision Maker Model	+	No	No

As follows from the table, all the requirements of the multi-agent business process model are met by the MARCP model. As the theoretical basis of the implemented method you can use the SIE-model, the advantage of which is the study of integration issues of simulation, expert and situational modeling.

4   Details of the Implementation of the MARCP Modification

To implement the simulation modeling service, it was decided to use the MARCP concept.

The simulation modeling service is based on ASP.NET Core technology in the C# programming language.

ASP.NET Core is a cross-platform, high-performance, open-source environment for building modern, cloud-based, Internet-connected applications.

ASP.NET Core provides the following benefits:

- A single solution for creating a web user interface and web API.
- Integration of modern client platforms and development workflows.
- Cloud-based configuration system based on the environment.
- Built-in dependency injection.
- Simplified, high-performance, modular HTTP request pipeline.
- Ability to host in IIS, Nginx, Apache, Docker or in your own process.
- Parallel version control of the application focused on .NET Core.
- Tools that simplify the process of modern web development.
- Ability to build and run on Windows, macOS and Linux.
- Open source and community oriented.

ASP.NET Core comes fully in NuGet packages. Using NuGet packages allows you to optimize applications to include only the necessary dependencies. ASP.NET Core 2.x applications targeting .NET Core require only one NuGet package. Due to the small size of the application's contact area, benefits such as higher security, minimal maintenance and improved performance are available.

Figure 1 shows the architecture of the simulation service.

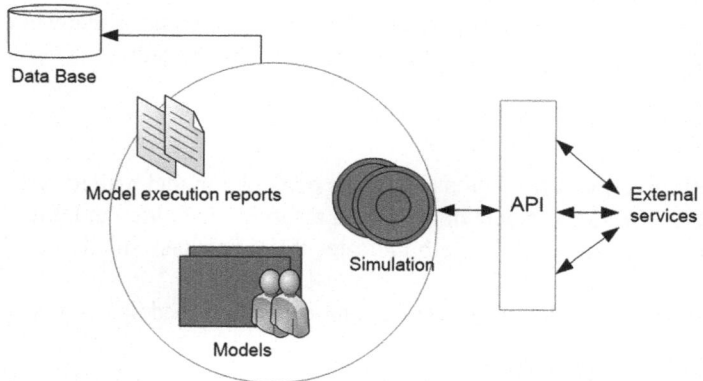

Fig. 1. Architecture of the simulation service.

The service manages 3 entities: models, simulation processes, and execution reports. It receives commands from the integration interface (API) and, depending on the command, receives or stores data in the database, performs internal transformations and calculations, and starts modeling.

5   WebAPI

The simulation modeling service has an interaction and integration interface in the form of cross-platform HTTP WebAPI. The HTTP protocol allows you to not only provide web pages. The simulation service describes a REST-style interface (RepresentationalStateTransfer). REST is an architectural style of software that defines the interaction of components of a distributed application on a network or the integration of multiple applications.

One of the requirements of REST is a unified programming interface for all entities with which the web service works. The CRUD (CreateReadUpdateDelete) interface of operations is described using the HTTP request verb (GET, POST, PUT, etc.), the names of entities and, if necessary, the identifiers of these entities.

Consider some possible queries on the models that the simulation service handles:

- GET model - get all models;
- GET model/{id} - get the model with the specified identifier;
- POST model - create a new model;
- PUT model/{id} - update the model;
- DELETE model/{id} - delete the model.

Here, all commands to the service have a single prefix "model". If there is an appeal to many models at once - to get all models, add a new one to many models - only the prefix is used. If you need an action associated with a specific model - get, change, delete - you must continue the request URL with the model identifier. An HTTP verb is used to determine the action to be performed on the request object.

In the REST style, a special approach is laid down for requests that work with some service entities at once. This is how the imitation task is created:

- POST model/{id}/task.

The URL describes the relationship of one particular model with its tasks. A service should take one from the model domain with a specific identifier and refer to its many tasks for simulation. The HTTP verb indicates that a new task should be added to this set.

The receipt of all tasks for simulating a model is described in a similar way:

- GET model/{id}/task;
- GET task/{id}/report.

However, work with many tasks for imitation can be carried out not in the context of any particular model, but immediately with the whole set. The following methods are used for this:

- GET task - get all simulation tasks;
- GET task/{id} - get information on a simulation task;
- DELETE task/{id} - stop simulation.

For each task, many reports are generated. The task report is strongly related to the essence of the task itself. Therefore, deleting a task deletes all reports for this task. The reports do not have unique identifiers and can be received by the whole set.

6 Data Storage

MongoDB was chosen as the data storage system of the SIM service.

MongoDB - DBMS that uses a document-oriented data model. This allows MongoDB to carry out CRUD operations very quickly, to be more prepared for changes in stored data and to be more understandable for the user. It is an open-source project that is written in C ++. All libraries and drivers for programming languages and platforms are also available in the public domain.

The storage method in MongoDB is similar to JSON (JavaScriptObjectNotation), although formally JSON is not used. MongoDB uses a format called BSON (binaryJSON) for storage. The BSON format has a certain structure and stores some additional information about a specific key and value pair (for example, data type and hash). Therefore, usually an object in BSON takes up a bit more space than JSON. However, BSON allows you to work with data faster: faster search and processing.

In MongoDB, each model is stored as a document. This document stores the entire structure of the model. Figure 2 shows the simulation model saved by the service in MongoDB.

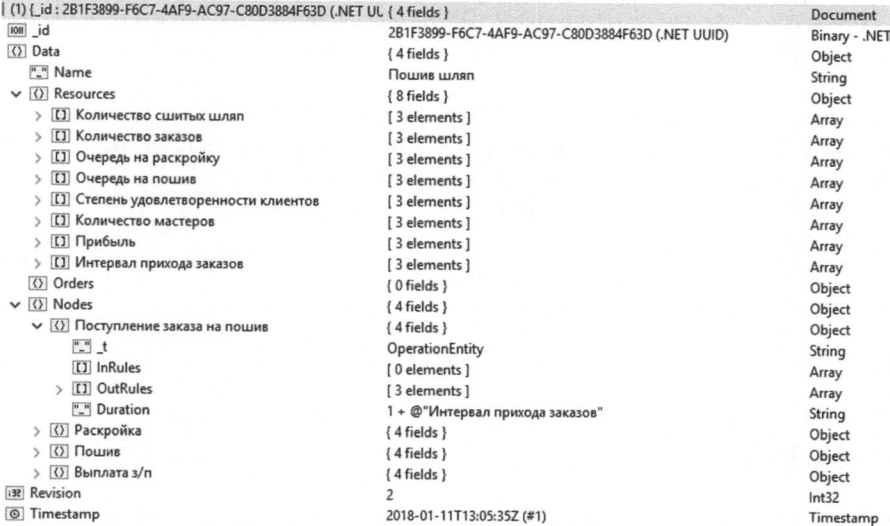

Fig. 2. Simulation model in MongoDB.

All models are saved in the Models collection. The structure of the model object itself, in addition to a unique identifier, consists of the following fields:

- Name - model name.
- Resources - an object in the form of a key-value, where key is the name of the resource, and value is the default value of the resource.
- Orders - the key-value object, where the key is the name of the request, and the value is an array of the names of the fields of the request.
- Nodes - a key-value object, where key is the name of the node, and value is a complex object that describes either the agent or the operation.

The "Agent" node has an array of global rules (GlobalRules) and a lot of knowledge (Knowledges). An array of rules stores the same rule entities as operations. Knowledge is a complex key-value object, where key is the name of knowledge, and value is an array of rules that describe this knowledge.

As mentioned earlier, simulation tasks also end up in the database. They are saved to the Tasks collection. The task consists of the following fields.

- ModelId - identifier of the model with which the task is associated.
- ModelRevision - version of the model by which the task was created. If the model has changed between the creation of the task and its immediate imitation, unforeseen incidents may occur.
- State - task state.
- SubjectArea - the subject area with which the simulation will occur.
- Configuration - the configuration with which the simulation will be launched. It stores information about when to stop the simulation, as well as some other information.
- Reports - an array of reports that were created for this task.

The task may be in one of the states. This is determined by the life cycle of the task. The states are as follows:

- 0 - Open - the task is created and ready to simulate;
- 1 - Scheduled - the task has already been planned, but has not yet been simulated (the engine is being prepared, objects are being created, etc.);
- 2 - Pending - the task is in simulation;
- 3 - Failed - the task failed;
- 4 - Successful - task completed successfully;
- 5 - Aborted - the task was interrupted;
- 6 - Deleted - the task was deleted before it was taken into imitation.

7 Simulation Process

The task created as a result of the HTTP request does not begin to be simulated immediately. It is saved to the database and enters the task queue. Service within a given period of time will check the queue for tasks. If there are no tasks for imitation, the cycle will be repeated after some time. If there is a task in the queue, imitation begins on it. The simulator can simulate several tasks in parallel. The degree of parallelism is not strictly defined and can be configured by the service settings. If the simulator does not have free resources to simulate, he does not look at the queue until they appear. As soon as some task completes the simulation, the simulator looks through the queue for new tasks.

When the task falls into the simulation, it saves to the database with the status 0 (Open). As soon as the simulator takes the task from the queue, it is set to status 1 (Scheduled). This is necessary so that a parallel process or another instance of the service does not begin to simulate the same task. When the simulator finishes preparations, he will begin the simulation, setting the task status 2 (Pending). Upon successful completion of the task, it will receive the status 4 (Successful), and if an error occurs - 3 (Failed). The task can be canceled by a special team. In this case, she will have the status 5 (Aborted) or 6 (Delete).

Figure 3 shows the pattern of product movement between the hot rolling mill LPC-10 and the cold rolling mill LPC-5.

The task is to recreate the production process of sheet steel coils and conduct a series of studies in which it is necessary to evaluate a set of key parameters within three 24-h working days. The parameters are as follows:

1. The minimum number of slabs in the warehouse of cast slabs at the beginning of the simulation, providing a continuous supply of slabs every three minutes.
2. The current, minimum, maximum and average number of objects in each warehouse of the system during the simulation time.
3. The load of all units in percent during the simulation time and the current load.

To create such a simulation model, you need to use the POST/api/v1/model service interface and put a JSON object describing model in the HTTP request body.

Figure 4 shows a small part of this object. You can see the first nodes of the model on it: two operations "Slab store" and "Batch generator" and the beginning of the description of the "In bake" agent.

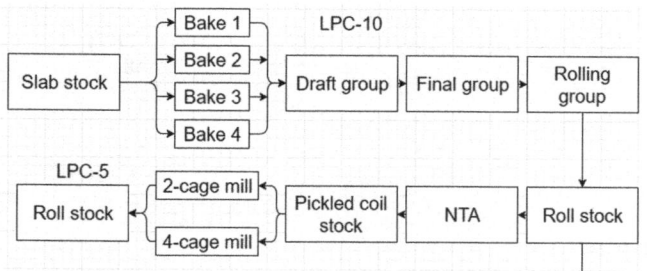

Fig. 3. Product flow chart between LPC-10 and LPC-5.

```
"name": "Cold and hot rolling shops",
"resources": {
"orders": {
"nodes": {
    "Slab store": {
        "InRules": [],
        "OutRules": [{
            "Expression": "@\"Initial slab\" = @\"Initial slab\" + Random(22, 89)",
            "Type": 0
        }],
        "Duration": "60"
    },
    "Batch generator": {
        "InRules": [],
        "OutRules": [{
            "Expression": "@\"Batch size\" = 2 + Random(1,3)",
            "Type": 0
```

Fig. 4. Part of the model description.

Nine experiments were conducted with the model. In each experiment, the minimum value of the slabs in the warehouse was changed. Table 3 presents a partial result of the experiments, including the minimum value of slabs in the warehouse, the final output of the model and the waiting time—the total idle time of the furnaces.

According to the results of the experiments, it was decided that the 6th experiment was the best. Starting from it, a continuous flow of slabs in workshops was obtained with the minimum quantity in the warehouse, the best effect was obtained.

Table 3. The results of experiments.

№	The min. number of slabs	Model output	Waiting time
1	310	776	234
2	350	628	133
3	390	538	69
4	410	543	65
5	430	529	48
6	477	503	11
7	490	517	13

8   Conclusion

The data obtained in the course of this work made it possible to analyze the current development of business process simulation systems (such as AnyLogic, ARIS, BPsim, G2) and highlight the requirements for a new system oriented to work on the Internet. A comparative analysis of the existing dynamic BP models was carried out and the model of the multi-agent resource conversion process was taken as a basis. A prototype web-service for BP simulation BPsim.Web was developed. The web service has been tested in solving the problem of analyzing the processes of two workshops.

Acknowledgment. The reported study was funded by RFBR according to the research project № 18-37-00183.

References

1. Devyatkov, V.V., Vlasov, S.A., Devyatkov, T.V.: Cloud technology in simulation studies, GPSS cloud project. In: Proceedings of the 7th IFAC Conference on Manufacturing Modeling, Management, and Control 2013, IFAC, vol. 7, pp. 637–641 (2013)
2. Solovyeva, I., Sokolov, B., Ivanov, D.: Analysis of position optimization method applicability in supply chain management problem. In: Proceedings of the Conference on Stability and Control Processes in Memory, pp. 498–500(2015)
3. Sokolov, B.V., Pavlov, A.N., Yusupov, R.M., Ohtilev, M.U., Potryasaev, S.A.: Theoretical and technological foundations of complex objects proactive monitoring management and control. In: Proceedings of the Symposium Automated Systems, pp. 103–110 (2015
4. Borodin, A., Kiselev, Y., Mirvoda, S., Porshnev, S.: On design of domain-specific query language for the metallurgical industry. In: Kozielski, S., Mrozek, D., Kasprowski, P., Małysiak-Mrozek, B., Kostrzewa, D. (eds.) BDAS 2015. CCIS, vol. 521, pp. 505–515. Springer, Cham (2015). https://doi.org/10.1007/978-3-319-18422-7_45
5. Aksyonov, K., Bykov, E., Aksyonova, O., Goncharov, N., Nevolina, A.: The architecture of the multi-agent resource conversion processes. In: Proceedings of the 11th European Modelling Symposium on Computer Simulation, pp. 61–64 (2017)

6. Aksyonov, K., Antonova, A., Goncharova, N.: Analysis of the electric arc furnace workshop logistic processes using multiagent simulation. In: Thampi, S.M., Krishnan, S., Corchado Rodriguez, J.M., Das, S., Wozniak, M., Al-Jumeily, D. (eds.) SIRS 2017. AISC, vol. 678, pp. 390–397. Springer, Cham (2018). https://doi.org/10.1007/978-3-319-67934-1_35

7. Cao, L., Zeng, Y., Symeonidis, A.L., Gorodetsky, V., Müller, J., Yu, P. (eds.): Agents and Data Mining Interaction. Lecture Notes in Artificial Intelligence, vol. 8316. Springer, Cham (2014). https://doi.org/10.1007/978-3-642-55192-5

8. Wooldridge, M.: Intelligent agent: theory and practice. Knowl. Eng. Rev. **10**(2), 115–152 (1995)

9. Hammer, M., Champy, J.: Reengineering the Corporation: A Manifesto for Business Revolutions. Harper Business, New York (1993)

10. Hartmann, S., Drexl, A.: Project scheduling with multiple modes: a comparison of exact algorithms. Netw. Int. J. **32**(4), 283–297 (1998)

11. Osaba, E., Carballedo, R., Diaz, F.: Simulation tool based on a memetic algorithm to solve a real instance of a dynamic TSP. In: Proceedings of the IASTED International Conference Applied Simulation and Modelling, pp. 27–33 (2012)

12. Dreżewski, R.: A model of co-evolution in multi-agent system. In: Mařík, V., Pěchouček, M., Müller, J. (eds.) CEEMAS 2003. LNCS (LNAI), vol. 2691, pp. 314–323. Springer, Heidelberg (2003). https://doi.org/10.1007/3-540-45023-8_30

13. Fillipovich, A.U.: Integration of Situational, Simulation and Expert Modeling Systems. Publisher "OOO Elix+", Moscow (2003)

14. Moskaliov, I.M.: System for analysis and optimization of resource conversion processes. Thesis, Russia, Ekaterinburg (2006)

15. Klebanov, B., Antropov, T., Riabkina, E.: The principles of multi-agent models of development based on the needs of the agents. In: Proceedings of the 35th Chinese Control Conference, pp. 7551–7555 (2016)

16. Klebanov, B., Antropov, T., Riabkina, E.: Bases of imitation model of artificial society construction accounting of the agents' needs recursion. In: Proceedings of the 16th International Multidisciplinary Scientific GeoConference, vol. 1, pp. 101–108 (2016)

Using of Open-Source Technologies for the Design and Development of a Speech Processing System Based on Stemming Methods

Andrey Tarasiev, Margarita Filippova, Konstantin Aksyonov, Olga Aksyonova, and Anna Antonova(✉)

Ural Federal University, 620000 Yekaterinburg, Russia
antonovaannas@gmail.com

Abstract. This article discusses the idea of developing an intelligent and customizable automated system for real-time text and voice dialogs with the user. This system can be used for almost any subject area, for example, to create an automated robot - a call center operator or smart chat bots, assistants, and so on. This article presents the developed flexible architecture of the proposed system. The system has many independent submodules. These modules work as interacting microservices and use several speech recognition schemes, including a decision support submodule, third-party speech recognition systems and a post-processing subsystem. In this paper, the post-processing module of the recognized text is presented in detail on the example of Russian and English dictionary models. The proposed submodule also uses several processing steps, including the use of various stemming methods, the use of word stop-lists or other lexical structures, the use of stochastic keyword ranking using a weight table, etc.

Keywords: Multi-agent · Design · Development · System · Decision-making · Real-time · Twin · Stemming · Postprocessing · Open-source

1 Introduction

At a present day technologies related to automated control processing systems are rapidly developing. As a part of these modern trends in the development of information technology the creation of effective and technologically advanced solutions for organizing the processing of incoming requests is required.

Data processing technologies are progressively evolving, with more and more systems replacing human resources every day. Automation and the creation of information systems are at the moment the most promising areas of activity of modern society. One of the reasons for the active development of these areas is that automation is the basis for a fundamental change in management processes that play an important role in the activities of companies.

Thus, there is a need to use a control system, whose operation is aimed at maintaining and improving the operation of the all business processes at all.

© IFIP International Federation for Information Processing 2020
Published by Springer Nature Switzerland AG 2020
V. Ivanov et al. (Eds.): OSS 2020, IFIP AICT 582, pp. 98–105, 2020.
https://doi.org/10.1007/978-3-030-47240-5_10

As an important part of this area an automation of call centers working process require the help of a control device (complex of means for collecting, processing, transmitting information, and generating control signals or commands).

The module of speech recognition in this system uses the two most developed at the moment existing solutions YandexSpeechKit and GoogleSpeech API. But integration with these third-party services and other related solutions can't provide complete accordance with system requirements including features, adequate recognition quality, scalability, flexibility and so on.

As previous part of this work the testing of the speech recognition systems using Russian language models including selecting and testing a speech recognition systems and designing architecture of the "Twin" automation system was conducted [5].

Based on the received information, we can conclude that the Yandex system is good at recognizing short expressive phrases, as well as numerals. On contrary, the Google API is good at recognizing long phrases and terms. The results of this research are being used in development of the automatic system that calls the customers of "Twin" [1, 2, 4]. At the same time, both systems have problems with recognition in terms of noise, uneasy speech tempo and voice defects of the interlocutor.

Development experience of answer and question automated systems are described in some works: based on frame approach [9], based on agent approach [10, 11, 15] and conceptual graphs [12–14]. This is due to the fact that both systems better recognize phonemes and phrases, and individual sounds are worse, especially if there are noises and other factors that distort the quality of the transmitted audio message. This observation is confirmed by the findings obtained by other independent researchers [3].

To eliminate such problems, it is necessary to include pre- and post-processing. These actions can provide requirements of recognition quality.

Pre-processing uses the dynamic selection of recognition services provided. Subsequent processing of the received textual information includes the lemmatization and normalization of individual words in the recognized speech and other methods. For example, in the case of processing numbers, this is the application of tokenization technology.

Also in previous part of this work the research and selection of methods for evaluating information about part of speech, word form and statistical relationships between words have been done.

As the conclusion of this research we can claim that the lemmatization method is most effective for solving the problems of dynamic text processing and recognition. However, to the same extent, this approach is extremely dependent on the exact definition of a part of speech (the lexical category of a word) and the language model.

Application of this algorithm leads to the fact that the analyzer module receives an array of words in primary form, due to which it is possible to easily recognize part of speech using the rules of the language model.

However, this information in practice may not be enough for the further work of the decision-making module and generating a response. In addition, there is the possibility of recognition errors associated with incorrect recognition of the lexical category of a word and its initial form.

To obtain a more accurate recognition and processing result, further post-processing mechanisms are used.

The implementation of the lemmatization mechanism in the system was performed through some open-source package solutions of morphological processing and lemmatization for the PHP language.

Within the framework of this work, the design and development of an automated system named "Twin" was carried out and details presents module of recognized text post-processing on the example of the Russian and English languages dictionary models.

2 Integration of Speech Recognition Functionality with Ranking and Database Generation Functionality

Since the approach of reducing the words to normal form and determining the parts of speech is insufficient for the voice robot to understand the interlocutor's speech and for further decision making, the system uses post-processing algorithms for normalized words. This is due to the presence of a number of problems, inaccuracies and recognition errors.

In addition, the lemmatization method can occur recognition errors since the lexical category of a word can be incorrectly determined. There is also a big problem with the correct recognition of numerals, which leads to difficulty to identifying numbers, dates, addresses, etc. To solve these problems, several additional processing algorithms are used.

Many researchers provide several methods to improve quality of natural language processing based on stemming methods.

When building the speech recognition module for voice system, we were guided for the most part not by coming up with conceptually new algorithms, but by focusing on the use and adaptation of existing and well-established approaches.

The most often usable method based on implementation of a large vocabulary speech recognition system for the inflectional languages such as Slavic group languages [8].

Based on this approach the following method for additional processing was proposed.

Conventionally, we can distinguish the following steps of the additional processing of the second stage.

- primary processing;
- introduction of a keyword system and the use of stochastic keyword ranking;
- introduction of a word stop-list system.

2.1 Primary Processing

Decisions on the basic additional processing of normalized words are determined on the basis of the given settings and information on the lexical category of the word (part of speech) as a preparatory stage for more serious text analysis methods.

The essence of the primary processing of the second stage of text analysis is the use of simple algorithms for automated morphological analysis.

To increase the accuracy of recognition of numerals, the information contains numerals goes through the tokenization procedure. Also, the system provides for the adjustment of language models, which allows you to customize the perception of numerals, dates, cases, as well as the need to use keywords. In addition, it is possible to configure the methods used for stemming.

2.2 Application of the Keyword System

The introduction of a keyword system allows for significantly more effective recognition of language units. Firstly, this is due to the fact that keywords can be tied to specific blocks of the dialogue script, which largely solves the problems associated with the context. This can be useful, for example, when processing paronyms.

When creating a script in a special interface, creator of the scenario can set keywords for each person's answer.

This dialogue scenario consists of various information blocks, most of which involve the interlocutor's response or expectation of a phrase.

Moreover, depending on the frequency of mentioning of certain words and phrases, further training takes place. The system, each time making a decision, increases the weight of a certain keyword in the expert table of stochastic data. Thus, the likelihood of a particular word appearing during further launches of this dialogue scenario increases depending on the frequency of its appearance and correct recognition earlier.

The processed text is transferred to the block of the analyzer of coincidence with keywords.

At the same time, both processed normalized words and initially recognized words are transmitted to the system. Keywords themselves can be set intentionally in various forms. Due to these two conditions, the recognition quality can be significantly improved, and the table of knowledge base weights for the stochastic ranking method will be more trained. A similar approach is widespread in systems using stochastic knowledge bases.

In addition, this makes it easy to solve the potential problem of the loss or distortion of the meaning of either a single word or the phrase itself as a whole.

That is, if several variants of the same word are specified in the system for a certain block of the script, and both coincide with the original and lemmatized recognized words, then the probability weights for both keywords will significantly increase, and the weight of the script branch will also increase by the weight of both keywords.

By default, the conditional weight of each keyword and each branch of the dialogue at the initial moment of execution time of a script is equal to one. When the lemmatized word coincides with the originally recognized word with the keywords, the weight of each keyword increases by one. In this case, the weight of the branch increases by two units. If only the keyword denoting the initial form and the lemmatized language unit coincide, then the weight of the script dialog branch increases by one.

Based on the dynamically calculated weights of each branch, at every moment a decision is made on the further development of the dialogue scenario taking into account the largest branch weight.

This approach allows the author of the script to work out the dialogue features important for the script, which are influenced by the degree and conjugation of the verb, etc.

As already mentioned, in addition to setting keywords the system provides for the use of tables of stochastic ranking of words by probability depending on the frequency of their appearance and correct recognition in dialogs.

Of course, to ensure the correct operation of such a system, it is necessary to implement and maintain a knowledge base. It is worth noting that this storage takes up much less volume than other knowledge base implementations for stochastic stemming methods would occupy. To ensure dynamic interaction, in the system it is implemented as a base tree.

The use of the stochastic method is primarily due to the fact that an approach that implements only lemmatization algorithms is not able to provide sufficient reliability for correct speech recognition and decision making, since it places great responsibility on the system operator itself, which may be mistaken due to the human factor or not take into account all the options, which can have a big impact on the course of the dialogue.

2.3 Application of the Stop-Word System

Similar to using the keyword system in a word processing module, stop words are also used. Their semantic load is similar to keywords. The essence of this idea is to strictly discard branches when the recognized word coincides with the stop word.

This approach allows us to simplify the writing of some dialogue scenarios by providing the user with the opportunity to work with negation and exceptional situations, or to write down fewer keywords and work out less on premediating of potential scenarios. It also allows to speed up the processing of text, due to the fact that some cases can be immediately discarded and not be considered in the future.

According to the implementation method, the process of recognizing stop words is practically no different from keywords. A lemmatized word and a primary word are transmitted to the handler in their original form recognized by an external open-source morphy system. These words are compared with stop words. If a match is found, the weight of the stop word in the knowledge base of stochastic rules increases, and the weight of the branch decreases to the minimum possible. Thus, during the execution of the further procedure for selecting a scenario vector, this branch cannot be selected in any way.

After applying all the rules and treatments, the search for a solution begins in accordance with the rules specified in the script, after which a response is generated.

2.4 Recognition Process Description

Based on everything described earlier, a simplified process of additional processing of a phrase recognized by third-party systems occurs as follows:

At the first step, the text recognized by a third-party system is transmitted to the post-processing module. This module analyzes this text in several stages.

First of all, the text goes through the procedure of splitting into separate linguistic units – words and statistical grouping by phrases. Each word is lemmatized, as a result of which the word in the initial form is returned at the output of the work of the stemming algorithms, and the lexical category of the word is also determined.

Next, the second stage of processing begins. Based on the part of speech defined in the previous step, initial processing is performed. In this case, the rules defined when setting up language models are used, such as processing numerals, tokenization, processing dates, cases for nouns, etc.

The processed words and words in their original form, recognized by third-party systems, are transferred to the next data processor, which deals with their comparison with keywords and stop words, which are pre-introduced to the system for the corresponding blocks of the dialogue script.

If the words transmitted to the input of the algorithm coincide with the ones specified in the system, the statistical weights of the keywords and corresponding branches of the script increase.

The weights of the words specified in the system are recorded in the production knowledge base of stochastic rules. Thus, the ranking of words is provided and the model is trained. The more often these or other words and phrases are used when executing a script during dialogs, the more likely it is the appearance of these words in these forms with other passages of this scenario. Accordingly, over time, these words will be more correctly recognized.

Finally, based on which branch, illustrating the possible choice of further development of the dialogue, is gaining the greatest weight, a decision is made and a response is generated.

This process can be visualized using the following sequence diagram (see Fig. 1).

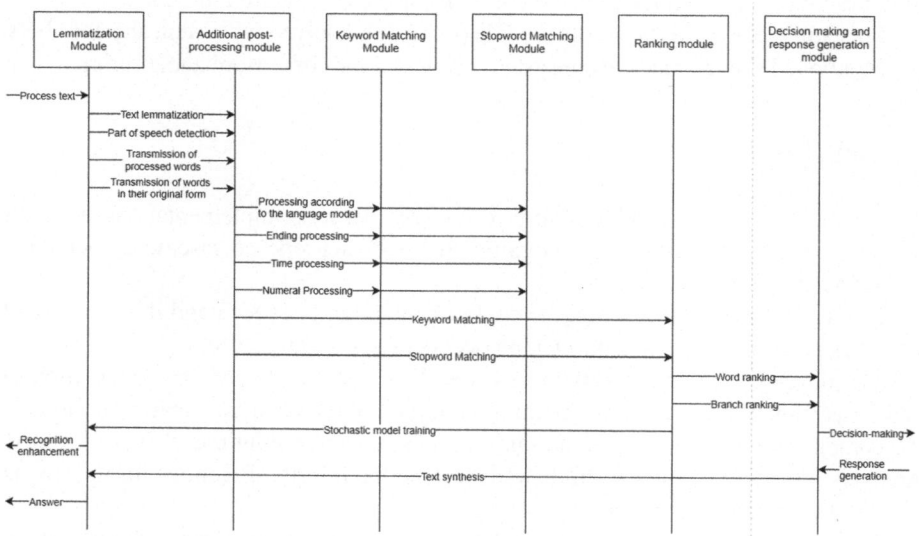

Fig. 1. Sequence diagram for additional post-processing of recognized text.

We are considering options for highlighting our own developments, such as a system of keywords, into separate freely distributed solutions.

3 Using of Open-Source Technologies to Development Post-processing System

The implementation of the lemmatization mechanism in the system was performed through an open-source package solution of morphological processing and lemmatization for the PHP language – PHP Morphy, which contains the corresponding knowledge bases - dictionaries for various language models. This solution easily integrates with the used development tool stack.

This library supports AOT and myspell project dictionaries. For the library to work, you need to compile a binary dictionary. When compiling, the dictionary is used in its original form.

Physically, the dictionary is presented in the form of several files, which are a data store in a key-value format, as well as storage of reference lexical information, grammatical information, end tables, grammes, etc.

Other word processing packages for processing declension cases, such as petrovitch library also are used. This package also allows to gender determination and develop and apply own linguistic rules.

It should be noted that using of open-source systems in not limited by mentioned solutions.

Flexibility of proposed application and modern technologies itself allows to simple scaling or replacing third-party modules or adding new.

Moreover, proposed dialogue systems use other open-source packages for different modules that are not limited to post-processing speech recognition module.

For example, we use Rasa Core module for speech-analyze subsystem and chat-bots.

Mentioned speech-analyze subsystem using as a part of customizable script.

4 Conclusion

Open-source solutions provide ability to integrate various implementations of exists methods, such as stemming text recognition methods in proposed case, with each other and own development.

Due to additional processing, the correct perception of speech and the meaning of what has been said and decision-making occurs in developing system.

The development of the system involves the development and implementation of additional functions, such as the sending of statistical data and the creation of hints in the compilation of the script. To do this exists open-source solutions also can be used. Analysis of internal statistics will help determine the priority directions for improving the interface and system features.

The range of use of the system can be extended, due to the initial flexibility of the structure and wide ability to integrate with third-party solutions, packages and so on.

It should be noted that proposed system Twin is used in teaching intellectual technologies at the Ural Federal University on a free basis.

We are considering options for highlighting our own developments, such as a system of keywords, into separate freely distributed solutions.

Acknowledgments. The work was supported by Act 211 Government of the Russian Federation, contract no. 02.A03.21.0006.

References

1. Aksyonov, K., et al.: Testing of the speech recognition systems using Russian language models. In: Proceedings of the 5th International Young Scientists Conference on Information Technologies, Telecommunications and Control Systems, ITTCS 2018. Yekaterinburg, Russian Federation, December 2018
2. Aksyonov, K., et al.: Development of decision making software agent for efficiency indicators system of IT-specialists. In: Proceedings of the 5th International Young Scientists Conference on Information Technologies, Telecommunications and Control Systems, ITTCS 2018, Yekaterinburg, Russian Federation, December 2018
3. The study of the reliability of speech recognition by the system Google Voice Search. Cyberleninka.ru. https://cyberleninka.ru/article/v/issledovanie-nadezh. Accessed 10 Mar 2020
4. Features of TWIN. https://twin24.ai/#features. Accessed 10 Mar 2020
5. Tarasiev, A., Talancev, E., Aksyonov, K., Kalinin, I., Chiryshev, U., Aksyonova, O.: Development of an intelligent automated system for dialogue and decision-making in real time. In: Proceedings of the 2nd European Conference on Electrical Engineering & Computer Science (EECS 2018), Bern, Switzerland, December 2018
6. Kartavenko, M.: On the use of acoustic characteristics of speech for the diagnosis of mental states of a person. https://cyberleninka.ru/article/v/ob-ispolzovanii-akusticheskih-harakteristik-rechi-dlya-diagnostiki-psihicheskih-sostoyaniy-cheloveka. Accessed 10 Mar 2020
7. Loseva, E., Lipnitsky, L.: Recognition of human emotions by spoken using intelligent data analysis methods. https://cyberleninka.ru/article/n/raspoznavanie-emotsiy-cheloveka-po-ustnoy-rechi-s-primeneniem-intellektualnyh-metodov-analiza-dannyh. Accessed 10 Mar 2020
8. Rotovnik, T., Maucec, M.S., Kacic, Z.: Large vocabulary continuous speech recognition of an inflected language using stems. https://hal.archives-ouvertes.fr/hal-00499182/document. Accessed 10 Mar 2020
9. Minsky, M.: A framework for representing knowledge in the psychology of computer vision. In: Winston, P.H. (ed.), McGraw-Hill (1975)
10. Greenwald, A., Jennings, N., Stone, P.: Guest editors' introduction: agents and markets. Intell. Syst. **18**, 12–14 (2003)
11. Dash, R., Parkes, D., Jennings, N.: Computationals-mechanism design: a call to arms. Intell. Syst. **18**, 40–47 (2003)
12. Sowa, J.F.: Knowledge Representation: Logical, Philosophical, and Computational Foundations. Brooks/Cole Publishing Co., Pacific Grove (2000)
13. Sowa, J.F.: Conceptual graphs for a database interface. IBM J. Res. Dev. **20**(4), 336–357 (1976)
14. Sowa, J.F.: Conceptual Structures: Information Processing in Mind and Machine. Addison-Wesley, Boston (1984)
15. Vittikh, V.A., Skobelev, P.O.: Multiagent interaction models for constructing the needs-and-means networks in open systems. Autom. Remote Control **64**, 162–169 (2003)

Combining Two Modelling Approaches: GQM and KAOS in an Open Source Project

Nursultan Askarbekuly[✉], Andrey Sadovykh, and Manuel Mazzara

Software Engineering Laboratory, Innopolis University, Innopolis, Tatarstan, Russia
n.askarbekuly@innopolis.university

Abstract. GQM is a software metrics method that produces meaningful and appropriate measurement metrics based on the specific goals of an organisation. KAOS goal modelling is a software engineering approach that allows to identify high level goals of an organisation, refine and expand them into lower-level more concrete goals and assign them to specific system agents. The two approaches can be combined, such that the goal modelling is used to derive specific goals rooted in the organisational context, policies and strategies of an organisation. The GQM, in turn, utilises the derived specific goals to produce appropriate and meaningful metrics that can be used to obtain valuable insights and track the state and progress of the formulated goals. Moreover, both models can be presented within a single diagram, thus providing an expressive and concise overview of the systems goals, actors and measurements. The suggested combination is then applied in the context of an open source project, followed by the discussion on potential benefits and drawbacks of using the two approaches.

Keywords: Goal Question Metric · GQM · KAOS · Goal model · Software metrics · Requirements engineering · Open source software

1 Introduction

Goal, Question, Metric (GQM) is a measurement modelling approach applicable in a wide variety of contexts ranging from assessing software reliability and validation of engineering techniques to evaluating the impact of business strategies [5–7].

It allows engineers to choose appropriate software measurement metrics. The GQM method takes a set of specific goals of an organisation as a basis, and connects them with metrics in order to measure their achievement and progress. Thus having a set of specific goals of an organisation is a prerequisite to applying the GQM model and extracting the metrics.

To produce the specific goals, understanding the higher-level strategic goals and the organisation environment is necessary and requires a substantial amount of effort, such as interviewing the stakeholders and working in close collaboration

© IFIP International Federation for Information Processing 2020
Published by Springer Nature Switzerland AG 2020
V. Ivanov et al. (Eds.): OSS 2020, IFIP AICT 582, pp. 106–119, 2020.
https://doi.org/10.1007/978-3-030-47240-5_11

with the organisation's team. However, the GQM in its essence does not reflect the context and high-level goals from which it was derived, and therefore requires other more general modelling approaches to reflect the bigger picture.

KAOS is a goal modelling approach used in requirements engineering [1,2]. It identifies high level system goals and proceeds top down to refine them, thus producing more concrete lower-level goals. The lower-level goals are then assigned to agents, such as software modules, external systems or individuals, responsible for the satisfaction of these goals. The diagrammatic notation used in the approach allows one to express and analyse various complex relations between the system goals and entities, and allows one to capture a system's functional and nonfunctional aspects and constraints.

The correspondence and complementary nature of the two approaches makes combination and interchange of their techniques and tools possible. In particular, the KAOS goal model's comprehensive diagrammatic notation can be used to reflect and facilitate the derivation process of the specific set of goals from the organisational context and higher level strategic goals. The GQM, in turn, can use the derived set of the specific goals to produce the set of appropriate metrics to measure and analyse the state and achievement of those goals. As a result, the two approaches produce a mapping of high-level strategic goals to more concrete lower-level goals, which are then assigned to agents, responsible for their fulfilment, and to appropriate metrics, that allows tracking, analysis and further interpretation.

In the following two sections a brief overview of the two modelling approaches is presented. Then in the fourth section an example of combining the two approaches is examined, and its main advantages are outlined. The fifth section is a case study on applying the combination of two approaches in the context of an open source software project. The authors demonstrate how the combination can be used for an actual project, and then list possible benefits and drawbacks to using the approach for the purposes of documenting requirments for an open source software (OSS) project.

2   Goal, Question, Metric (GQM) Method

One way for an organisation to have some valuable insights regarding itself, its assets and processes is to conduct some appropriate measurements and interpret them correctly. The question of what comprises appropriate measurements is critical. The GQM method helps one to arrive at those measurements, provided there is a set of specific goals for that organisation [2]. To get from each specific goal to a measurement the method defines three levels (Fig. 1), each representing a step on the way from the goal to a metric:

- *Goal:* Conceptual level, where each of the specific goals is represented.
- *Question:* Operational level, at which questions are posed against the goal in order to assess its achievement and identify some of its aspects through which the progress can be observed and measured.

- *Metric:* Quantitative level, at which appropriate metrics is selected to answer the questions posed at the operational level in a quantitative manner.

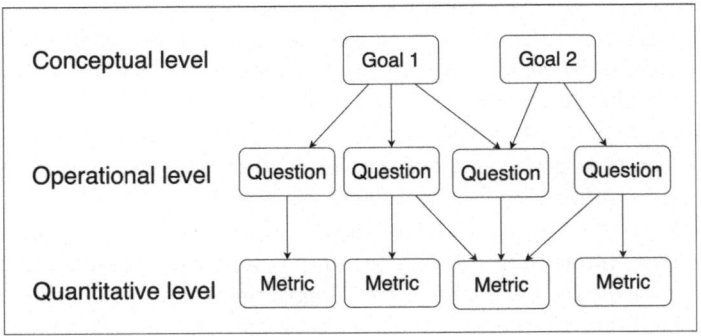

Fig. 1. Levels of the GQM model

Following is an example of the GQM process using a simple example of a web application of a company selling airplane tickets. The process starts with a specific goal. It has to be formulated in a particular way and be associated with an object, which in the context of software development could be an artefact, process or resource. Within the goal a purpose is defined, together with a particular quality issue of the object and a viewpoint from which it is looked at. The example goal is to improve usability of the ticket booking feature from the point of view of a person booking a ticket (end user). The object of the goal is the ticket booking feature. The purpose is to improve, the quality issue is the usability and the viewpoint is that of a person booking a ticket.

Once the specification of the goal is ready, questions can be posed against the goal and metrics can be proposed to answer the questions. Looking at the example goal above, its purpose and quality issue one can deduce following questions:

- What are the completion rates of the feature?, i.e. what portion of users actually accomplishes booking a ticket.
- What is the average user task time?, i.e. how much time does it normally take a user to accomplish booking a ticket.
- How satisfied are the end users with the feature's usability?

Each of the questions can have one or several metrics answering it. The whole GQM can be presented in a tabular format [2], as in the Table 1. Often, there is a set of specific goals and a GQM is produced for each one of them. Evidently, having these set of specific goal is what makes deriving metrics possible. The question arises then of how the set of specific goals for an organisation is actually produced.

Table 1. Exemplary GQM

Goal	Improve the usability of the ticket booking feature from the point of view of a person booking a ticket (end user)
Purpose	Improve
Quality issue	Usability
Object	The ticket booking feature
Viewpoint	End user
Question	Q1: How long does it take a user to complete the booking?
Metrics	M1: Average task time
	M2: Standard deviation from the average
	M3: Percentage of cases exceeding the average maximum limit
Question	Q2: What are the completion rates of the feature?
Metrics	M4: Percentage of successfully completed bookings
Question	Q3: How satisfied are the users with the feature?
Metrics	M5: Average subjective rating by users grading the feature

In fact, the team constructing GQMs needs to accomplish a thorough work of understanding the context of the organisation itself, its mission, strategy, policy and high level goals. The team also needs to understand the local context of the object being measured, which can be a product or some process within a project. Finally, viewpoints of various stakeholders need to be taken into consideration to serve as another important element formulating the goals. The whole process involves interviewing stakeholders, analysing the environment and collaboration between the corporate management, project and GQM team. The derived goals need to be analysed with regards to their relevancy and relation to the high level goals [2].

Evidently, deriving the specific goals is a lengthy and nontrivial process. Therefore presenting only the specific goals and their corresponding GQMs is insufficient to understand the greater context and the relationship between specific goals, the environment and strategic high level goals of the organisation. So the question arises, what techniques and approaches can be used to simplify the process of deriving the set of specific goals? Furthermore, can the context and its relationships with the specific goals be represented in a concise and comprehensive manner?

Yet one more important aspect related to the metrics is related to the actors involved. Does the measurement process involve personnel, devices or software? Who or what is responsible for accomplishing the goal and gathering the measurement data?

The GQM's tabular format above is in fact only a concise output of the work preceding it, while the context and the actors involved with the system can be conveyed through text or by using other modelling approaches [2]. The KAOS goal modelling approach provides tools and techniques necessary to reflect the strategic context and actors involved. In the following section, KAOS and its tools are introduced, and the benefits of combining it with GQM is elaborated upon based on an example.

3   Goal Modelling: Keep All Objectives Satisfied (KAOS)

Goal modelling is an approach widely used in requirements engineering, and it allows to capture requirement by analysing a software system's high-level goals and contextual environment.

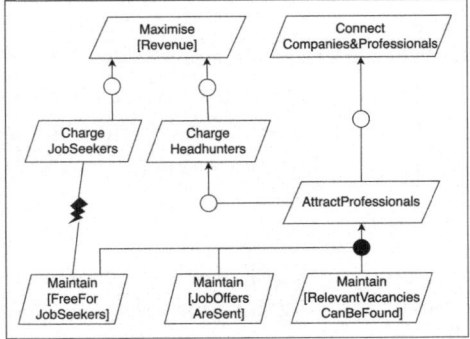

Fig. 2. Goal model for a professional social network

The specific approach being introduced here is KAOS. The abbreviation stands for Knowledge Acquisition in automated specification or Keep All Objectives Satisfied, but within this paper it will be interchangeably referred to it as KAOS and the goal model. The goal model uses expressive and concise diagrammatic notation to convey the flow and refinement of a system's high level strategic goals into lower-level technical goals. Moreover, it can conve various complex relations between the goals at different levels [1].

Figure 2 demonstrates a simple example of applying goal model in the context of building a social network for professionals. This fairly simple diagram contains several aspects that worth noting:

1. The top level element are the high level strategic goals of the system being built. There are two high-level goals: to generate revenue, and to connect companies with professionals. The strategic goals are then broken down into finer-grained goals in a top down fashion, such that the goals on the third level in the diagram are actually describing the technical design objectives of the system.
2. Relationships between goals at different levels can be identified and denoted. The first type is the relationship between a parent goal and its direct children.

Does the system need to achieve all of the child goals in order to satisfy a parent goal, or the child goals are actually alternatives, and fulfilling only one of them is sufficient? The KAOS notation uses something called or- and and-refinement to expressing that, and the refinements are denoted by the blank and solid circles serving as connection between the goals (Fig. 3).

The solid black circle denotes that all child goals have to be fulfilled, and is call complete and-refinement, as in *AttractProfessionals* goal and its children [1].

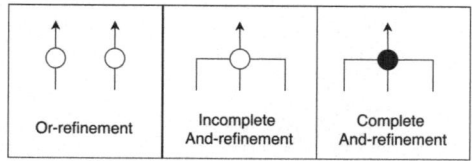

Fig. 3. Refinement types

If there are two or more blank circle coming out of a single goal, like in the case of the *GenerateRevenue* goal, it denotes that the children connected through the circles are alternative ways of satisfying the goal. It is referred to as or-refinement.

The case in-between, not present in the example diagram, is referred to as incomplete and-refinement, which has the meaning that only some and not all the child goals need to be achieved in order to satisfy the parent goal. It is denoted by a single blank circle pointing an arrow at the parent goal, with several lines coming out of it and connecting the circle with the child goals.

3. Having system goals in one place, allows one to analyse the goals and to identify and denote the conflict between the goals on different levels. A lightning bolt shape connection is used for that, as can be observed in the case of two apparently conflicting goals from the example: *ChargeJobSeekers* and *Maintain[FreeForJobSeekers]*. Together with identifying conflict, the goal model approach suggest various mechanisms of resolving the conflicts [1].

4. As can observed, the goals on the third level have the prefix Maintain before them. This comes from the notion of behavioural and soft goals used in KAOS. Behavioural goals are preceded by prefixes such as Achieve, Maintain and Avoid, and denote some logical constraints on the behaviour of the system. Achieve means that the goal has to be achieved at some point, and often comes with a conditional close dictating when it should be achieved. Maintain defines that some desirable state needs to be up-kept in the system at all times, while avoid means the opposite, i.e. that some state must never occur. Soft goals, in turn, denote other less stringent conditions on the system, and use prefixes such as maximise, minimise. This technique of defining various types of goals provides an expressive and fairly flexible tool of conveying constraints on the system and its environment through the goal statements.

For some goals, a different refinement strategy can be used. Instead of defining subgoals, an obstacle preventing the goal from being achieved can be defined. Figure 4 represents an example of such a case.

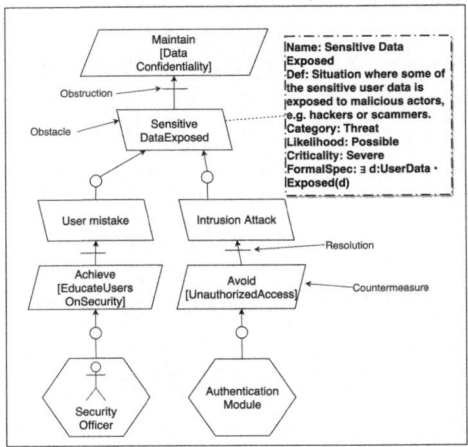

Fig. 4. Goal model obstacles and agents

There are several important aspects in this example too:

1. A goal common to most software systems dealing with personal user data is keeping the user data confidential. An obstacle obstructing that goal, i.e. preventing its satisfaction, would be exposure of some sensitive user data. The obstacle is further refined into two alternative sub-obstacles, and then countermeasures for both of them are found. According to the notation the crossed arrows denote obstruction and resolution relationships. An attentive eye will also notice that obstacles are represented inside a horizontally flipped parallelogram, which signals that obstacles are opposite of goals.
2. There is a table on the right of the *SensitiveDataExposed* obstacle, providing additional details such as the definition, category, likelihood, criticality and even a formal specification expressed using predicate logic. Such tables can be provided for any goals or obstacles, that need an extra level of detail or clarification.
3. Yet, the aspect of biggest interest is the fact that the lowest level goals are attached to hexagons, which represent agents. Agents can be software modules, individuals or devices. Individuals are normally denoted with a human figure, while non-human agents are denoted with titles only. This is one of the key aspects of the goal model, since it allows to attach each goal on the lowest level to an agent, thus connecting the strategic goals with the system or environmental elements responsible for satisfying them. Normally, each low-level goal will have one agent responsible for fulfilling it. In cases when a goal has several agents, the possibility of further refining the goal should be

considered. On the other hand, if an agent is responsible for too many goals, the refinement and better definition of the agent should be considered too.

It is worth noting that the examples in Fig. 2 and Fig. 4 had both business and human related goals (e.g. *GenerateRevenue* and *EducateUsersOnSecurity*), which were included on purpose. The purpose of including such goals is to demonstrate that the goal model approach can be used in various context, not limited to technical requirements specification. In fact goal modelling can be used to reconcile and align technical project decision with the business goals [4]. The goal model diagram in its essence is a mind map, which allows one to visualise the goals and the context, analyse how the elements relate and synchronise between each other, expand the solution, spot conflicts and obstacles.

To summarise, goal modelling allows one to define strategic goals, expand and refine them into lower-level finer-grained goals, and express their breakdown structure and flow. The concise and expressive notation tools such as or-/and-refinements, conflict and obstacles identification allow one to express various relations between goals and subgoals, and identify possible barriers on the way of achieving them. The notion of agents allows to explore and define the actors involved with the system, and to allocate and assign their responsibilities. Altogether, it comprises a powerful tool allowing one to convey the strategic and environmental context, technical and business constraints and actors involved.

4   Combining GQM and KAOS

In this section, an example of combining the two approaches is presented based on the case of the ticket booking company's web application from the second section.

Before building a GQM, the company's high level strategic goals need to be analysed and understood. Increasing revenue is a high level goal shared by many companies. The techniques and tools introduced in the previous section will be used to derive lower level specific goals from the strategic goal, and reflect the thought and derivation process (Fig. 5).

As was mentioned in the previous section, the goal model diagram is normally constructed in a top down manner. Despite the fact that the diagram in the example (Fig. 5) is of relatively small size, there is a number of techniques used to describe various relationship between the goals:

1. The top goal has two subgoals connected by using an or-refinement. The or-refinement signals that the two subgoal are alternatives, i.e. the company can either try to *IncreaseNumberOfBookings*, which is the central function of the web application, or try to *SellBannerAdvertising* for third parties and extra services.

2. Following the refinement of the *IncreaseNumberOfBookings* goal, one can see that it has two subgoals itself. Thus in order to have more bookings the company needs to acquire new customers or retain the existing ones. The corresponding goals are *Maintain[CustomerAcquisition]* and *Maximise[CustomerRetention]*.

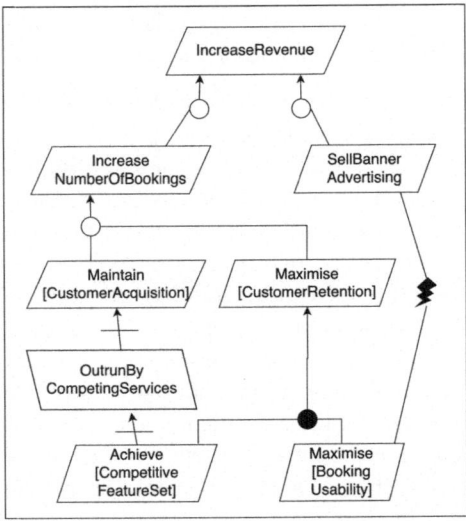

Fig. 5. From strategic to specific goals

3. At the bottom level, there are two goals: *Achieve[CompetitiveFeatureSet]* and *Maximise[BookingUsability]*. Both of them need to be fulfilled to satisfy the parent goal of retaining customers. The relationship between the parent goal and two subgoals is conveyed through the and-refinement, denoted by the solid black dot connecting the two levels.
4. Two more aspects that should be noted are the following: the of maintaining the CompetitiveFeatureSet is the countermeasure to the obstacle of losing customers to competing services, and the conflicts is identified between the goals BookingUsability and SellBannerAdvertising.

The diagram in the Fig. 5 describes the process of arriving at the specific goal of maximising the booking feature's usability, the GQM of which has been constructed in the second section of this paper, and has another specific goal next to it, for which a GQM can be constructed in a similar manner. The most important thing to note, is that the goal model diagram provides a concise and comprehensive way of visually conveying the context and derivation process of the low-level specific goals used for constructing GQMs.

Interestingly, GQMs can also be constructed for higher level goals, in particular for *Maximise[CustomerRetention]*, *IncreaseNumberOfBookings* and *Achieve[CustomerAcquisition]*. For example, the customer retention goal calls for a question of "Do the users come back to make repeat bookings through the service?", for which a simple metric can be provided as an answer, namely "Percentage of returning users making repeat bookings". The fact that the GQM can be used to measure the achievement and state of goals at various levels, implies that the GQM metrics can enhance the goal model approach, especially when it comes to soft goals. The very formulation of soft goals using verbs such as

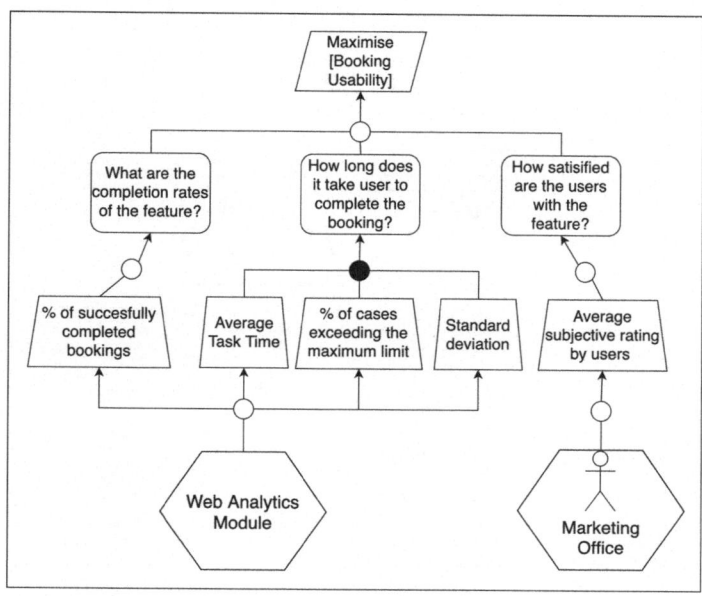

Fig. 6. Integrating GQM into the Goal model

Maximise, Minimise and Optimise calls for metrics to be used in order to track the state of the system, and declare concrete satisfaction criteria for these goals.

Another important point is that GQM can be integrated into the diagrammatic notation of the Goal model. Figure 6 exemplifies the case of the GQM constructed in the Sect. 2.

The notation introduced is a rounded-rectangle for questions and a trapezoid for metrics. This way the GQM can be integrated into the diagrammatic format of the goal model. The advantage of it is two-fold. Firstly, the exact placement of the GQM within the greater context can be observed. Secondly, and more importantly, the agents responsible for gathering particular metrics can be identified and denoted, as in the case of ascribing the user satisfaction metrics to the Marketing Office, and the rest of the metrics to the Web Analytics module.

5   Applying the Technique to an Open Source Project

The combination of the two modelling approaches has been tried and tested by the authors on an open source software project called KinApp [8]. KinApp is a mobile application that helps users to keep in touch with their family and friends while being away.

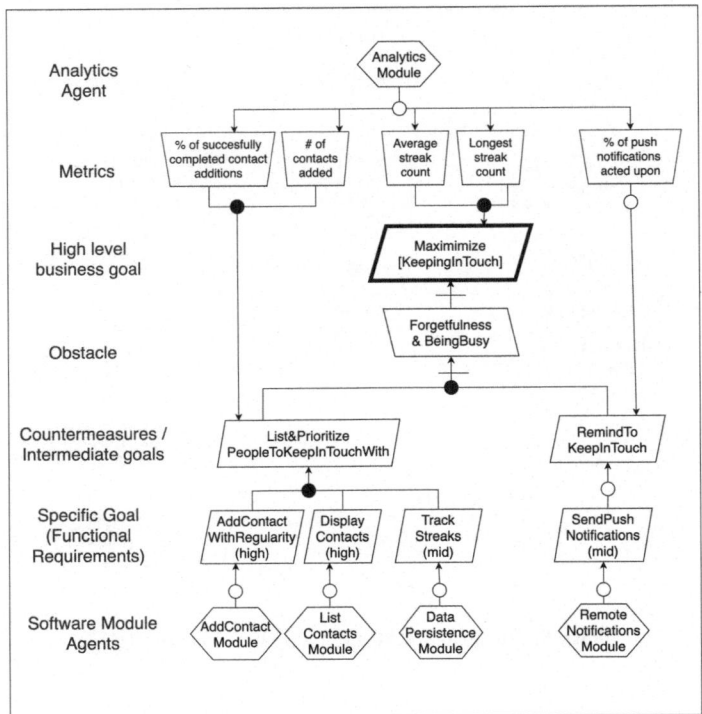

Fig. 7. KinApp's combined GQM and KAOS models

During user research stage preceding requirements elicitation, the authors were able to establish that there is a segment of potential users who would like to keep in touch with their relatives, but for various reasons are not able to do so. The most common reason named was forgetfulness due to being busy and having other priorities to take care of. Based on these findings, the authors developed and implemented a concept for the KinApp mobile application. It is a simple reminder app where users can add people they want to keep in touch with, and configure the desired frequency of contacting for each of them. The application will send reminders, and keep track of streaks (unbroken sequence of successfully contacting the family member or friend on a regular basis).

KAOS approach is used to produce specific goals, corresponding to functional requirements within the app. GQM in turn provided a way of measuring the effectiveness of the tool in achieving the high and intermediate level goals by providing measurement metrics.

Figure 7 demonstrates the process of applying KAOS and GQM to the high level goal of *Maximize[KeepingInTouch]*, right in the middle of the graph. As has been established during user research, the most common preventer is forgetfulness due to having other responsibilities. This can be represented as the *Forgetfulness&BeingBusy* obstacle within the goal model. The two countermeasures are 1) having a prioritized list of people to contact and 2) to remind users to keep in touch. We introduce them as the two intermediate goals. The prioritized list represents the main functionality of the app. It will require several essential features:

- Adding people to list
- Configuring regularity of contact, i.e. how often does the user want to contact each person
- Displaying the list of added people

This translates into two specific goals with the highest implementation priority: *AddContactWithRegularity* and *DisplayContacts*. Another intermediate goal *RemindToKeepInTouch* translates into a specific functional requirement of sending push notifications to the user as reminders that sufficient time has passed since the last contact with a particular person.

Table 2. GQM for *Maximize[KeepingInTouch]*

Goal	Maximize keeping in touch with family and friends from the point of view of a person affected by forgetfulness and being busy (end user)
Question	Q1: Is the person able to follow up with the configured regularity for each added contact?
	Q2: What is the longest streak (an unbroken sequence of successfully contacting an added person in accordance with the regularity)?
	Q3: What is the average streak for all added contacts?
Metrics	M1: Longest streak count
	M2: Average streak count

GQM is then applied to make the above goals measurable. Table 2 demonstrates the process of arriving to metrics for *Maximize[KeepingInTouch]*.

Other metrics are similar to the ones demonstrated in the previous sections, and for the sake of keeping the example concise will not be delved into. Noteworthy, the introduced streak metrics necessitate a new functional requirement of having to track streaks for users. The corresponding specific goal is placed under the intermediate *ListAndPrioritize* goal, due to being closely related to the functionality within the goal. This points to the fact, that GQM and KAOS can complement each other and help to reveal implicit requirements during an early stage of a project's timeline.

Importantly, the resulting diagram also demonstrates the reasoning behind each of the specific goals, and serves as a concise and readable way to present the requirements for the project to both end-users and developers willing to join the effort. This can be especially valuable in the context of an open source project, as readability of requirements is one of the important characteristics for the success and adoption of a project by the open source community [9]. Moreover, the presence of high-level goals can allow the community to suggest alternative ways of achieving the goal, and could facilitate ideation process.

On the other hand, a possible drawback is that maintaining the diagrams relevant can become difficult as the project evolves, which is a common reason the open source projects tend to keep a minimally possible amount of informal documentation [9].

6   Conclusion

In summary, the GQM and KAOS goal model can be used together to derive and represent a system's high- and low-level goals, actors, relationship between them and appropriate metrics to measure various important aspect of the system.

The goal model can facilitate and reflect the extensive process of mapping the strategic goals and concrete specific goals of the system, which are a prerequisite to implementing GQM.

The GQM, in turn, provides a quantitative perspective on this mapping in the form of appropriate metrics rooted in the system's strategic context, and can provide quantification for goals at different abstraction levels. The complementary union of the two models enables a more comprehensive and encompassing approach to defining, analysing and refining software systems.

The combination of two approaches has been tried in the context of an open source mobile application, and allowed the authors to arrive at a set of specific functional requirements and metrics to measure the effectiveness of these functionality in achieving the high level business goal.

Moreover, the inter-complementary effect of both approaches was demonstrated, such that the KAOS serves specific goals to GQM, which simplify producing metrics. Whereas GQM facilitates discovery of implicit low-level goals through the questioning process of making high-level goals measurable.

Potential benefits and drawbacks of applying the combination in the context of an open source project were suggested. The benefits include increased readability and transparency of requirements to the open source developers community and the ability to see the origin and intent of each particular functionality. The latter can allow to suggest alternative or complementary ways of achieving high goals. A possible drawback is the difficulty of maintaining the diagrams and prose up-to-date as the project progresses and evolves. Future studies of applying the two models and those similar to them could allow to further analyze and identify the advantages and disadvantages of using the suggested combination.

References

1. Van Lamsweerde, A.: Requirements Engineering, pp. 287–349. Wiley, Chichester (2013)
2. Basili, V.R., Caldiera, G., Rombach, H.D.: The Goal Question Metric Approach. In: Encyclopaedia of Software Engineering, Wiley (1994)

3. Ullah, A., Lai, R.: Modeling business goal for business/IT alignment using requirements engineering. J. Comput. Inf. Syst. **51**, 21–28 (2011)
4. Ellis-Braithwaite, R., Lock, R., Dawson, R., Haque, B.: Towards an approach for analysing the strategic alignment of software requirements using quantified goal graphs. Int. J. Adv. Softw. 119–130 (2013)
5. Ivanov, V., Reznik, A., Succi, G.: Comparing the reliability of software systems: a case study on mobile operating systems, Innopolis University (2017)
6. Ivanov, V., Succi, G., Pischulin, V., Yi, J., Rogers, A., Zorin, V.: Design and validation of precooked developer dashboards (2018)
7. Basili, V.R., et al.: Determining the impact of business strategies using principles from goal-oriented measurement, Internationale Tagung Wirtschaftsinformatik, Books OCG, Vienna, Österreichische Computer Gesellschaft, Austria (2009)
8. KinApp, Github Repository, KinApp Mobile Open Source Application. https://github.com/nurlingo/adabi, 12 Mar 2020
9. Scacchi, W.: Understanding the requirements for developing open source software systems. IEE Proc. Softw. **149**(1), 24–39 (2002)
10. Scacchi, W.: Understanding requirements for open source software. In: Lyytinen, K., Loucopoulos, P., Mylopoulos, J., Robinson, B. (eds.) Design Requirements Engineering: A Ten-Year Perspective. LNBIP, vol. 14, pp. 467–494. Springer, Heidelberg (2009). https://doi.org/10.1007/978-3-540-92966-6_27

An XQuery Specification for Requests with Preferences on XML Databases

Maurice Tchoupé Tchendji[1] and Patrik Joslin Kenfack[2]($\boxtimes$)

[1] Department of Mathematics and Computer Science, University of Dschang,
Dschang, Cameroon
maurice.tchoupe@univ-dschang.org
[2] Department of Computer Science and Automated Systems, Belgorod State
Technological University, Belgorod, Russia
kenfackjoslin@gmail.com

Abstract. An exact query is a query in which the user specifies precisely what to retrieve from a database (XML or relational database). For these queries only data that strictly respect all user's conditions is returned. XML documents are generally semi-structured. Due to the non-existence or lack of knowledge of the model of the document being queried, when exact queries are used, there is a high risk of obtaining an empty result (in the case of too specific queries) or too large (in the case of too vague queries). In contrast to exact queries, requests with preferences aim to return only the most relevant results in order to avoid empty or too important results as much as possible. To achieve this goal, requests with preferences generally consist of two parts: the first part is used to express strict constraints and the second part to express preferences or wishes. The satisfaction of both parts increases the relevance of the corresponding results. This paper presents *XQuery preference*, an extension of the XQuery language, that allows to express requests with preferences relating to both the values and the structure of an XML document. A representation model of such requests based on the Generalized Tree Pattern (GTP) model is also proposed in order to allow an evaluation of these requests through a tree pattern matching process. Integration of the proposed language in open source implementations of XQuery like BaseX, Berkeley DB XML, eXist-db, Galax and much more, will allow users to get much more relevant responses to their concerns.

Keywords: Semi-structured documents · XQuery · XQuery preference · XML · Open source

1 Introduction

One of the consequences of the proliferation of online information today is data diversity. XML is widely used as a core technology for knowledge management within companies and the dissemination of data on the Web (such as product catalogues), as it allows semi-structured data to be organized and manipulated.

V. Ivanov et al. (Eds.): OSS 2020, IFIP AICT 582, pp. 120–130, 2020.
https://doi.org/10.1007/978-3-030-47240-5_12

A collection of XML documents is considered to be a forest of trees with labelled nodes. To manipulate the data stored in XML and extract the relevant information in terms of structure and/or content, many query languages have been proposed such as XPath [6] and XQuery [7]. Indeed, these query languages take into account both the content and the structure of underlying documents, as it can completely change their relevance and adequacy with regard to the needs expressed by the user. However, it is important to note that in order to query a document using these languages, the user must a priori know its structure. This requirement is difficult to meet in an open environment such as the Web, where document structures are not always available. Thus, due to the non-existence or lack of knowledge of the model of the document being queried, the documents are queried almost blindly. Query writers in this context do so according to an imaginary document structure they believe to be that of the document. Such queries would generally return either no results (cases of too specific queries having little or no match with the content or structure of the document in question) or, in the extreme, too many results (case of too general queries intensively using wildcards).

The problems of absence or very large number of results of a query have also emerged within the classical database community. *Requests with preference* aims to be a solution to this problem. Intuitively, a request with preferences specifies the user's wishes and consists of two parts specifying on the first one, the mandatory requirements called *constraints* and on the second part, the optional requirements called *wishes or preferences*. However, a result of a request with preferences must necessarily satisfy the first part and possibly the second; if there is at least one answer satisfying the first and second part of the query, only the answers satisfying both parts must be returned as a result.

Some specific languages (generally extensions of SQL or XPath) have been proposed for the formulation of queries with preferences: *SQLf* [2], *Preference SQL* [10], *Preferences Queries* [5], ... for relational databases (RBD), *XPref* [1], *Preference XPATH* [9], *PrefSXPath* [13], ... for XML databases (XML BDs). Generally, proposed extensions of XPath language for importing the concept of preferences are only interested in either value based preferences [1,9] or structure based preferences [13]. Our approach takes into account these two types of preferences in order to better satisfy user requirements.

The rest of this paper is organized as follows: Sect. 2 presents some concepts related to XML documents, queries languages and open source implementations, we detail our specifications by presenting in Sect. 3, a grammar for the language *XQuery preference* and the representation model. And we finally end with a conclusion and future work.

2   XML Document and Queries Languages

An XML document is commonly considered as a tree where nodes are the elements or attribute names, and edges represent the child node's membership of the parent node and where leaves are the contents of the elements or attribute values. An XML database is a forest of XML document trees. The Fig. 2 illustrates an example of a tree representation of an XML document (Fig. 1).

```
<?xml version="1.0" encoding="UTF-8"?>
<persons>
  <person id="122">
    <profile>
      <name>Joel Dongmo</name>
      <email>joeldongmo@gmail.com</email>
    </profile>
    <experience>3</experience>
    <diploma>MSc</diploma>
    <skills>
      <java>3</java>
      <spring-mvc>4</spring-mvc>
      <symfony>4</symfony>
    </skills>
  </person>
</persons>
```

Fig. 1. XML document.

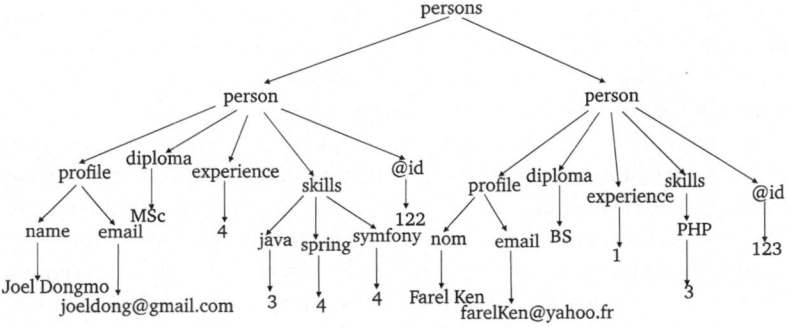

Fig. 2. Tree representation of an XML document.

The use of XML documents requires the ability to extract information and reformulate it for applications. Thus, there are many languages to retrieve information from a semi-structured document. Here we present the most popular: XPath and XQuery.

2.1 XPath

XPath allows to designate one or more nodes in an XML document, using path expressions. Thus, an XPath expression is a sequence of steps. $[/]step_1/step_2/.../step_n$. An XPath step consists of an axis, a filter and a predicate (optional): $axe :: filtre[predicat]$ The axis indicates a search direction. The most used axes are parent-child (represented by A/B) and descendant axis $(A//B)$. The filter selects a node type. For example the expression A/B returns all elements B children of an element A. Predicates select content.

2.2 XQuery

XQuery [7] is the query language recommended by the W3C to extract information from many types of XML data sources. XQuery is the XML equivalent of

SQL language, for retrieving data contained in relational databases and inherits the properties of several other languages. From XPath it uses the path expression syntax for addressing elements in XML documents. From SQL it takes up the idea of a series of clauses based on keywords that provide a model for data restructuring (the SQL SELECT-FROM-WHERE model). XQuery queries have several expression forms, the most famous is the FLWOR form. The acronym FLWOR comes from the reserved words of the language which make help to define the main clauses of this type of expression: **For - Let - Where - Order By - Return**.

Each clause in a FLWOR expression plays a particular role in the query and some of these clauses are optional. Thus, a FLWOR instruction consists of the following parts:

- **For:** iteration on an XML document part list
- **Let:** allows the assignment of values to a variable
- **Order by:** sorting results
- **Where:** restriction clause (constraints)
- **Return:** form of the expression to be returned

An example of this type of request is given in Fig. 3. This query select the email addresses and skills of people who have a Java skill level above 3 and have more than two years of experience.

```
FOR $p IN document("candidat.xml")//persons, $c IN $p/skills
WHERE $c/java >= 3 AND $p/experience > 2
RETURN <result> {$p//profile/email} {$c}</result>
```

Fig. 3. Example of an XQuery query

2.3   Open Source Implementations of XQuery

There are many open source implementations of XQuery. We present here a non-exhaustive list of them:

- BaseX is a very light-weight, high-performance and scalable XML Database engine and XPath/XQuery 3.0 Processor, including full support for the W3C Update and Full Text extensions all developed in Java. It comes with interactive user interfaces (desktop, web-based) that give users great insight into their data [8].
- eXist-db is a high-performance open source native XML database - a NoSQL document database and application platform built entirely around XML technologies. A Browser-based IDE allows managing and editing all artifacts belonging to an application. Syntax-coloring, code-completion and errorchecking help to get it right. Being a complete solution, eXist-db tightly integrates with XForms for complex form development [12].

- Galax is an open-source implementation of XQuery, the W3C XML Query Language. It includes several advanced extensions for XML updates, scripting, and distributed programming. Implemented in O'Caml, Galax comes with a state of the art compiler and optimizer. Most of Galax's architecture is formally documented, making it ideal for users interested in teaching XQuery, in building new language extensions, or developing new optimizations [11].
- Oracle Berkeley DB XML is an open source, embeddable XML database with XQuery-based access to documents stored in containers and indexed based on their content. Implemented in C, Oracle Berkeley DB XML is built on top of Oracle Berkeley DB and inherits its rich features and attributes.

XML queries (XPath or XQuery) to be evaluated on XML documents (trees), need to be represented in a model (a tree representation) in order to facilitate their evaluation. Therefore, evaluating the query is equivalent to apply the corresponding model to the XML tree trough a *tree pattern matching* process.

2.4 Generalized Tree Pattern (GTP)

The concept of the generalized tree model (GTP) is introduced in [4] and allows to express more precisely the semantics of XQuery. The arcs of a GTP may be Parent-Child (PC), Ancestor-Descendant (AD) or optional. They are indicated by solid edges, double solid edges and dotted edges, respectively. A mandatory arc links an sub-expression corresponding to clauses *FOR* and *WHERE* with the rest of the query. An optional arc links an subexpression corresponding to clauses *LET* and *RETURN* with the rest of the query.

Definition 1. A generalized tree pattern is a couple $G = (T, F)$ where T is a tree and F a Boolean formula such as.

- Each node in the tree T is labeled with different variables and has a group number.
- To each arc of T is associated a pair of labels $< x, m >$, where $x \in \{PC, AD\}$ specifies the axis (parent-child and ancestor-descendant, respectively) and $m \in \{mandatory, optional\}$ specifies the arc's status.
- F is a Boolean combination of predicates applicable to nodes.

Zhimin Chen et al. [4] also propose an algrithm for translating an XQuery expression[1] in GTP. The request is put in a canonical form and is then parsed clause by clause while the GTP is progressively built up to the last clause, we invite you to read [4] for more details. The GTP is intended to be mapped (*Pattern matching*) to the XML tree.

Definition 2. A *Pattern Match* of a GTP $G = (G, F)$ in a tree collection C is a subtree h partial: $h : G \rightarrow C$ such that:

---

[1] The GTP model deals with a very significant subset of the XQuery language and supports nesting, quantizer, grouping and aggregation.

- h contains at least group 0 of G.
- h preserves the relational structure of G. This means that whenever h is defined on two nodes u, v and there is a PC arc (respectively AD) (u, v) in G, then h(v) is a son (respectively a descendant) of h(u).
- h satisfies the Boolean formula F of G (Fig. 4).

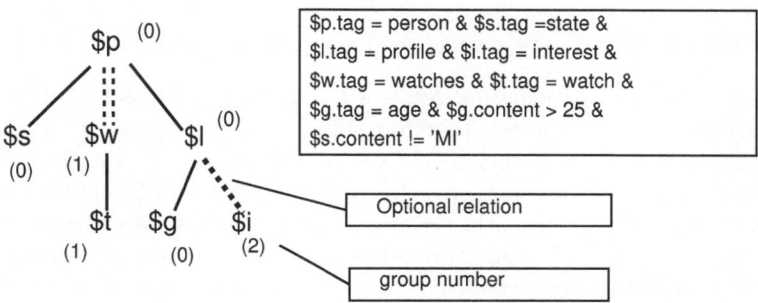

```
FOR $p IN document("auction.xml")//person, $l In $p/profile
WHERE $l/age > 25 AND $p//state != 'MI'
RETURN<result> {$p//watches/watch} {$l/interest}</result>
```

Fig. 4. Example of an XQuery expression and corresponding GTP query.

3 XQuery Preference: A Language for Expressing XQuery Requests with Preference

In order to take into account the two types of preferences, namely on values based and structure based, we propose an extension of XQuery at two levels: an extension of XPath language for the integration of structural preferences, through the use of the operator "!" introduced in [13] and the addition of a new clause (the **Pref** clause) for the expression of preferences on content.

3.1 Grammar of the Language *XQuery Preference*

Based on the grammar given in [4] to describe a significant subset of the XQuery language, we consider the following grammar for XQuery preference expressions (Fig. 5).

FLWR ::= (ForClause | LetClause) + WhereClause **PrefClause** ReturnClause.
ForClause ::= FOR f_{v1} IN E_1 , ..., f_{vn} IN E_n.
LetClause ::= LET l_{v1} := E_1 , ..., l_{vn} := E_n.
WhereClause ::= WHERE $\varphi(E_1, ..., E_n)$.
PrefClause ::= Pref $\varphi(E_1, ..., E_n)$
ReturnClause ::= RETURN $E_1...E_n$.
E_i ::= FLWR | XPATH.

Fig. 5. Syntax of XQuery preference expressions

For simplicity, we make other assumptions about our grammar as follows.

- The atomic predicates allowed in the boolean formula φ are the integrated relop predicates ($<, \leq, >, \geq, =, \neq$) or the integrated predicate $empty(FLWR)$. The operand of a relop predicate can be one of the following: constant c, XPath expression XPE, or $agg(XPE)$, where agg is one of the integrated aggregate functions, namely, avg, $count$, min, max, or sum [4].
- The XPath expressions used are expressions extended by the operator "!" except for the **Pref** clause.

3.2   Expression of Preferences on Values and Structure

XPath language is a component of XQuery and is used to extract nodes from the XML document. This language therefore allows you to browse the structure of the document. We use the notation "!" (a unary operator) introduced by Tchoupé et al. [13] for expressing preferences in an XPath (sub)path. For example, in the path $Q_1 = /a/b!/c$, the subpaths $/a$ and $/c$ represent the *constraints*, while $/b$ represents a *preference*. Q_1 is interpreted as a request returning all occurrences c_i of the node c such that the path from the root to c_i must have an occurrence of a and possibly an occurrence of b. The occurrences c_i candidates to be included in the solution are the sub-trees of the form $/a_i/b_i/c_i$ or $/a_i/c_i$. For simplification purposes, we assume that operator "!" can only be applied on a single node and not on an XPath subpath for example $(a/b/c)!$. In other words, this operator does not take into account parentheses.

We introduce a new clause in the XQuery language: the **Pref** clause. A Boolean clause to define preferences (wishes) on results. Just like the clause *Where*, *Pref* will define the constraints on the values but with the only difference that, it will not accept an embedded XQuery expression.

In this way, requests for *XQuery preference* language are composed of two parts: one to express mandatory constraints (the *Where* clause), and the other to express preferences or wishes (the *Pref* clause). The language *XQuery preference* therefore follows the bipolar model. Thus, the answers satisfying constraints and wishes are returned in priority to the user. But if such answers do not exist then results that satisfy only the constraints are delivered. The example below shows an example of an XQuery request with preferences on values and structure.

Example 1. *XQuery query with preference on values and structure:* Let's consider a query in witch, a user is looking for a candidate with Java skills and at least a diploma level above 3. But would like this person to have at least two years of experience, and skills with the framework Sping-boot would be a plus. The user also wants the returnees to have filled in the information on their profiles.

In this example, the condition on Java skills and diploma level above 3 is a constraint while the condition on the number of years of experience and Spring-Boot skills is a wish whose satisfaction increase relevance of the associated result.

The Fig. 6 illustrates how this request can be expressed in the language *XQuery preference*.

For this request, people with only Java skills and a diploma level above 3 represent potential responses but are dominated by candidates who have in addition, an experience of more than 2 years and Spring-Boot skills. However, if no answer respects all the constraints of the **Pref** clause, only those that best integrate the user's preferences are returned: They are called *undominated solutions*. The operator "!" present in the XPath expression $p/profile!//name$ specifies that the *person* elements with a *profile* sub-element are preferred. For now, we have imposed certain restrictions on *XQuery preference* expressions. For example, we require that XPath paths defined in the clause *Pref* do not include a preference element for the simple reason that all these paths are already preferential since they appear in the pref clause.

For $p in document('candidate.xml')//persons
Where $p/skills/Java > 1 AND $p/diploma > 3
Pref $p/experience > 2 AND $p/skills/Spring-Boot > 1
Return <result> {$p/profile!//name} </result>

Fig. 6. An example of XQuery request with preference on structure and values

In the Sect. 2.4 we presented a model for XPath and XQuery queries. Indeed, these model considerably reduce the complexity of evaluating requests. In the following section, in the same vein we propose a query model for *XQuery preference* requests based on the GTP model of Chen Zhimin et al.

3.3 GTP Request with Preference

As previously stated, GTP model is used to represent exact XQuery queries. We adapt this model as follows for the representation of XQuery requests with preferences:

– to the GTP tree we add a new type of arc called *preference arcs*. A preference arc can be of the type AD (Ancestral-descending), PC (Parent-child) or PP (Preference Path).
– the Boolean formula F verifying the predicates applicable to nodes is divided into two groups of formulas S and P:
  • group S defines the mandatory constraints.
  • and group P the preferential constraints (wishes).
– A set of nodes forms a group if they are connected to each other by non-optional or preferential relationships.

The Fig. 7 illustrates an example of a GTP request with preference (see Fig. 8), distinguishing between the different types of arcs to take preferences into account:

- The arcs *preferences of type ancestor-descendant (APN)*. This type of arc allows to represent a structural preference between an element and its descendant for example $a//b!$
- The arcs *of type parent-child preferences (PPN)*. For the representation of a structural preference between an element and its child for example $a/b!$
- Finally, arcs of the type *preference path (PP)* for the representation of preferences on values. This type of arc will be generated for XPath expressions found in the Pref clause.

The formula group S defines constraints on mandatory nodes while the group P defines constraints on preference nodes. All the nodes of the tree are part of the same group because they are all connected to each other by optional arcs or preference. More formally, a GTP with preference is defined as follows:

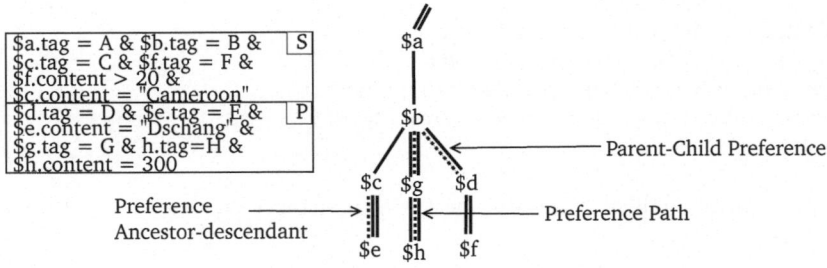

Fig. 7. Example of representation of a GTP request with preference

Definition 3. A generalized tree pattern with preference is a couple $G = (T, F)$ where T is a tree and F a Boolean formula such as:

- Each node in the tree T is labeled with a different variable and has a group number.
- to each arc of T is associated a tag e, where $e \in \{PC, AD, OP, PN, APN, PP\}$
    • **PC, AD:** specify the parent-child and ancestor-descendant axis
    • **PN, APN:** specify respectively the parent-child preference and ancestor-descendant preference axes.
    • **OP, PP:** specify the optional axes and preference path respectively.
- F is a group of formula S and P specifying respectively a Boolean combination of predicates applicable to non-preferential nodes and to *preferential nodes*.

Definition 4. A node is said to be a preference if it is located at target of a preference arc.

FOR $p IN document("doc.xml")//A, $b IN $a/B
WHERE $b/D!/F >= 20 AND $b/C = "Cameroon"
PREF $b/G/H = 300 AND $b/C//E = "Dschang"
RETURN <result> {$b/C//E!} </result>

Fig. 8. XQuery preference request corresponding to the GTP with preference of the Fig. 7

The model thus presented integrates the different elements for the representation of preferences in the GTPs. The GTP with preference is obtained by a *parsing* of the query *XQuery preference* as in [4]. The process for parsing a request is as follows: We have a global analysis environment ENV to manage information collected from the request analysis i.e The association variable name-nodes. The query is parsed clause by clause. We also use a help function $buildTPQ(xp)$ where xp is an extended XPath expression[2], which constructs part of GTP with preference from xp. This function is described as follows:

- Each time that xp starts with the built-in document function, a new GTP is added to ENV.
- If xp begins with a variable, the node associated with this variable is searched for in the tree and the new part resulting from xp starts from it.
- When xp contains the operator "!", The arcs associated with the nodes considered are of PN or APN type, depending on the axis (/ or // respectively) and the constraints linked to these nodes are placed in group P of the GTP formula.

During the analysis of a Pref clause, the arcs created are of type PP and the constraints linked to these nodes are placed in group P.

4 Conclusion

In this paper, we have made two major proposals: *XQuery preference* an extension of the XQuery language for the expression of requests with *preferences* which can relate to both the structure and the content; the GTP model with preference an extended version of the GTP model for the representation of XQuery preference queries; The examples given show that the proposed language is quite expressive and thus makes it possible to meet a variety of needs. We have carried out a study for the evaluation of GTPs requests with preference by an adaptation of the algorithm $Twig^2Stack$ [3] for the evaluation of exact GTPs requests. Due to the limitation of the number of pages in this paper, we could not describe it here, but it is accessible via the open repository on Github[3]. The results obtained

---

[2] An extended XPath expression is an expression containing the notation $ and the operator "!".

[3] https://github.com/patrikken/PrefTwig2Stack.

are very interesting and show that we can extend the existing algorithms with a very small loss in performance but an improvement in terms of quality of the results delivered to users.

Furthermore, this work serves as the foundation for a much larger body of work, which could be the subject of further study. Among which, integration and experimentation of XQuery preference in the presented open source sources implementations, an in-depth study of the nested XQuery preference queries and the search for the best algorithms for evaluating queries with preferences.

References

1. Agrawal, R., Kiernan, J., Srikant, R., Xu, Y.: XPref: a preference language for P3P. Comput. Netw. **48**, 809–827 (2005)
2. Bosc, P., Pivert, O.: SQLf query functionality on top of a regular relational database management system. In: Pons, O., Vila, M.A., Kacprzyk, J. (eds.) Knowledge Management in Fuzzy Databases. Studies in Fuzziness and Soft Computing, vol. 39, pp. 171–190. Physica-Verlag HD, Heidelberg (2000). https://doi.org/10.1007/978-3-7908-1865-9_11
3. Chen, S., Li, H., Tatemura, J., Hsiung, W., Agrawal, D., Candan, K.: Twig$_2$stack: bottom-up processing of generalized-tree-pattern queries over XML documents. In: Proceedings of the 32nd International Conference on Very Large Data Bases (VLDB 2006), pp. 283–294 (2006)
4. Chen, Z., Jagadish, H.V., Lakshmanan, L.V.S., Paparizos, S.: From tree patterns to generalized tree patterns: on efficient evaluation of XQuery. In: Proceedings of the 29th International Conference on Very Large Data Bases (VLDB 2003), vol. 29, pp. 237–248. VLDB Endowment (2003). http://dl.acm.org/citation.cfm?id=1315451.1315473
5. Chomicki, J.: Preference formulas in relational queries. ACM Trans. Database Syst. **28**(4), 427–466 (2003). https://doi.org/10.1145/958942.958946
6. Consortium, W.: XML path language (XPath) 2.0 (2006). http://www.w3.org/TR/XPath20
7. Consortium, W.: XQuery 1.0: an XML query language, October 2004. (w3C Working Draft)
8. Database, T.U.K., Group's, I.S.: Implements the XQuery update facility; full-text support (since 2006). http://www.basex.org
9. Kießling, W., Hafenrichter, B., Fischer, S., Holland, S.: Preference XPATH: a query language for e-commerce. In: Buhl, H.U., Huther, A., Reitwiesner, B. (eds.) Information Age Economy, pp. 427–440. Physica-Verlag HD, Heidelberg (2001). https://doi.org/10.1007/978-3-642-57547-1_37
10. Kießling, W., Endres, M., Wenzel, F.: The preference SQL system - an overview. IEEE Data Eng. Bull. **34**, 11–18 (2011)
11. Mary Fernàndez, J.S.: Galax: an XQuery implementation, 1 October 2009. http://galax.sourceforge.net
12. Meier, W.: The high-performance native XML database engine (since 2000). http://exist-db.org
13. Tchoupe Tchendji, M., Nguefack, B.: XPath bipolar queries and evaluation. In: Revue Africaine de la Recherche en Informatique et Mathématiques Appliquées, Special issue CARI 2016, vol. 27, October 2017

The Strategic Technical Debt Management Model: An Empirical Proposal

Paolo Ciancarini[1]($\boxtimes$) and Daniel Russo[2]

[1] University of Bologna - Italy and Innopolis University, Innopolis, Russia
`paolo.ciancarini@unibo.it`
[2] Department of Computer Science, Aalborg University,
Selma Lagerlöfs Vej 300, 9000 Aalborg, Denmark
`daniel.russo@cs.aau.dk`

Abstract. Increasing development complexity in software applications raises major concerns about technical debt management, also in Open Source environments. A strategic management perspective provides organizations with an action map to pursue business' targets with limited resources. This article presents the Strategic Technical Debt Management Model (STDMM) to provide practitioners with an actionable roadmap to manage their technical debt properly, considering both social and technical aspects. To do so, we pursued a theoretical mapping, exploiting a set of interviews of 124 carefully selected and well-informed domain experts of the IT financial sector.

Keywords: Technical debt · Strategic management · Empirical software engineering

1 Introduction

Software development is a complex social task, undertaken by groups of people who have to cope with existing legacy requirements, which need to evolve according to market expectations. Software is rarely developed from scratch, and its design integrity is shared among different people; moreover it changes in time, according to new and unpredictable requirements.

A primary concern of each organization which uses software is typically related to the maintenance of its assets, and the evolution of its products to deal with market competition [8]. This is the most common situation were shortcuts are undertaken for several reasons, typically related to budget or schedule constrains. Long-term software maintainability is often neglected, and a short-term perspective is pursued. Architectural layering and code smells are the typical results of such management, which drifts to poor software quality. This kind of pattern is well-known: it was named by Cunningham as *Technical Debt* (TD) [4]. A growing community holds that software quality practices to improve systems'

V. Ivanov et al. (Eds.): OSS 2020, IFIP AICT 582, pp. 131–140, 2020.
https://doi.org/10.1007/978-3-030-47240-5_13

sustainability (e.g., refactoring) is ultimately a business decision [10]. Even in the domain of open source software there is a trend into exploiting the concept of technical debt as intentional, hence strategic: see for instance the study on self-admitted technocal debt found in [7].

A support model is needed to allow developers and managers to make choices, i.e., whether or not to refactor [18]. The idea itself of *debt*, taken from finance, implies to manage with limited resources and make the best out of it. This has the following implications.

Firstly, it relates to a rational **trade-off** between quality and budget. This idea is deeply rooted in software managers. Maturity models (e.g., CMMI) are valuable frameworks to predict software quality according to the minimal software process requirements. Typically, for critical software, a CMMI level of 4 or 5 is required by contract. It should assure the customer that the software house undertakes full refactoring. Accordingly, the price per LOC incorporates this effort, increasing the value of software. On the contrary, to secondary software systems, which will be replaced soon, will be devoted less budget. Indeed, there is no economic rationality to assign the same relevance to a system's application or component. Thus, in a situation of limited resources, ones have to make choices and assign priorities. This means that not all software components will receive the same amount of resources, leading to different levels of quality within the same information system. Hence, it needs to be adequately managed, making such choices rational. Technical debt may arise from random processes and poorly managed development. Therefore, a management model helps to identify the sources of technical debt, so to assign them the respective priority.

Secondly, it is **quantifiable**. Once you take a bank loan, you have to repay it with interest rates. Interests are not always negative when the need is to deploy some secondary code good-enough-to-work and focus on strategic applications. Nevertheless, it should also be clear that, at a certain point in time, one has to repay the debt with its interests.

Thirdly, it permits to **make investments**. We do not always have enough budget or time to implement all requirements. However, if stakeholders consider one application of strategic value to exploit competitive advantages, organizations need to make investments. So, they will earn much more than they have to pay for interests. Subsequently, software houses are willing to deploy some applications, also with high technical debt, since the earnings from their use will fully repay their later refactoring, letting make them profit.

Fourth, **debt management** needs to be considered. Issuing any debit note has its cost because it implies some operations which have to be undertaken to grant the loan. Typically, the investment needs to be planned, the debt traced, repaid, and managed. It is the same for software projects. Once the need for investments emerges, what does it mean in terms of technical debt management? So, questions like *where* is the debt, *how* and *when* are we going to repay it, and *who* should do that - have to be taken into great care.

In our research journey, we experienced all those issues in highly complex banking information systems [16,17]. Also, we modeled those concerns in an ontology to make such knowledge representation inter-operable with other similar systems [1].

It is quite usual for a large organization to exploit different software houses for the evolution and maintenance of the information systems. This is a typical situation were technical debt emerges for several reasons:

- Architectural stratification as a consequence of a lack of conceptual integrity.
- Applications become rapidly outdated, afflict by high maintenance cost, and difficult to evolve.
- Market competition pushes for new applications.
- Core System Optimization is costly, and the skills to evolve old mainframes are lacking.

The management of an information system's quality is, with such a setting, a challenging effort. Still, it is a pivotal task.

From a software management perspective, the four outlined financial implications suggest that the literature about technical debt [9,12] is unable to provide enough explanatory power of this phenomenon since the social part is missing. The reason is that technical debt is a socio-technical matter, and as such comprehensive handling is needed to address its complexity. In the end, managing technical debt means to control people.

To get a deep understanding of this crucial issue, we developed an innovative research design and involved 13 top managers of the IT banking industry for the items identification and 124 IT banking domain for the item validation and construct definition. We asked them to outline the most relevant *software quality concerns* related to banking information systems. We obtained 28 unique factors through the Delphi-like research design, which we mapped in the proposed managerial model.

The main contribution of our paper is the Technical Debt Management Model, gathered by highly relevant empirical research to provide the practitioner's community with a valuable tool to manage technical debt in a structured way.

In the rest of this paper, we will contextualize the metaphor of technical debt through the Agile triangle in Sect. 2. Moreover, we will briefly explain how we elicited software quality concerns by a high-level panel of banking industry experts in Sect. 3. After mapping the items, we propose a model to manage technical debt in Sect. 4. Finally, we conclude our study in Sect. 5.

2   The Technical Debt Triangle

The idea of technical debt is not a radically new one. In software engineering, we are well aware of software deterioration problems, where the complexity of software raises along with its evolution [11], and reuse [2,3]. Similarly, software ages when it is not able to cope with new requirements due to irreconcilable technology paradigms [15].

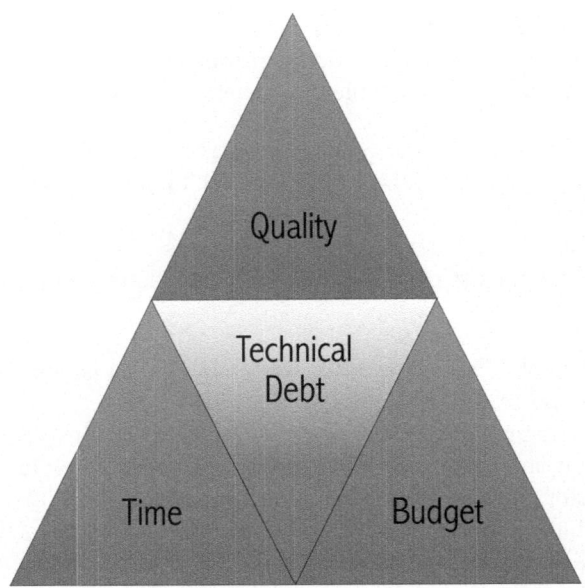

Fig. 1. Technical Debt Triangle

To better explain the concurrent drivers of technical debt, we elaborate on the idea of the Agile Triangle [6]. The three different dimensions of technical debt are budget, time, and scope. They are conflicting since it is not feasible to develop high-quality software with a low budget in a short time. This assumption is the baseline for any strategic software development model since you typically have to deal with limited resources. In an ideal situation, where resources are unlimited, there is no need for any strategic management effort, since strategic choices are simply not necessary. So, if we are focused on one corner, we are going to weaken the other two. If we are concerned about the scope, the relevant budget must be planned and sufficient time should be devoted to the project. If we need some new functionalities in a short time, it will have a high cost (since unplanned tasks require the organization to reschedule the work-flow), and quality will suffer from necessary fine-tuning before deployment, e.g., minor bug fix or refactoring. Finally, in case of a low budget, the project will last reasonably for an extended period, since few people can work on it. Moreover, the quality will also probably decrease since the most skilled (and paid) developers will work on other projects (Fig. 1).

These last two cases, which are the most frequent ones, typically lead to technical debt. Often, technical debt is beneficial because it permits to make investments in case of a project's budget, which is lower than that effectively needed. It is a continuous trade-off between long and short term perspectives. However, it needs to be a strategic (i.e., rational) decision. Often, technical debt is caused by subsequent uncontrolled, unplanned, and irrational tasks, which led to an explosion of its interests. At that point, organizations typically struggle because they feel to be on a sinking ship, were new applications just increase the debt, and no exit strategy is planned because they often do not know where to start to repay it [16].

A strategic management model is a roadmap, where any organizations, according to its internal and external constraints, plan the (i) what, (ii) how, (iii) when, and (iv) where the technical debt should be managed.

Several mapping studies of the literature have been pursued, to identify and analyze the elements required to manage technical debt [5]. These studies have proposed some taxonomies, which could be useful to understand the most impelling issues while dealing with technical debt. However, a taxonomy is not a management model.

Other scholars introduced a maturity model for technical debt management, where they identified three levels of awareness in software factories; see for instance [20]. Still, a proposal for a strategic management model is missing.

3   Research Design

Defining technical debt is hard [10]. In our research we identified the proxy-construct of *Software Quality Concern*. Our domain experts were able to express openly, in a structured scientific procedure, all concerns regarding the software quality of the information systems they were working on.

To do so, we first identified 13 top managers of the IT financial industry to cover in, a representative way, the entire the addressed problem. Those experts were able to elicit several concerns, and, using the Delphi methodology, they were able to reach full consensus about the solicited items. Afterward, we identified other 124 domain experts through a stratified random sampling technique and asked them to express their level of agreement with the proposed items and to add personal opinions on every single item.

In that way, we were able to identify the 28 concerns, namely: (1) Module interfaces complexity, (2) Interfaces architectural complexity, (3) Custom software quality, (4) Increase of maintenance costs, (5) Quality vs. Time & Budget, (6) Quality vs. System analysis, (7) System analysis vs. Documentation, (8) Documentation vs. Time & Budget, (9) New packages functionalities vs. complexity, (10) Packages vs. Documentation, (11) Packages documentation vs. System analysis, (12) Application & Maintenance contracts vs. Documentation, (13) International applications vs. Quality & Maintainability, (14) Domestic applications vs. Quality & Maintainability, (15) Measurement of software quality, (16) Lower developers' expertise and professionalism, (17) Contracting & Skills, (18) Lacking tools & Methodologies, (19) Establishment of internal and external development processes, (20) Developer's professionalism vs. Skills, (21) Developer's professionalism vs. Rates, (22) Web technologies vs. Methodologies, (23) Quality vs. Requirements, (24) Requirements vs. Methodologies, (25) Requirements vs. Technical jargon, (26) Data analysis vs. Functional analysis, (27) Functional analysis vs. Data modeling, (28) Documentation standards and tools. For a better understanding of the concerns and the research design, refer to [16, 17] (Fig. 2).

Fig. 2. Software Quality Concerns

After the elicitation and validation of the relevant concerns, we mapped them within an established technical debt management taxonomy [13]. Interestingly, the technical one has already been explored and led to the development of the SQALE method [12]. Indeed, SQALE identifies several technical sub-dimension and their related software metrics. However, we did not find in the scientific literature any similar framework addressing the social dimension. Therefore, we proposed a comprehensive managerial model. We pursued a theoretical mapping of the items within their related sub-dimensions. The outcome of the theoretical mapping for both technical and social dimensions is listed in Table 1.

Table 1. Technical Debt type mapping

Social		Technical [13]	
TD type	Items	TD type	Items
Staffing & Seniority	20, 21	Requirements	6, 14, 23, 24, 25
Skills & Training	16, 17, 21, 22	Design & Architecture	1, 2, 4, 6, 9, 11, 26, 27
Risk & Contracting	3, 5, 12, 17, 19, 20	Code	1, 4, 5, 10, 19, 23
Stakeholder involvement & Outsourcing	14, 17, 19, 25	Test & Defect	3, 4, 5, 6, 13, 15, 16
		Build & Versioning	4, 15, 18
		Documentation	4, 7, 8, 10, 11, 12, 28

Finally, we were able to relate the empirically gathered items within a relevant managerial concept, which is the base of our Strategic Technical Debt Management Model, described in the next section.

4   Strategic Technical Debt Management Model

The essential elements of any strategic management model are: situation analysis, strategy formulation, strategy implementation, and evaluation & control [19]. Such a model is typically non–linear since the surrounding environment changes more or less rapidly according to exogenous market-related factors. Consequently, we build our STDMM on such assumptions, fine–tailoring the evaluation and control phase, as represented in Fig. 3.

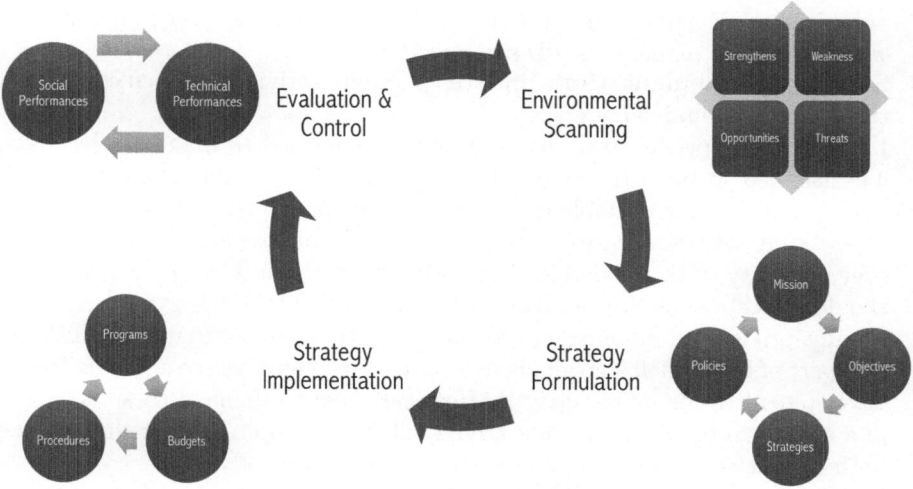

Fig. 3. Strategic Technical Debt Management Model

Thus, to strategically manage technical debt means to take into account:

1. **Situation analysis (Environmental Scanning).** The first step should raise awareness within the organization about its external and internal environment. Benchmarking competitors is always a good idea since there is no such absolute baseline. Indeed, markets that experience continuous requirements adaptations at high velocity may generate more TD concerning those who have to follow standardized quality processes (e.g., CMMI). Therefore, identifying *External Opportunities & Threats* supports effectively management decisions. This enables an organization to position itself to the market. Relevant questions might be: how does the market manage TD? Or where do competitors invest their debt? Afterward, *Internal Strengths & Weaknesses* have to be analyzed. In particular: how good is my organization in managing TD, or where go my investments, are fundamental questions to scan the internal environment. Typically, the first quantification of the already existing debt happens in this phase.

2. **Strategy Formulation.** After the assessment phase, the organization should draw its strategy to manage technical debt. Each strategy has four main pillars [19]. To make it self-evident, we propose key questions, useful to draw a strategy:
   - *Mission*: why should an organization exploit TD?
   - *Objective*: which results do we want to accomplish, and by when?
   - *Strategy*: which plan do we define to achieve mission & objectives?
   - *Policies*: which internal guidelines for TD decision making do we want to have?

   Of course, these are high-level questions, which need to be tailored to any organization. However, they provide good–enough fit for every organization which aim is to manage its TD strategically.

3. **Strategy Implementation.** Once the planning activity has been concluded, the strategy should carry on.

   In particular, specific *programs* and activities needed to manage effectively, TD has also to be outlined and followed. Continuous code inspection with quality metrics is a valuable example of this step.

   These kinds of plans have a price, which needs an ad hoc *budget*. Notably, every activity with no budget is poorly effective; thus, every organization should allocate enough resources. Otherwise, an STDMM is rather useless.

   Finally, *procedures*, intended as a sequence of steps needed to manage TD, are also part of the model. The aim is to leverage on TD to finance urgent software development needs or to repay it. However, *how* to manage these decisions in a complex organization is not trivial. Therefore, internal procedures guide both developers and management to use TD strategically.

4. **Evaluation & Control.** The last phase accounts for the continuous follow up of the strategy. Although the technical dimension of TD is a well known one [14], we introduced here also social aspects, which are equally important for an effective management strategy. We were able to elicit and validate through or research journey [16,17] relevant social dimension regarding TD management, which is described in Table 1.

   In particular, *staffing and seniority* impacts on TD, since a right mix of senior and junior developers enhances code quality. Moreover, the project team should be as stable as possible in time, as also suggested by Brook's law. *Skilled developers* on *ongoing training* are educated to deal with new complex tasks and technologies. For example, the presence of a training plan is a positive software quality indicator. *Risk mitigation through contracts*, which transfer TD to contractors (like Service Level Agreement), is a common practice for most organizations. These aspects poorly relate to technical assessment techniques of TD, although they have an impact on organizations. Thus, to effectively manage TD means to include risk and contracts within the strategy. Finally, any software is a collective product, which can be developed in different ways (e.g., internally or externally to the company). The involvement of *stakeholders*, especially *outsources* is a key quality issue. Continuous interaction is an effective way to have a complete overview of the development process and the use of TD. This is even more important for an outsourced project, where the customer typically has poor visibility about what is happening.

5   Conclusions

To conclude, this paper provides three main contributions. Firstly, it maps the social dimension of TD. Secondly, it proposes a strategic approach to manage TD. Finally, STDMM is a first attempt to include the social dimension of TD within a strategic technical debt management model.

Future works will focus on the extension and validation of the proposed model.

Acknowledgments. This work was partially funded by the Institute of Cognitive Sciences and Technologies (ISTC) of the Italian National Research Council (CNR), and the Consorzio Interuniversitario Nazionale per l'Informatica (CINI).

References

1. Ciancarini, P., Nuzzolese, A.G., Presutti, V., Russo, D.: Squap-ont: an ontology of software quality relational factors from financial systems. arXiv preprint arXiv:1909.01602 (2019)
2. Ciancarini, P., Russo, D., Sillitti, A., Succi, G.: A guided tour of the legal implications of software cloning. In: Proceedings of the 38th International Conference on Software Engineering Companion, ICSE 2016, pp. 563–572. ACM (2016)
3. Ciancarini, P., Russo, D., Sillitti, A., Succi, G.: Reverse engineering: a European IPR perspective. In: Proceedings of the 31st Annual ACM Symposium on Applied Computing, pp. 1498–1503. ACM (2016)
4. Cunningham, W.: The WyCash portfolio management system. ACM SIGPLAN OOPS Messenger **4**(2), 29–30 (1993)
5. Fernández-Sánchez, C., Garbajosa, J., Yagüe, A., Perez, J.: Identification and analysis of the elements required to manage technical debt by means of a systematic mapping study. J. Syst. Softw. **124**, 22–38 (2017)
6. Highsmith, J.: Agile Project Management: Creating Innovative Products. Pearson Education, London (2009)
7. Huang, Q., Shihab, E., Xia, X., Lo, D., Li, S.: Identifying self-admitted technical debt in open source projects using text mining. Empirical Softw. Eng. **23**(1), 418–451 (2017). https://doi.org/10.1007/s10664-017-9522-4
8. Khadka, R., et al.: How do professionals perceive legacy systems and software modernization? In: Proceedings of the 36th International Conference on Software Engineering, pp. 36–47. ACM/IEEE (2014)
9. Kruchten, P., Nord, R., Ozkaya, I.: Technical debt: from metaphor to theory and practice. IEEE Softw. **29**(6), 18–21 (2012)
10. Kruchten, P., Nord, R., Ozkaya, I.: Technical Debt: Reducing Friction in Software Development. Addison-Wesley, Boston (2019)
11. Lehman, M.M., Belady, L.A.: Program Evolution: Processes of Software Change. Academic Press Professional Inc., Cambridge (1985)
12. Letouzey, J., Ilkiewicz, M.: Managing technical debt with the SQALE method. IEEE Softw. **29**(6), 44–51 (2012)
13. Li, Z., Avgeriou, P., Liang, P.: A systematic mapping study on technical debt and its management. J. Syst. Softw. **101**, 193–220 (2015)

14. Li, Z., Liang, P., Avgeriou, P.: Architectural technical debt identification based on architecture decisions and change scenarios. In: 2015 12th Working IEEE/IFIP Conference on Software Architecture (WICSA), pp. 65–74. IEEE (2015)
15. Parnas, D.: Software aging. In: Proceedings of the 16th International Conference on Software Engineering, pp. 279–287. ACM/IEEE (1994)
16. Russo, D., Ciancarini, P., Falasconi, T., Tomasi, M.: Software quality concerns in the Italian bank sector: the emergence of a meta-quality dimension. In: Proceedings of the 39th International Conference on Software Engineering, pp. 63–72. ACM/IEEE (2017)
17. Russo, D., Ciancarini, P., Falasconi, T., Tomasi, M.: A meta model for information systems quality: a mixed-study of the financial sector. ACM Trans. Manag. Inf. Syst. **9**(3), 1–38 (2018)
18. Tempero, E., Gorschek, T., Angelis, L.: Barriers to refactoring. Commun. ACM **60**(10), 54–61 (2017)
19. Wheelen, T.L., Hunger, J.D.: Strategic Management and Business Policy. Pearson, London (2017)
20. Yli-Huumo, J., Maglyas, A., Smolander, K.: How do software development teams manage technical debt?-An empirical study. J. Syst. Softw. **120**, 195–218 (2016)

How the Cathedral Embraced the Bazaar, and the Bazaar Became a Cathedral

Terhi Kilamo[1], Valentina Lenarduzzi[2(✉)], Tuukka Ahoniemi[3], Ari Jaaksi[1],
Jurka Rahikkala[4], and Tommi Mikkonen[5]

[1] Tampere University, Tampere, Finland
terhi.kilamo@tuni.fi, ari@linux.com
[2] LUT University, Lahti, Finland
valentina.lenarduzzi@lut.fi
[3] Tuxera, Espoo, Finland
tuukka.ahoniemi@iki.fi
[4] Vaadin, Turku, Finland
jurka.rahikkala@vaadin.com
[5] University of Helsinki, Helsinki, Finland
tommi.mikkonen@helsinki.fi

Abstract. Over the past 20 years, open source has become a widely adopted approach to develop software. Code repositories provide software to power cars, phones, and other things that are considered proprietary. In parallel, proprietary development has evolved from rigid, centralized waterfall approaches to agile, iterative development. In this paper, we share our experiences regarding this co-evolution of open and closed source from the viewpoints of tools, practices, and organizing the development work, concluding that today's bazaars and cathedrals have much more common characteristics than those that separate them.

Keywords: Open source · Development tools · Software business

1 Introduction

In 1997, Eric S. Raymond [1] juxtaposed two ways of software development: the cathedral and the bazaar. The differences of the two have from the beginning been in the development approach instead of the source code alone. The cathedral model develops the software within a closed group of developers, and the product is only released in structured intervals; in contrast, the bazaar keeps the development process fast and visible to any interested party all the time.

Originally, the bazaar marked open source, and the cathedral proprietary. Over time, things have changed however, making proprietary development resemble open source software and its development models. In parallel, open source has grown to the level of importance where it has adopted many of the centralized development schemes traditionally associated with proprietary software. Moreover, open source quality increased year after year [2–4], and producers started to apply similar marketing models of proprietary [5]. As a result,

© IFIP International Federation for Information Processing 2020
Published by Springer Nature Switzerland AG 2020
V. Ivanov et al. (Eds.): OSS 2020, IFIP AICT 582, pp. 141–147, 2020.
https://doi.org/10.1007/978-3-030-47240-5_14

companies started to consider open source as trustworthy of proprietary ones [6], and opening proprietary software has become a viable option [7–9].

We approach this evolution with a retrospective view of the past 20 years of software development, and find that the cathedral has turned into "a babbling bazaar" while the bazaar has evolved towards "reverent cathedral-building" [1].

2   Background

The origins of open source software can be traced back to 1974, when US Commission on New Technological Uses of Copyrighted Works (CONTU) [10] decided that software is a proper subject matter of copyright to the extent that it embodies its authors' original creation [11]. While previously code had been liberally shared among different stakeholders largely ignoring IPR, this was no longer an option, concerning in particular modifying program source code. This initiated the movement to regain the original 'freedoms' of programmers, eventually resulting in forming the Free Software Foundation (https://www.fsf.org).

The early years of open source software revolved around infrastructure software, including operating systems, windowing systems, programming tools and compilers, and other software that is commonly used to operate or program any computer. A key milestone in this era is year 1989, when the first version of the GNU General Public License (GPL) was published. It governs the use of open source software, taking open source to the league of a "serious" software system, where formal governance and ruling existed.

By year 2000, as witnessed by Raymond's essay [1], the focus was shifting to development models where proprietary software was compared to carefully crafting a pre-designed cathedral and open source was evolving organically based on individuals' desires in bazaars. In parallel, using open source as a part of business and proprietary software gained widespread interest [12]. Soon, open source become a viable business model [13], and it was adopted by various companies.

Today, open source is characterized by three key elements: (i) code comprising the implementation, (ii) the licence under which the software is distributed, and (iii) the community that maintains the code. Furthermore, open source is viewed through its meritocratic nature of collaboration where anyone can contribute, contributions are judged based on merit and the development is self-organizing [14]. This characterization does not consider the cathedral and the bazaar metaphor, and over time, the difference between the two has become a fine line – companies extensively participate in open source development [15] and open source communities and projects are organized and governed [16,17]. The beginning of this transformation was documented by Fitzgerald [18]; the trend has since continued, making cathedrals embrace bazaars and bazaars to become cathedrals.

3   Why the Cathedral Embraced the Bazaar?

Pre-open source software industry habits were very similar to the rest of the industry, consisting of large enterprises that had very established ways and elaborated processes, to the brink of a disaster in their inability to adopt new practices [19]. For software development companies, this meant rigorous inspections [20] to improve quality and process models such as CMM [21], where the organizational capabilities were being improved without paying much attention to the interests of individuals.

Open source development challenged all the above. Since its humble origins, the power of open source has stemmed from programmers who choose to contribute to projects of their interest, not by management control. To support voluntary cooperation across the Globe, various tools were introduced, including source control management tools such as Subversion and later Git. Distributed version control systems have enabled the development through pulling code from repositories to create software locally as a combination of several code sources. The range of components from operating and windowing systems to tiny, almost self-evident snippets have made open source systems an integral part of systems [22], many of which we do not consider as open source, and these are also visible in software architecture of many systems [23].

Open source also helped to shape new development processes, such as introducing the pull requests mechanism and the concepts of continuous integration, deployment and delivery, as means for handling new contributions to the code base. Similarly, issue tracking tools such as Bugzilla and review tools such as Gerrit for collaborative handling of issues and reviewing code contributions in turn stem from open source projects. New tools are continuously introduced into the market, with the goal of supporting the developed product and the development process [24]. Since these tools have largely been about 'scratching one's own itch', the developers working on proprietary software have quickly realized that these tools really empower the developers. Hence, tools and processes made familiar by open source development are used to distribute the development effort globally, to manage quality, and to enable agile development, manifesting transparency in every development phase.

Furthermore, companies do not only apply open source tools and associated methods in their internal development, but also contribute directly to open source projects. To this end, big closed source players such as Microsoft, Google, Oracle, Facebook and Amazon are nowadays major open source contributors, with a large open source codebase of their own [25]. For many companies, this has meant a complete transformation from their organizational perspective and operational culture – so-called agile transformation [26], increasing transparency and empowering the developers in particular.

Finally, there are also more unscrupulous motives to embrace open source than those above. For instance, large companies may contribute to OSS just because they no longer see viable business around a product, to white-wash their public picture of becoming a Linux/OSS lover, or simply because they have to, as someone accidentally misused a GPL component.

4 How the Bazaar Turned into a Cathedral?

While anyone can start an open source project without commercial interests, the fact is that many of the projects work well because someone is funding the work. A common model is that an open source project is mainly a product of one company that is hosting the infrastructure needed by the project, contributing the biggest chunk and then inviting others to join in. Naturally, as the company seats most of the maintainer spots, it has a wide influence on what gets in to the main branch of the project and what does not. Typically, the funder has its own interests, although based on contributions also other stakeholders' interests can be identified – for instance, with respect to the Qt framework and open source Qt Project, one can clearly see from the contribution timeline when eg. different phone vendors have had their time in adopting the GUI framework to their own platform-specific needs.

Today, it is easy to find big names in open source software. Linux has risen as the de-facto OS for clouds, servers, and mobile and embedded devices alike, and web browsers are predominantly open source due to the rise of Chromium next to Firefox, and Microsoft letting go of their closed-source implementation [27]. With Linux at its core, Android now has the largest market share of smartphone ecosystems. Recently Microsoft purchased the largest host of code repositories GitHub (https://blogs.microsoft.com/blog/2018/10/26/microsoft-completes-github-acquisition/). This rise to a key position in commercial settings has strengthened the corporate role in open source. As the direction of each project has significant commercial meaning, business stakes have become too high for the development to take unexpected turns, following individual developers' itch.

When growing in size and importance, many open source projects have started to lose their bazaar development model. Decision-making has become centralized, and processes are decided within a small group. For instance, in the Linux community, which has been an example of the centralized approach from its start, there is a well-defined governance model instead of everyone directly contributing to the code base. Similarly, open source foundations such as the Apache Software Foundation and the OW2 Consortium have set rigorous "cathedral-like" processes to developers who want to have their software in the foundation – a quality control process to follow, a program of incubation, and an "attic" to keep track of unmaintained projects (https://www.apache.org/foundation/how-it-works.html). In general, it is difficult to imagine any large-scale open source project that goes completely ungoverned.

Finally, stakeholder needs include ensuring the sustainability of the project as several stakeholders have significant business based on key open source software [28]. The recognition of IPR and the licence model are such key mechanisms. This has resulted in acts that are based on business reasons rather than the software itself. The selected licence itself acts as a cathedral-building mechanism and the licence and the licencing model can have major business impacts. Especially as not all licences can coexist within the same software, business drivers affect the software [29].

5   What to Look for Next?

During the recent years, we have seen open source and proprietary software come closer to each other and at the same time switch places. As a consequence of this convergence, the hybrid nature of open source is thriving. When the open source community starts the development as a bazaar – like Linux for example has – they evolve towards cathedrals as they grow, gain business impact, and need to get organized to support the business stakeholders. On the other hand, communities that originate from business needs move to the opposite direction and adopt in part the bazaar model to get contributions from a wider contributor community. Similarly, the distribution of contributors in open source has turned towards corporate employed contributors instead of a buzzing group of volunteers, and in some of the open source projects, it is not possible for a volunteer to contribute any more [30] – you can fork individually but not join back as the company managing the software does not embrace contributions from other stakeholders, no matter how good they are. The issue is not only about controlling the individual developers' itch but also a wider perspective – what is the general direction of the project?

The modern way of accepting contributions is no longer through a monolithic project model but more from a distributed ecosystem marketplace resembling an appstore of modules/features. Perhaps the most vital communities that truly embrace participation of everyone are the likes of the NodeJS ecosystem (https:// nodejs.org), where one can easily reuse or modify existing components, contribute new ones, and mash them together to create new systems [31]. These are modern bazaars where "capitalism of code" really rules – the most well-received modules/add-ons thrive and get additional contributors (if allowed), whereas individual hobbyist experiments can still co-exist but will eventually perish. Another example of this is the Microsoft VSCode (https://code.visualstudio. com/) where the actual open source project is the core platform, but the idea is actually not about the OS project (of developing a dull code editor) but about the very inclusive ecosystem where everyone can have a shot at creating an add-on. So, forget cathedral-like strict rules and CLAs (contribution license agreements) and bully-like maintainers, but just create your own "app" to the "store" and let's have the markets decide what will work.

Finally, changes in the value chain have had an impact to open source. Today, in many cases data, open APIs, and cloud services are far more important than the code, which has become a commodity. This attitude is backed by the fact that going for full open source means that one does not need to worry about issues such as licence compatibility, liberating companies from considering them.

6   Conclusions

By now it is obvious that open source software has realized its fundamental reuse promise. The many facets of software in general, together with the availability of readily reusable open source components in particular, have woven open source so deep in software industry that they are next to inseparable. The different kinds of software endeavors can start from opposite ends of being open or closed, but by now it seems that over time, the benefits of both worlds is something to seek for both small companies as well as giant enterprises.

References

1. Raymond, E.: The cathedral and the bazaar. Knowl. Technol. Policy **12**(3), 23–49 (1999)
2. del Bianco, V., Lavazza, L., Morasca, S., Taibi, D., Tosi, D.: The QualiSPo approach to OSS product quality evaluation. In: International Workshop on Emerging Trends in Free/Libre/Open Source Software Research and Development, pp. 23–28 (2010)
3. del Bianco, V., Lavazza, L., Morasca, S., Taibi, D., Tosi, D.: An investigation of the users' perception of OSS quality. In: Ågerfalk, P., Boldyreff, C., González-Barahona, J.M., Madey, G.R., Noll, J. (eds.) OSS 2010. IAICT, vol. 319, pp. 15–28. Springer, Heidelberg (2010). https://doi.org/10.1007/978-3-642-13244-5_2
4. Rudzki, J., Kiviluoma, K., Poikonen, T., Hammouda, I.: Evaluating quality of open source components for reuse-intensive commercial solutions. In: 2009 35th Euromicro Conference on Software Engineering and Advanced Applications, pp. 11–19. IEEE (2009)
5. del Bianco, V., Lavazza, L., Lenarduzzi, V., Morasca, S., Taibi, D., Tosi, D.: A study on OSS marketing and communication strategies. In: Hammouda, I., Lundell, B., Mikkonen, T., Scacchi, W. (eds.) OSS 2012. IAICT, vol. 378, pp. 338–343. Springer, Heidelberg (2012). https://doi.org/10.1007/978-3-642-33442-9_31
6. del Bianco, V., Lavazza, L., Morasca, S., Taibi, D.: A survey on open source software trustworthiness. IEEE Softw. **28**(5), 67–75 (2011)
7. Kilamo, T., Hammouda, I., Mikkonen, T., Aaltonen, T.: From proprietary to open source—growing an open source ecosystem. J. Syst. Softw. **85**(7), 1467–1478 (2012)
8. Kilamo, T., Hammouda, I., Mikkonen, T., Aaltonen, T.: Open source ecosystems: a tale of two cases. In: Software Ecosystems. Edward Elgar Publishing (2013)
9. Sirkkala, P., Aaltonen, T., Hammouda, I.: Opening industrial software: planting an onion. In: Boldyreff, C., Crowston, K., Lundell, B., Wasserman, A.I. (eds.) OSS 2009. IAICT, vol. 299, pp. 57–69. Springer, Heidelberg (2009). https://doi.org/10.1007/978-3-642-02032-2_7
10. US Congress: National commission on new technological uses of copyrighted works. Final report of the National Commission on New Technological Uses of Copyrighted Works (CONTU) (1978)
11. Keplinger, M.S.: Computer software-its nature and its protection. Emory L. J. **30**, 483 (1981)
12. DiBona, C., Ockman, S.: Open Sources: Voices From the Open Source Revolution. O'Reilly Media, Inc., Nweton (1999)
13. Rolandsson, B., Bergquist, M., Ljungberg, J.: Open source in the firm: opening up professional practices of software development. Res. Policy **40**(4), 576–587 (2011)
14. Riehle, D., et al.: Open collaboration within corporations using software forges. IEEE Softw. **26**(2), 52–58 (2009)
15. Johri, A., Nov, O., Mitra, R.: "Cool" or "monster"? Company takeovers and their effect on open source community participation. In: Proceedings of the 2011 iConference, pp. 327–331 (2011)

16. Di Tullio, D., Staples, D.S.: The governance and control of open source software projects. J. Manage. Inf. Syst. **30**(3), 49–80 (2013)
17. Sadowski, B.M., Sadowski-Rasters, G., Duysters, G.: Transition of governance in a mature open software source community: evidence from the debian case. Inf. Econ. Policy **20**(4), 323–332 (2008)
18. Fitzgerald, B.: The transformation of open source software. MIS Q. 587–598 (2006)
19. Kanter, R.M.: When Giants Learn to Dance. Simon and Schuster, New York (1990)
20. Ackerman, A.F., Buchwald, L.S., Lewski, F.H.: Software inspections: an effective verification process. IEEE Softw. **6**(3), 31–36 (1989)
21. Paulk, M.C.: The Capability Maturity Model: Guidelines for Improving the Software Process. Addison-Wesley Professional, Boston (1995)
22. Mikkonen, T., Taivalsaari, A.: Software reuse in the era of opportunistic design. IEEE Softw. **36**(3), 105–111 (2019)
23. Lokhman, A., Mikkonen, T., Hammouda, I., Kazman, R., Chen, H.M.: A core-periphery-legality architectural style for open source system development. In: 2013 46th Hawaii International Conference on System Sciences, pp. 3148–3157. IEEE (2013)
24. Sbai, N., Lenarduzzi, V., Taibi, D., Sassi, S.B., Ghezala, H.H.B.: Exploring information from OSS repositories and platforms to support oss selection decisions. Inf. Softw. Technol. **104**, 104–108 (2018)
25. Hoffa, F.: Who contributed the most to open source in 2017 and 2018? Let's analyze GitHub's data and find out. FreeCodeCamp, 24 October 2017. https://www.freecodecamp.org/news/the-top-contributors-to-github-2017-be98ab854e87/
26. Fry, C., Greene, S.: Large scale agile transformation in an on-demand world. In: Agile 2007 (AGILE 2007), pp. 136–142. IEEE (2007)
27. Warren, T.: Microsoft is building its own Chrome browser to replace Edge. The Verge, 4 December 2018. https://www.theverge.com/2018/12/4/18125238/microsoft-chrome-browser-windows-10-edge-chromium
28. Nyman, L., Mikkonen, T., Lindman, J., Fougère, M.: Perspectives on code forking and sustainability in open source software. In: Hammouda, I., Lundell, B., Mikkonen, T., Scacchi, W. (eds.) OSS 2012. IAICT, vol. 378, pp. 274–279. Springer, Heidelberg (2012). https://doi.org/10.1007/978-3-642-33442-9_21
29. Hammouda, I., Mikkonen, T., Oksanen, V., Jaaksi, A.: Open source legality patterns: architectural design decisions motivated by legal concerns. In: 14th International Academic MindTrek Conference: Envisioning Future Media Environments, pp. 207–214. ACM (2010)
30. Mäenpää, H., Kilamo, T., Mikkonen, T., Männistö, T.: Designing for participation: three models for developer involvement in hybrid OSS projects. In: Balaguer, F., Di Cosmo, R., Garrido, A., Kon, F., Robles, G., Zacchiroli, S. (eds.) OSS 2017. IAICT, vol. 496, pp. 23–33. Springer, Cham (2017). https://doi.org/10.1007/978-3-319-57735-7_3
31. Hartmann, B., Doorley, S., Klemmer, S.R.: Hacking, mashing, gluing: understanding opportunistic design. IEEE Pervasive Comput. **7**(3), 46–54 (2008)

An Open Source Environment
for an Agile Development Model

Paolo Ciancarini[1,2(✉)], Marcello Missiroli[1], Francesco Poggi[3],
and Daniel Russo[4]

[1] DISI, University of Bologna, Bologna, Italy
paolo.ciancarini@unibo.it
[2] Innopolis University,
Innopolis, Russian Federation
[3] DCE, University of Modena and Reggio Emilia, Modena, Italy
francesco.poggi@unimore.it
[4] Department of Computer Science, Aalborg University, Aalborg, Denmark
daniel.russo@cs.aau.dk

Abstract. Tools are of paramount importance in automating software
engineering tasks; although the Agile Manifesto prefers *"individuals and
their interactions over processes and tools"*, some agile development
activities make no exception and can be automated effectively and successfully. In process frameworks like Scrum or similar ones some activities
are in fact quite structured and need specific tool support. Hence, it is
interesting to study the combination of specific agile practices with OSS
tools.

In this paper we introduce the Compositional Agile System (CAS),
an environment created to support iAgile and automate some of its tasks
using OSS tools. iAgile is a Scrum-like model designed to develop critical
systems in the military domain.

1 Introduction

The relationship between a development method and the tools which compose its
programming environment has been debated for a long time. In a seminal paper
Osterweil introduced the idea that software processes should be programmed just
like applications [27], since they *"are software, too"*. This idea is powerful and had
the consequence to foster the study of the so called "process engines", namely environments programmed in order to support specific development methods [2,15].

The Agile era inaugurated by the Agile Manifesto gave less importance to
tools, in fact the first of the four Agile values says: *"(...we have come to value...)
Individuals and interactions over processes and tools"*.

However the development of modern, complex software needs a lot of careful effort; several specific activities can and should be automated. For instance,
the management of the product backlog in Scrum is well supported by digital
taskboards like Trello [26]. Even the concept of *Definition of Done* can be partially automated [16] using for instance some tool for checking the quality of code

© IFIP International Federation for Information Processing 2020
Published by Springer Nature Switzerland AG 2020
V. Ivanov et al. (Eds.): OSS 2020, IFIP AICT 582, pp. 148–162, 2020.
https://doi.org/10.1007/978-3-030-47240-5_15

and measuring the technical debt, like SonarQube. Moreover, the globalization of the software industry has fostered the development of collaborative platforms - like Jira - in multi-site environments to reduce costs and increase productivity.

Thus, it is still interesting to study what are the most appropriate approaches and tools to support agile developments. Another, complementary, question is if the interactions necessary to any team-based software development method suggest to design specific ad-hoc platforms.

In this paper we introduce the Compositional Agile System (CAS in short), an environment created to support iAgile, an improved agile development model introduced to develop critical systems in the military domain.

The structure of this paper is the following: in the next Sect. 2 we describe the iAgile method for developing critical systems in specific domains; in Sect. 3 we discuss the requirements of CAS, an open source development environment supporting a Scrum-like model called iAgile; in Sect. 4 we describe the CAS architecture. In Sect. 5 we compare CAS with other environments and services for agile developments. Finally, in Sect. 6 we describe our future plans and draw our conclusions.

2   iAgile: An Improved Agile Development Model for the Military Domain

Eisenhower is attributed the following quote: *"In preparing for battle I have always found that plans are useless, but planning is indispensable"*. This applies to Agile approaches like Scrum, where planning the overall project is forbidden, however planning sprint-by-sprint is mandatory. iAgile is a model for empirical project management of software developments. Inspired by the Agile Manifesto, it has been derived from Scrum, and has been especially tailored for Command and Control (C2) critical systems in the military domain [23]. A C2 system in this domain includes functional military areas to cope with humanitarian assistance, stability operations, counterinsurgency operations, and combat operations [25].

The transition to Agile was needed to support faster adaptation to changes to operational needs and quality and security requirements but was also mandated by a drastic reduction in the budgets experienced in Italian public administration. The continual evolution of the operational environment in conflict theaters generates instability of the C2 requirements; this means that their developers have to work at all times with unstable and unconsolidated mission needs. Thus, planning a C2 system using the old, strongly planned, waterfall approach became unsuitable [9].

The initial idea was to experiment an in-house development of some novel functions of an established, waterfall-based, C2 system. The results using Scrum with some developers rented for specific enhancements were encouraging, however the stakeholders felt that some productivity analysis was necessary. In fact, some aspects of Scrum were not satisfactory for the context of C2 systems developed and operated in-house.

The introduction of an Agile approach in the development of critical software required the solution of many problems and the construction of a solid structure based on four principles: user community governance, specific Agile training, new Agile CASE tools and custom Agile development doctrine.

Thus for the new developments a method called iAgile was introduced [23]. Table 1 shows how the Agile principles[1] have been embedded in iAgile.

Table 1. iAgile embeds agile principles

Agile principles	iAgile
Our highest priority is to satisfy the customer through early and continuous delivery of valuable software	iAgile has been introduced in order to develop LC2EVO, a military C2 system, aiming at shortening the "time-to-the-field" of new functions [24]
Welcome changing requirements, even late in development. Agile processes harness change for the customer's competitive advantage	iAgile systematically developed new incremental versions which were immediately tested on the field [25]
Deliver working software frequently, from a couple of weeks to a couple of months, with a preference to the shorter timescale	Sprints lasted 4 weeks + 1 for certification [6]
Business people and developers must work together daily throughout the project	Developers and users worked daily together [3]
Build projects around motivated individuals. Give them the environment and support they need, and trust them to get the job done	iAgile has been quite successful, exploiting the enthusiasm of both civil and military developers [7]
The most efficient and effective method of conveying information to and within a development team is face-to-face conversation	Daily meetings and physical shared taskboard were used systematically [4]
Working software is the primary measure of progress	The LC2EVO project executed about 30 sprints, each delivering a working increment [17]
Agile processes promote sustainable development. The sponsors, developers, and users should be able to maintain a constant pace indefinitely	The project lasted 18 months, produced several releases with a string reduction of development costs [8]
Continuous attention to technical excellence and good design enhances agility	iAgile requires excellent technical capabilities [14]
Simplicity–the art of maximizing the amount of work not done–is essential	The "lean" approach implicit in iAgile shortened the workflow necessary to implement critical requirements [18]
The best architectures, requirements, and designs emerge from self-organizing teams	The quality of the final system is high and is still being used [17]
At regular intervals, the team reflects on how to become more effective, then tunes and adjusts its behavior accordingly	Projects based on iAgile used systematically retrospectives [14]

---

[1] https://agilemanifesto.org/iso/en/principles.html.

3   Requirements of a Development Environment for iAgile

The project we were involved consisted in defining a development environment supporting the iAgile development model. For security reasons we could not use commercial software online in the cloud. The target of the project was to develop an open source development environment suitable to be deployed either on a private network or in a hybrid cloud keeping complete control on its implementation and extensions.

We identified the following user stories (or epics) for CAS:

1. As a stakeholder, I am interested in estimating and monitoring the effort required by a new function to be added to the system, in order to know how many people are necessary and their productivity.
2. As a Product Owner during the project I need to check productivity data in order to predict when a release will be possible, so that *delivery on time* is ensured.
3. As a developer or stakeholder I need to communicate easily, fast, and safely with all other developers or stakeholders.
4. As a PO I need to check the code delivered by the team with respect to the Product Backlog (*percentage of adopted work*), including the Definition of Done.
5. As a developer I need tool support for asymmetric pair programming in order to get help from senior developers or domain experts.
6. As a developer I need tool support to check the quality of my code in order to satisfy the Definition of Done.
7. As a developer I need tool support to monitor defects in libraries and open source components.
8. As a PO I need to track how the user stories of the Product Backlog evolved into code in order to plan the next release.

These User Stories do not cover the whole spectrum of iAgile roles and activities, however we have found them useful as an initial reference that now can be expanded.

3.1   Mapping the Requirements on Open Source Components

The above user stories were suggested by interviewing the stakeholders involved in the development of a critical system. In particular, the introduction of the COSYSMO estimation framework [28] was suggested by some military stakeholders who were interested in matching system engineering estimation with agile development of software-intensive components.

In the meantime in the same project we had proposed a survey to the agile community; the results of such survey are reported in [10]. According to the survey, Jira is currently the most popular tool for agile developments. Also Trello and Slack are very popular. However these tools are not adequate for the context of our project, since they are commercial and based on proprietary clouds.

Table 2. Mapping the user stories and main iAgile roles on some open source tools

#	User story	Tool	iAgile roles
US1	Estimating and monitoring	COSYSMO, COCOMO	AD
US2	Checking the team productivity	Taiga, GitInspector, logger plug-in	PO, SM, team, AD
US3	Supporting communication among all stakeholders	Mattermost	team, PO, AD
US4	Check the code	Taiga, Git (GitLab CE), Junit	PO, team
US5	Asymmetric remote pair programming	Saros (plugin Eclipse)	team, SM
US6	Check code quality and technical debt	SonarQube server	team, SM, (PO)
US7	Issue tracking and library monitoring	Bugzilla, SonarLint (plugin Eclipse)	team, (PO, AD)
US8	Track user stories into code and releases	Taiga	PO, team

Thus we searched the open source market and identified a number of open source components useful to satisfy the user stories listed above. The result of our study is shown in Table 2.

We decided to include these components as services in the CAS back end. We also added a front end in the form of an IDE like Eclipse [19] or IntelliJ IDEA [20].

4   Architecture of CAS

The Compositional Agile System (CAS) is based on two subsystems: the *CAS server*, whose architecture is based on microservices, and the *CAS client*, a normal IDE like Eclipse or IntelliJ IDEA (we are working also on an Atom client) enriched with some plugins.

Figure 1 shows the CAS architectural stack, available on any operating system able to host dockerized services. Each CAS server service (e.g. SonarQube, Taiga, GitLab, etc.) - represented by its own logo - has its own container, which includes a locale storage system. The environment architecture is compositional in the sense that each service is separate and new services can easily be added, following the approach to *agile software architecture* suggested in [5].

4.1   The CAS Client

By CAS client we mean any IDE that developers use as the front end of the development environment. We have integrated two IDEs with CAS: Eclipse and IntelliJ IDEA. We are also working at integrating other IDEs such as Atom, an IDE developed and integrated with GitHub.

The integration of each client consists of an original plug-in we developed for collecting developers data, in order to monitor productivity [13], plus other plugins available for the main CAS server services and necessary to support some user story.

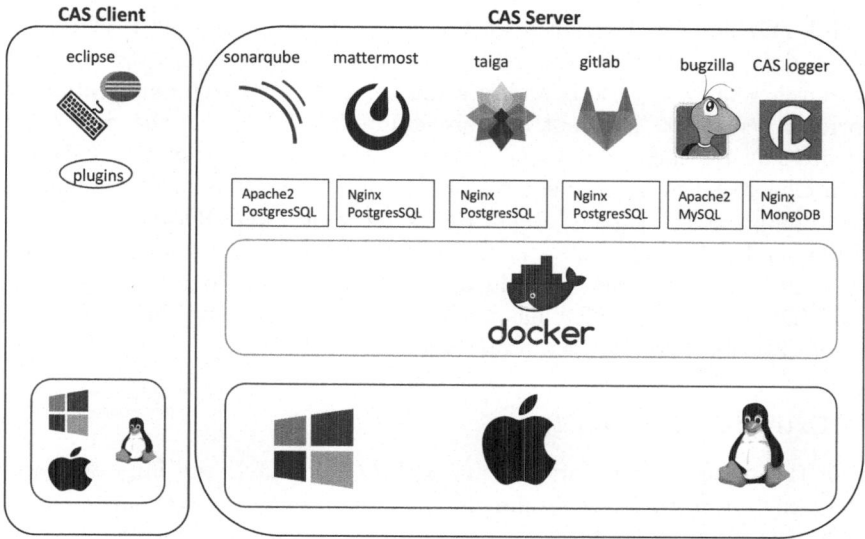

Fig. 1. CAS client-server architecture: the CAS server lower layer is the operating system, then the docker layer, and finally the services, each with its own web server and storage dbms. The CAS client components (i.e. Eclipse, which is shown in the figure, or IntelliJ IDEA) and their plugins are not dockerized. They rely on CAS server components to store and analyze developers' data.

Eclipse: Eclipse is an integrated multi-language and cross-platform development environment. It is designed by a consortium called the Eclipse Foundation, which includes large companies such as IBM, Ericsson, HP, Intel, SAP. Eclipse is a free and open source software distributed under the terms of the Eclipse Public License.

Eclipse can be used for the development of a huge variety of software products. It can be used as a complete IDE for several programming languages, for instance: Java Development Tools (JDT) for the Java language, C/C++ Development Tools (CDT) the C/C++ language. Similarly, through plugins it is possible to manage XML, JavaScript, PHP, as also designing graphically a GUI for a Java application (i.e., Window Builder). Eclipse is considered an environment for Rapid Application Development.

The platform is focused on the use of plugins, which are software components designed for a specific purpose. Indeed, the whole platform is a set of plugins, including the basic version, and anyone can develop and edit the different plugins. In the basic version it is possible to program in Java, taking advantage of help functions such as automatic completion ("Code completion"), suggestion of the types of parameters of the methods, direct access to git and automatic rewriting of the code ("Refactoring function") in case of changes in the classes.

Finally, since Eclipse has been written in Java, it is portable and available for Linux, macOS, Windows and other platforms.

IntelliJ IDEA: IntelliJ IDEA (it was once known simply as IntelliJ) is an integrated development environment for the Java programming language. It has been developed by JetBrains and is available in both Apache and commercial proprietary editions. The first version of IntelliJ IDEA was the first IDE to integrate features such as code navigation and *code refactoring*. In a 2010 ranking, IntelliJ received the highest test score among the four most popular Java programming tools: Eclipse, IntelliJ IDEA, NetBeans and JDeveloper[2].

In December 2014, Google announced version 1.0 of Android Studio, an open source IDE for developing Android apps, based on the Community edition of IntelliJ IDEA[3]. IntelliJ IDEA has two editions: Community Edition (OSS) and Ultimate Edition (which is the proprietary version).

4.2   Extending a CAS Client

One of the main reasons for choosing Eclipse/IntelliJ is the large amount of plugins existing for both environments. The main examples are *saros*, *egit* and *sonarlint*.

Another reason is that every developer can build specific plugins in order to add new functions to her IDE. For example, we have introduced a keylogger plugin to record data concerning the actions performed by the developers.

The *saros* plugin allows remote pair programming, and supports synchronous text editing on a document shared by up to five devlopers.

The *egit* plugin integrates either GitLab or GitHub directly inside Eclipse or IntelliJ.

The *sonarlint* plugin allows to analyze the quality of the source code and it reports any problems during the editing.

The *logger* plugin helps developers to record and then to monitor and summarize their actions. Accordingly, the PO can analyze the productivity of the team or individual developers.

4.3   CAS Services

GitLab: Git is an open source Version Control System (VCS), also used as Software Configuration Management (SCM) tool. Git allows to keep track of the changes made to the files of a project, keeping the history of all the changes made, so that it is always possible to access the different versions of the project's artifacts [22]. Git is more precisely a system for distributed version control (DVCS), since it allows a group of people to collaborate on the same file system, sharing it and keeping track of who does what.

It is always possible to restore, partially or completely, the structure of the base directory of a project so that there is a version of the files and subfolders with the changes that had been made at some time in the past.

---

[2] www.infoworld.com/article/2683534/infoworld-review--top-java-programming-tools.html.

[3] www.venturebeat.com/2014/12/08/google-releases-android-studio-1-0-the-first-stable-version-of-its-ide.

Git is especially useful when working with plain text files, such as source code. In fact, it provides various tools to compare the different versions of a file and see what changes have been made between one version and another. Although numerous graphical interfaces are available, Git is usually used via the command line interface. For this reason it mostly suggested for software development, but could be also used in other areas. For example, it can be useful if a group of people write a book collaboratively using Microsoft Word or Latex.

The CAS server includes GitLab, a Git-repository manager providing a rich set of functionalities such as tools for DevOps lifecycle support, issue-tracking, and Continuous Integration/Continuous integration Deployment (CI/CD) pipeline features.

Bugzilla: Bugzilla is an issue tracker, a program that creates a service to record and manage problem reports. Bugs can be submitted to the system by anyone, and will be assigned to the developer who has been associated with the bug. Bugs can have various types of status associated with them, along with user comments and examples of the error itself.

Mattermost: Mattermost is a scalable messaging system for team communication. It allows both direct and group-based communication. It supports topic or meeting-based channels. It offers string search functionality in messages and channels. Mattermost facilitates communication between teams by keeping all messages in one place. Those can be easily searched within the repository and are available for every team member everywhere. It is also possible to create an own chat solution hosted on a private cloud service.

In CAS, Mattermost is the main communication system, useful for the various iAgile ceremonies, especially if they are performed remotely and e.g., the PO is not co-located with the team such as in some sprint planning, daily meeting, sprint review or retrospective events.

SonarQube: An important issue in iAgile - just like in Scrum - is the concept of Definition of Done. We have introduced in iAgile the concept of *Definition of Done* based on a tool for checking the quality of code. The tool we have chosen is SonarQube.

Traditional approaches to software quality management tend to postpone code testing until after its completion, and to complete it at the end of the development of the entire software. This kind of approach, at best, generates delays and the need to review the whole work, when even the smallest bug is found. In the worst case scenario, on the other hand, it pushes the delivery of low quality software with several defects, and difficult to maintain. To address this issue, Continuous Inspection is the goal of SonarSource, a company that focuses on software quality analysis, which goal is to enhance software quality along the entire development process. Accordingly, the tool SonarQube which is a service for the ongoing management of the technical debt has been developed to support Continuous Inspection.

SonarQube is an open-source program for continuous analysis of code quality. It is able to perform automatic static analysis of code to detect bugs, code smells, and security vulnerabilities on several programming languages. It offers reports on duplicated code, coding standards, unit tests, code coverage, code complexity, comments, bugs, and security vulnerabilities. It also integrates with Eclipse and IntelliJ IDEA through the SonarLint plug-in.

A way to enrich a Definition of Done is via coding rules, namely rules that developers have to follow when writing their code. There are two ways to extend coding rules in SonarQube. The first is by writing coding rules using Java via a SonarQube plugin; the second is by adding XPath rules directly through the SonarQube web interface. The Java API is richer than the XPath one.

SonarQube might therefore be considered as a reference tool for analyzing the quality of software both continuously during development and postmortem at the end of the project.

The tool can be used both as a cloud service (i.e., SonarCloud) and as an open source package that can be hosted on own proprietary servers. In CAS we used the open source version, that has been included as a component of the CAS server. One of the most interesting advantages of SonarQube is the ability to track the evolution of a project's quality metrics over time. Every time an inspection is performed, users have a visual representation of the project's quality. It provides a snapshot of the code quality, including lagging indicators (problems already present) and leading indicators (problems that may arise in the future). Furthermore, it also provides services to address future issues, such as the code-review tools.

Taiga: Taiga is a free and open-source project management system able to host a product backlog and the related items of agile processes, like sprint backlogs and burndown charts. Backlogs are shown as a running list of all User Stories and related tasks belonging to the project. It is released under GNU Affero General Public License.

Taiga tracks the progress of a project using a taskboard whose template can be either Kanban or Scrum, or both. For iagile we use the Scrum template.

Taiga integrates chats and video conferencing functions with the use of third party services. The on-premise version of Taiga can be downloaded from its github repositories and used for free. This project management system can interface with web-based version control repositories like GitHub and Bitbucket. Taiga also provides several importers to facilitate migration from other proprietary software platforms, like Trello.

The project template can be configured using the following modules: Epics, Backlog, Kanban, Issues, Wiki, Meet Up. For Scrum active are: Backlog, Issues and Wiki; for Kanban the Kanban Board suffices. Combining the Backlog module and the Kanban Board we get a valid template for Scrumban.

The roles supported are: Product Owner, UX, Design, Front, Back, Stakeholder, External User. All roles except External User must be registered users.

Each role gets specific access privileges: Epics, Sprints, User story, Tasks, Issues, Wiki. Access rights are read-only, new-item, modify-item, comment-item, delete-item.

4.4   CAS Administration

Currently, the CAS administration consists mainly in controlling accesses to CAS services. Each service in CAS has its own access protocol. We plan to overcome this weakness in the next version.

Figure 2 shows the configuring process for CAS. First the server settings are defined, then a CAS View is added to the IDE Eclipse, then a new CAS instance can be used.

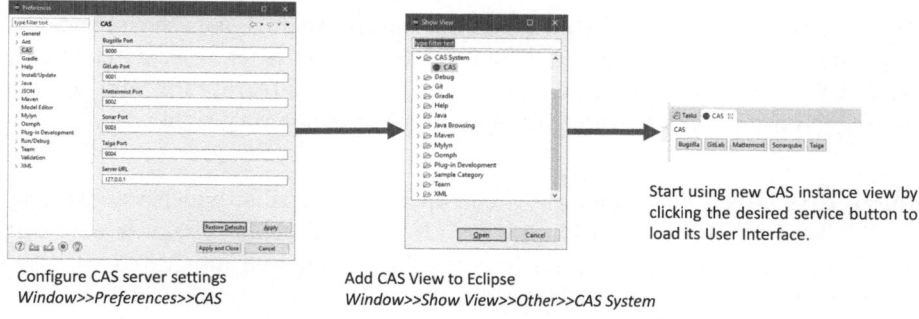

Configure CAS server settings
Window>>Preferences>>CAS

Add CAS View to Eclipse
Window>>Show View>>Other>>CAS System

Fig. 2. Configuring CAS

5   Comparison

We can compare CAS to other tools chosen by agile teams for software developments. The main contender is Jira, that is arguably the most comprehensive and popular tool used in software project management.

Jira: Jira is a comprehensive issue tracking and project management system. It is, however, neither free nor open source.

It can be accessed either as a cloud service or installed locally. Jira provides a variety of services and, on top of it, one can add a series of tightly integrated tools to further expand. To have a meaningful comparison, we chose the Jira+Helpdesk offer, the one that maps CAS services more precisely.

Given the tight integration and the single sign-on features, installation and setup is far easier and straightforward with respect to CAS, which currently requires separate access configurations for the various services.

Taiga vs Jira: Like Taiga, Jira also offers both Kanban and Scrum taskboard support. It is possible to setup User Stories, estimate them, assign them to specific persons. Thereafter, it is possible to start a Sprint or the Kanban board. It also offers a "Roadmap" page that presents a higher level of abstraction (Epics, for example). Several reporting options are avaialable. However, Taiga got inspiration from Trello. Both value simplicity and creativity and require low learning effort from the users. Moreover Taiga supports interactions via its telephone app for iOS, Android, and Windows devices.

GitLab vs Bitbucket: Bitbucket is one of the main Git-based service for cooperative source management recommended for Jira; its features match closely those of GitLab and other similar services. It can be integrated in Jira using a single sign-on mechanism, though the integration is not very tight.

Bugzilla vs Jira: Jira's name is a corruption of bugzilla, which was used by the Jira team before they produced Jira. In fact, originally Jira was a ticking service, and therefore this section is very mature and well integrated with the project management section compared to bugzilla.

Sonarqube and Mattermost vs Jira: These services have no direct equivalent in the Atlassian platform. Sonarqube can be configured to work with Jira, using procedures similar to CAS, but no tight integration is possible. After discontinuing its internal instant communication services (Hipchat) Atlassian suggests to use Slack, arguably the most famous and mature service of its kind which is however not open source or free.

6   Conclusions and Future Works

The CAS environment has been developed in four months, and is currently used in research projects [11,12] and by groups of students. So it has been tested for a very short time: the preliminary evaluations by the students are encouraging.

An important question that we should answer closing this paper is: which is the difference between iAgile and Scrum, and which impact has on development tools? This is a relevant question that has been already partially answered in [6,7]. We now offer a new discussion after having built CAS.

Table 3. Comparing Scrum vs iAgile/CAS

Scrum	iAgile
Roles: PO, SM, team	New roles: Requirement Owner, Operative PO, PO team, expert in cybersecurity
ScrumMaster	Military Facilitator
Self organizing team	Team with both civil and military personnel, including at least one cybersecurity expert
Contract: free	Contract: in-house or outsourced
Simple user stories	Structured user stories
Most popular tool: Jira (commercial)	Main tool: CAS (open source)
Shared physical taskboard	Digital taskboard (Taiga)
Face to face communication	Digital channels (Mattermost)
Metrics: chosen by the team	COSYSMO + development metrics
Definition of Done: defined by the PO	Definition of Done including SonarQube analysis
Various scalability models	LeSS-based scrum of scrums
Product certification: difficult	Product certification in each sprint

Table 3 shows a comparison between Scrum and iAgile. After we built CAS we have appreciated how strongly connected are a development model and its environment. For instance, we have yet to solve the problem of supporting scrums of scrums according to the LeSS model [21] using Taiga.

Another important issue is the combination of OSS licenses. The tools we have used have the licenses listed in Table 4.

Table 4. OSS licenses used in CAS

Component	License	Version	Link
Eclipse	EPL	4.10	www.eclipse.org/eclipse/news/4.10/
Taiga	GNU AGPL v3	4.0.0	github.com/taigaio/
GitLab	MIT	11.11	about.gitlab.com/releases/
Egit	BSD	5.3	www.eclipse.org/egit/
Gitinspector	GPL v3	0.4.4	github.com/ejwa/gitinspector/releases
Mattermost	Apache 2.0	5.11	docs.mattermost.com/administration/changelog
Saros	GNU v2	15.0	www.saros-project.org/releases/
SonarQube	LGPL v3	7.7	www.sonarqube.org/downloads/
bugzilla	GPL (MPL)	5.0.6	www.bugzilla.org/releases/
PostGres	PostgreSQL	9.5/9.6	dev.mysql.com/doc/relnotes/mysql/8.0/
docker	Apache 2.0	18.09.6	docs.docker.com/engine/release-notes/

We note that all these licenses are different, so we have to study their composition [1].

Another issue that we have to study is how the evolution of the different services proceeds smoothly under Docker and with respect the other services included in the CAS. For instance, SonarQube evolves rapidly and its API changes.

Acknowledgements. We thank prof. gen. Angelo Messina (rit.) for the interviews and the lively constructive discussions we had concerning iAgile. We thank for the support obtained with the project PNRM AMINSEP from CINI and from CNR/ISTC.

References

1. Alspaugh, T.A., Asuncion, H.U., Scacchi, W.: Analyzing software licenses in open architecture software systems. In: ICSE Workshop on Emerging Trends in Free/Libre/Open Source Software Research and Development, pp. 54–57. IEEE (2009)
2. Ambriola, V., Ciancarini, P., Corradini, A.: Declarative specification of the architecture of a software development environment. Softw. Pract. Exp. **25**(2), 143–174 (1995)
3. Arseni, G.: Role of the design authority in large scrum of scrum multi-team-based programs. In: Ciancarini, P., Sillitti, A., Succi, G., Messina, A. (eds.) Proceedings of 4th International Conference in Software Engineering for Defence Applications. AISC, vol. 422, pp. 181–189. Springer, Cham (2016). https://doi.org/10.1007/978-3-319-27896-4_15
4. Aslam, H., Brown, J.A., Messina, A.: Affordance theory applied to agile development: a case study of LC2EVO. In: Ciancarini, P., Mazzara, M., Messina, A., Sillitti, A., Succi, G. (eds.) SEDA 2018. AISC, vol. 925, pp. 24–35. Springer, Cham (2020). https://doi.org/10.1007/978-3-030-14687-0_3
5. Babar, M., Brown, A., Mistrik, I. (eds.): Agile Software Architecture. Morgan Kaufmann, Boston (2014)
6. Benedicenti, L., Messina, A., Sillitti, A.: iAgile: mission critical military development. In: Proceedings of IEEE International Conference on High Performance Computing and Simulation, pp. 545–552. Genoa, Italy (2017)
7. Benedicenti, L., Ciancarini, P., Cotugno, F., Messina, A., Sillitti, A., Succi, G.: Improved agile: a customized scrum process for project management in defense and security. In: Mahmood, Z. (ed.) Software Project Management for Distributed Computing. CCN, pp. 289–314. Springer, Cham (2017). https://doi.org/10.1007/978-3-319-54325-3_12
8. Chang, S.J., Messina, A., Modigliani, P.: How agile development can transform defense IT acquisition. In: Ciancarini, P., Sillitti, A., Succi, G., Messina, A. (eds.) Proceedings of 4th International Conference in Software Engineering for Defence Applications. AISC, vol. 422, pp. 13–26. Springer, Cham (2016). https://doi.org/10.1007/978-3-319-27896-4_2
9. Ciancarini, P., Messina, A., Poggi, F., Russo, D.: Agile knowledge engineering for mission critical software requirements. In: Nalepa, G.J., Baumeister, J. (eds.) Synergies Between Knowledge Engineering and Software Engineering. AISC, vol. 626, pp. 151–171. Springer, Cham (2018). https://doi.org/10.1007/978-3-319-64161-4_8

10. Ciancarini, P., Missiroli, M., Sillitti, A.: Preferred tools for agile development: a sociocultural perspective. In: Mazzara, M., Bruel, J.-M., Meyer, B., Petrenko, A. (eds.) TOOLS 2019. LNCS, vol. 11771, pp. 43–58. Springer, Cham (2019). https://doi.org/10.1007/978-3-030-29852-4_3
11. Ciancarini, P., Poggi, F., Rossi, D., Sillitti, A.: Improving bug predictions in multicore cyber-physical systems. In: Ciancarini, P., Sillitti, A., Succi, G., Messina, A. (eds.) Proceedings of 4th International Conference in Software Engineering for Defence Applications. AISC, vol. 422, pp. 287–295. Springer, Cham (2016). https://doi.org/10.1007/978-3-319-27896-4_24
12. Ciancarini, P., Poggi, F., Rossi, D., Sillitti, A.: Analyzing and predicting concurrency bugs in open source systems. In: Proceedings of International Joint Conference on Neural Networks (IJCNN), pp. 721–728. IEEE (2017)
13. Coman, I.D., Sillitti, A., Succi, G.: A case-study on using an automated in-process software engineering measurement and analysis system in an industrial environment. In: Proceedings of 31st International Conference on Software Engineering, pp. 89–99. IEEE (2009)
14. Cotugno, F.R.: Managing increasing user needs complexity within the ITA army agile framework. In: Ciancarini, P., Sillitti, A., Succi, G., Messina, A. (eds.) Proceedings of 4th International Conference in Software Engineering for Defence Applications. AISC, vol. 422, pp. 1–11. Springer, Cham (2016). https://doi.org/10.1007/978-3-319-27896-4_1
15. Cugola, G., Ghezzi, C.: Software processes: a retrospective and a path to the future. Softw. Process Improv. Pract. 4(3), 101–123 (1998)
16. Diebold, P., Ostberg, J.-P., Wagner, S., Zendler, U.: What do practitioners vary in using scrum? In: Lassenius, C., Dingsøyr, T., Paasivaara, M. (eds.) XP 2015. LNBIP, vol. 212, pp. 40–51. Springer, Cham (2015). https://doi.org/10.1007/978-3-319-18612-2_4
17. Galantini, L., Messina, A., Ruggiero, M.: Software requirements complexity analysis to support the "advisory network in to the nation forces build-up". In: Ciancarini, P., Mazzara, M., Messina, A., Sillitti, A., Succi, G. (eds.) SEDA 2018. AISC, vol. 925, pp. 187–197. Springer, Cham (2020). https://doi.org/10.1007/978-3-030-14687-0_17
18. Gazzerro, S., Marsura, R., Messina, A., Rizzo, S.: Capturing user needs for agile software development. In: Ciancarini, P., Sillitti, A., Succi, G., Messina, A. (eds.) Proceedings of 4th International Conference in Software Engineering for Defence Applications. AISC, vol. 422, pp. 307–319. Springer, Cham (2016). https://doi.org/10.1007/978-3-319-27896-4_26
19. Holzner, S.: Eclipse Cookbook. O'Reilly, Sebastopol (2004)
20. Krochmalski, J.: IntelliJ IDEA Essentials. Packt Pub (2014)
21. Larman, C., Vodde, B.: Large-Scale Scrum: More with LeSS. Addison-Wesley, Boston (2016)
22. Magana, A., Muli, J.: Version Control with Git and GitHub. Packt (2018)
23. Cotugno, F.R., Messina, A.: Adapting SCRUM to the Italian army: methods and (open) tools. In: Corral, L., Sillitti, A., Succi, G., Vlasenko, J., Wasserman, A.I. (eds.) OSS 2014. IAICT, vol. 427, pp. 61–69. Springer, Heidelberg (2014). https://doi.org/10.1007/978-3-642-55128-4_7
24. Messina, A., Fiore, F.: The Italian Army C2 evolution: From the current SIAC-CON2 land command & control system to the LC2EVO using agile software development methodology. In: Proceedings of International Conference on Military Communications and Information Systems (ICMCIS), pp. 1–8. Brussels, Belgium (2016)

25. Messina, A., Fiore, F., Ruggiero, M., Ciancarini, P., Russo, D.: A new agile paradigm for mission critical software development. Crosstalk J. Def. Softw. Eng. **29**(6), 25–30 (2016)
26. Naik, N., Jenkins, P., Newell, D.: Learning agile scrum methodology using the groupware tool trello through collaborative working. In: Barolli, L., Hussain, F.K., Ikeda, M. (eds.) CISIS 2019. AISC, vol. 993, pp. 343–355. Springer, Cham (2020). https://doi.org/10.1007/978-3-030-22354-0_31
27. Osterweil, L.: Software processes are software too. In: Proceedings of 9th IEEE International Conference on Software Engineering, pp. 2–13 (1987)
28. Valerdi, R.: The Constructive Systems Engineering Cost Model (COSYSMO). Ph.D. thesis, University of Southern California (2005)

InnoMetrics Dashboard: The Design, and Implementation of the Adaptable Dashboard for Energy-Efficient Applications Using Open Source Tools

Shokhista Ergasheva, Vladimir Ivanov, Ilya Khomyakov, Artem Kruglov, Dragos Strugar$^{(\boxtimes)}$, and Giancarlo Succi

Innopolis University, Innopolis, Tatarstan Republic 420500, Russian Federation
s.ergasheva@innopolis.university,
{v.ivanovov,i.khomyakov,a.kruglov,d.strugar,g.succi}@innopolis.ru

Abstract. Increasing amount of data the organizations worldwide have at their disposal lead to the need to structure, organize and present the information obtained from it. That is because, in today's rapid-changing business environment, managers and executives need to be able to gain crucial insights about the ongoing project in as little time as possible. Recently, energy efficiency has become a greater field of research, and companies started concentrating on monitoring energy-related metrics. In addition, many of them have built their own internal tools (dashboards) to do just this. However, one of the major drawbacks of building specialized tools is the lack of adaptability. That is, they are often tailored to only one person (e.g. CEO), or a small group of them (e.g. board of directors, managers). Furthermore, the combination of metrics that is displayed to them does not change over time. This is a problem because most likely there exists a better metric combination that would allow users to get the crucial insights faster. To fill this gap, our ongoing research focuses on making the dashboards adaptable to multiple roles within the organization while optimizing for a certain goal. In some scenarios the dashboard's goal may be to detect defects, in others it may be to generate the most profit. As our primary research interest is to amplify energy efficiency, we have chosen that to be our dashboard's goal. Our previous work suggests that in order to handle compound metrics at scale it is needed to represent the dashboard as a complex system. This paper presents the design and the architecture of our proposed solution synergizing the notions from complexity theory, software architecture and user experience (UX) design.

Keywords: Dashboards · Energy efficiency · Adaptable systems

1 Introduction

Due to modern-day rapid-changing business requirements, especially in the mobile space, and the advent of agile methodologies for tracking project status

© IFIP International Federation for Information Processing 2020
Published by Springer Nature Switzerland AG 2020
V. Ivanov et al. (Eds.): OSS 2020, IFIP AICT 582, pp. 163–176, 2020.
https://doi.org/10.1007/978-3-030-47240-5_16

came need to continuously monitor the overall picture of energy consumption. At the beginning, it was assumed that only hardware metrics influence energy efficiency levels [1]. Lately, more focus has been given to software (code) and process related metrics [2,3]. In order to achieve the products' continuous delivery it is necessary in each step of software development process to help the development team to assess energy efficiency levels and suggest ways of potentially improving it. Therefore, our research tries to pinpoint the software, process and project-related metrics that have the influence on energy efficiency, and then optimizing these metrics. This paper highlights the steps we took to design, architect and develop a dashboard specifically made for the use case of monitoring energy efficiency and optimizing the set of parameters needed to be displayed to different users.

1.1   Outline of the Paper

We start by mentioning the importance of the problem we are trying to solve as well as the research hypothesis by giving a literature review in Subsect. 1.2. The primary sections containing the majority of paper's novel contributions are Sects. 2, 3 and 4 where we decomposed our action plan and outlined all the metrics we used, and major design and architecture decisions. Here we talk at length about the aspects like technology choice, design style guide, layout, widgets, charts, security, complex systems and more. As the solution we have developed is still in its infancy, Sect. 5 pinpoints the key ways our research is going to progress with the dashboard being one of the central tools. Finally, Sect. 6 brings out some reflections.

1.2   Related Work

The field of effective dashboard design has gained traction at the beginning of the new millennium thanks to Stephen Few, among others. His "Information dashboard design" [4] is still being referenced by many. He starts by arguing that dashboards in the 1990s had major flaws, and that their root problem was in the inability to effectively communicate. Few also said that dashboards have to hold a balance between clarity and complexity [5]. With recent advances in the field of User Experience (UX) and User Interface (UI) design, dashboards started getting significantly more traction [6–10]. This resulted in dashboards being way more able to focus on the communication aspect, thus increasing use cases, leading to their wide-spread adoption [4]. Dashboard are becoming also of strategic importance in lean and agile environments [11,12], to spread knowledge across workers [13,14], and in distributed development environments [15–17].

Meanwhile, with the increasing popularity of mobile devices, energy efficiency has become an ever-growing concern. Recent research by Pinto et al. [2] pinpointed that energy efficiency has to be addressed at all levels of the software stack. More specifically, they argue that it is due to the developers having the lack of knowledge and lack of tools. These bottlenecks prevent software developers from identifying, fixing, refactoring, and removing energy consumption hotspots [18].

Finally, it would be advisable to take an open source approach to this topic, since it would ensure a larger diffusion of the dashboard [19–21].

2   Energy-Efficiency Related Metrics

In this section we describe the importance of metrics included in the dashboard we are developing. We start by providing an overview of the project as well as additional information to place the system in context. Firstly, the dashboard we are building is mainly concerned with monitoring the energy efficiency of software artifacts. The goal is to make it easy and convenient for managers as well as other users to track the energy consumption of the software. Overall, energy consumption metrics referring to the energy consumption can be divided into:

- Process metrics
- Project metrics
- Product metrics

We provide several Process and Product metrics throughout this paper that encapsulate the functionality of the dashboard.

Dashboard's primary purpose is to share important information in terms of different metrics to the end user. Determining what it is that is *important* to the user is the most critical part of designing the dashboard. By considering the metrics provided one would gain crucial insights, allowing them to make more educated decisions faster.

By working closely with the industry representatives, as well as consulting the literature in this field (data and findings revealed in [22–26]), we have come up with the list of metrics that the potential users would find most valuable [27–29] (Table 1).

These metrics are of paramount importance in qualifying the results of the work so that developers can judge objectively the development status. The main contribution can be directed into the energy efficient development of software in teams and individually. The proposed metrics were computed by applying rules common to the existing hierarchical measures of other internal software attributes. For example, by knowing the Number of classes in the source code we can easily calculate other metrics like: Number of Immediate sub-classes of a Class, Response for a Class, Weighted methods per Class as well as the Number of Children metric. It can be followed by better development estimates and more qualified product that can maintain the customers expectations. As it was stated in the paper [25], developers need a set of valid indicators in assisting the developers for better applications. Thus, the study results showed that Cyclomatic complexity, Number of classes, LOC, number of parameters, nested block depth, number of methods, weighted methods per class and method lines have direct relationship with power consumption of mobile applications. Authors of the paper [22] demonstrated specific coding practices for reading array length information, accessing class fields and performing invocations help to lower the overall energy consumption and improve the usability of the software.

Expanding the list of energy consumption metrics is already on our research agenda. However, not only obtaining additional metrics is of high significance. Combining the already existing ones, as well as easily modifying them is very important. Thus, Sect. 4 describes how we utilized these metrics in greater detail.

Table 1. Code metrics for the energy efficiency measurement

#	Name of the metric	Description
1	Performance tips	Strategies that can be used to conserve and extend the battery life
2	Code size	The length of the code and row column weight in the form
3	Loops	Number of For and While loops in the source code
4	Code smells	Internal Setter, Leaking Thread, Member ignoring method and Slow Loop consume up to 87 times more
5	Cyclomatic complexity	It counts the number of flows through a piece of code
6	Classes	The number of classes used in the source code
7	LOC (XML)	Lines of code in XML
8	LOC (Java)	Lines of code in Java
9	Collections types in Java	Number of frameworks that provide an architecture to store and manipulate the group of objects in Java
10	Invocation	Number of invocations of a program or a function

3   Design, Visualization and Development

3.1   Design

S. Few in his [4,5,30,31] pointed out several key characteristics that all dashboard should have. This section makes a bridge between the Sect. 2 and the design guidelines. As he (Few) puts it,

"A dashboard is a visual display of the most important information needed to achieve one or more objectives; consolidated and arranged on a single screen so the information can be monitored at a glance."

We strongly agree with the majority of his guidelines. First, all elements of a dashboard have to have a purpose and only the most important information that truly contributes to a specified goal should be shown to the end user. A dashboard is a mean of communication, and in order to effectively convey the message to the user, the message has to be clear, concise and goal-oriented.

Message has to be Clear. The information presented on a dashboard is most commonly a combination of graphics and text, with the emphasis on visual representations. The reason is that visuals can communicate with richer meaning than text on its own. Having clear, easy to understand graphics is one of the crucial requirements from the design perspective.

Message has to be Concise. It is highly advisable to fit the main metrics of the dashboard to one screen and one screen only, without horizontal and vertical scrolling. The users should be able to easily scan through all the visuals effortlessly and obtain the insights they are looking for. If the system consists of dozens and even hundreds of smaller metrics and they all need to be shown, the ones that are less important should be moved elsewhere. Only the metrics with high level of importance should appear on the main page.

Message has to be Goal-Oriented. Whether it is to gain an important business insight, or to successfully finish a project on time, dashboard's goal is to get users as close to their objectives as possible. What we have found is that a feedback loop, where users would report which metrics are more relevant to the goal than others, is one of the most valuable insights we could get to improve the set of metrics that get shown. This approach will be thoroughly examined later.

3.2   Visualization

As mentioned in the previous subsection, the visual representation and layout play a crucial role in designing a goal-oriented dashboard. Hence, visuals like widgets [32], graphs, charts all require special attention. Thus, we needed to develop a style guide, a set of standards and styles that all of our visual elements would conform to. It would enforce style to improve communication via consistency and clarity. The fully developed style guide can be viewed at: https://innometrics-12856.firebaseapp.com/.

Here is a comprehensive list of visual elements and containers chosen for the style guide:

- Colors
- Typography
- Container Elements (cards, carousels, modals, tables, etc.)
- Functional Elements (forms, menus, etc.)
- Charts

We have divided colors into three parts: theme colors, grays, and additional colors. This way the theme could be changed, and the users could tune the settings to their liking. Next, typography for headings one through six, as well as **bolded**, *italicized* and underlined text has also been defined. In addition, cross-functional and organizational elements such as forms (with buttons and input fields), tables (with cells), and different types of containers also needed a well-defined set of styling rules (Fig. 1).

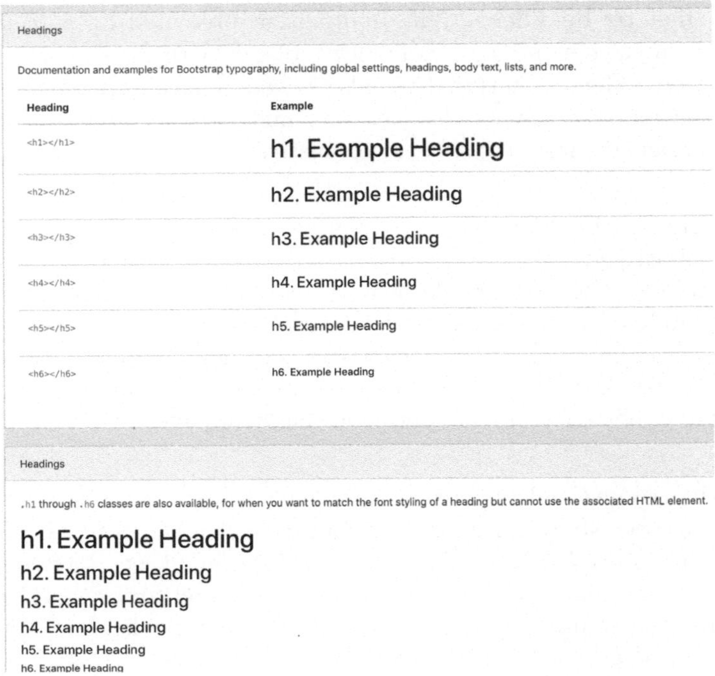

Fig. 1. Typography - headings 1 through 6

However, the main page of the dashboard consists almost entirely of widgets and charts. As we noted earlier, it is crucial to keep the main page free of clutter and not have to scroll or click elsewhere to get to the crucial information. That is why, due to their effectiveness and expressive power, we chose to fine tune their visual appearance. Taking multiple existing charting libraries into consideration and comparing their advantages and disadvantages, we decided to go with *ChartJS*. It has all the visuals we wanted, such as bar, line, and area charts and allows for editing when needed. Figure 2 depicts some of them that we decided to include in our prototype.

3.3 Technology

Considering the architectural decisions from Sect. 2 and design decisions from Sects. 3.1 and 3.2, choosing the platform was relatively straightforward, it had to be a web application. That means that the main programming language for development should be *JavaScript (JS)*.

However, choosing the appropriate JS framework/library was a challenging task. There are numerous options, and all of them offer similar functionality that we need. The one that stood out and ultimately we ended up choosing is *ReactJS*. The primary reason being that its Virtual DOM (Document Object Model) is optimized for real-time applications and that it facilitates the overall process

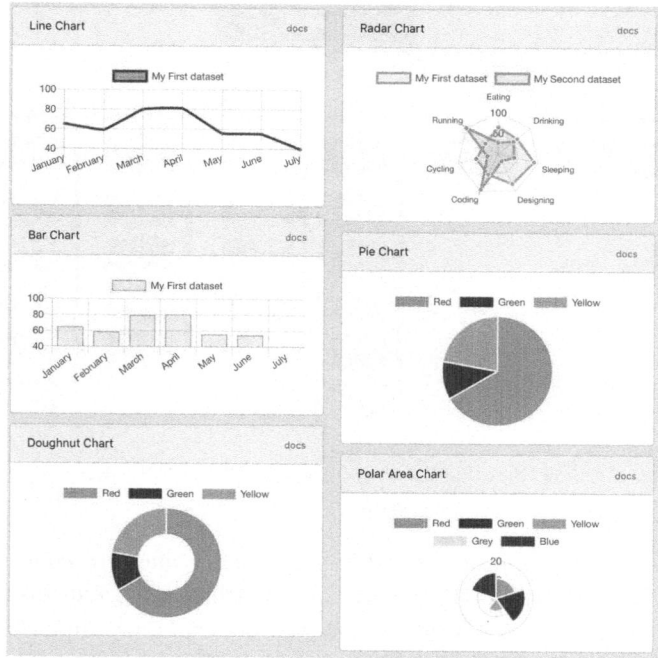

Fig. 2. Different types of charts from ChartJS

of writing components. Our system could potentially consist of hundreds of metrics, and reusing existing components while at the same time having impressive performance is critical.

In addition, file structure in *ReactJS*, although not opinionated, could be organized in very practical and clear ways. Consider, for example, our code structure, shown in the Fig. 3. It captures almost all the functionality while still remaining organized. Notice that we have left some of the implementation parts due to the lack of space.

To manage application's state we use *Redux*, a flexible, and predictable state container. It allows us to easily handle user input, authentication and authorization, as well as storing the results from REST API calls. One of the main benefits of using a state container is the centralization, where application's state and logic enable capabilities like undo/redo, state persistence and much more.

4   Dashboards as Complex Systems

As mentioned in the Subsect. 3.1, all dashboards must be optimized for a certain objective. As energy efficiency became a greater problem in recent years [33], our research agenda encapsulated that. It was immediately noticeable that the majority of state-of-the-art energy efficient software solutions had a very limited and strictly defined set of metrics to optimize for.

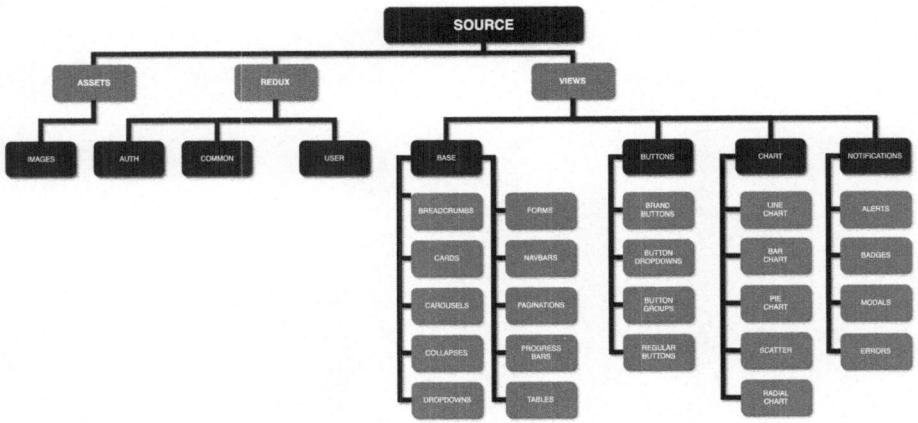

Fig. 3. File structure of the implementation

We took a different approach to addressing energy efficiency concerns. Instead of having a fully deterministic system, one in which each and every metric is manually chosen to be displayed, we opted for a system where an algorithm would decide whether or not to display a certain metric. The system would still take into consideration the manually entered metrics, albeit not relying on them heavily. All of this would be supported by a feedback loop, where users would rate the importance of the metrics they have been shown.

4.1   Self-adaptable Systems and Energy-Efficiency Dashboards

Self-adaptable systems (systems with behavior just mentioned) have recently gained traction [34], and they could be used as an abstraction to represent the software artifact, such as a dashboard. The rationale behind choosing Complex Systems (CS) to perform the self-adaptation is the following; by definition, a CS is a system with components particularly difficult to model. As it has not yet been fully investigated which factors (metrics) influence the efficiency the most, one approach would be to try and make all combinations of metrics and record the results. However, one may notice that as the number of metrics significantly increases, generating all combinations becomes unfeasible. In addition, metrics do not necessarily need to interact with others in linear fashion [35]. In fact, most of the interactions in CS are nonlinear, and often stochastic.

Therefore, we argue that dashboards for energy efficiency applications should be represented as a Complex System. Metrics (presented in Sect. 2), key components of dashboards, become agents within the system. That allows us to closely monitor the relationships each metric has with the other. It became apparent that almost no metrics are isolated, i.e. energy saved depends on a vast majority of software metrics that interact with each other. Thus, carefully monitoring and reacting to change is critical.

By embracing feedback loop and adaptation, these metrics are able to synchronize their internal states with the other metrics in the system. Additionally, the system should be able to recognize these changes and self-adjust with the emergence of globally coherent patterns of adjustment developing. This way the system would notice a change, and adapt to it.

So far we have only discussed the interactions between the metrics contributing to the global state. However, a major part of any CS is the ability of the system to feed back the globally coherent patterns to micro-level agents. These patterns are discovered either by the system or the dashboard user. An example of a system-discovered pattern in the energy efficiency context would be battery drainage per minute. The system, if noticed irregularities, would notify the agents, and they would adjust to that situation. The next section showcases the implementation details of such an approach.

4.2   Application of Evolutionary Algorithms

To be able to achieve the self-adaptation needed from our dashboard, a mechanism for handling the fittest metrics is needed [36,37][1]. The goal can be derived from the fitness function, which we define as follows:

Definition 1. *An agent has a higher contribution/fitness to the overall system if and only if a slight change in a specific metric would yield a significant change in the amount of energy saved, the difference between the expected energy efficiency level and the current level diverge significantly, or a metric answers custom energy-related questions that users may have.*

With this in mind, by applying the fitness function to each of the metrics inside the system we would get a numeric score for each of them. This tells the system how much does each individual metric influence the overall energy efficiency level of system as a whole. Furthermore, the user would be shown only the metrics particularly relevant to the current state of the system. Thus, by choosing this exact fitness function, these would follow:

- metrics that deviate from the mean are more likely to be shown to the user;
- metrics whose improvement may result in other metrics' fitness are more likely to be shown to the user;
- metrics of all sizes whose improvement would not yield a substantial increase/decrease in energy efficiency levels, have less change of being shown to the user.

The final algorithm would then run as follows:

1. **assign** a fitness score to each agent in the system (according to the fitness function defined above)

---

[1] Notice the use of the word *fittest*, indicating the usage of natural selection as a mean of choosing the metrics that tell the most about the specified goal.

2. **select** members to act upon using some variation operators (crossover and mutations) [38][2]
3. **replace** certain members of the population with these children from variation operators
4. **keep** some members from the previous population in the new population

The next step would be then to perform the *natural selection* between the metrics. More specifically, we chose the tournament-like contest in which the winner would continue to breed, and the loser would be most likely eliminated [39,40].

4.3 Dynamic Equilibrium

As energy efficiency monitoring solutions became larger, stakeholders operating such systems would have significant difficulties determining which metric to display and optimize for, and which to ignore. Such a system is said to be deterministic, as all the change has to be manually done and the system has no means of improvement.

Advances in the field of big data and machine learning indicate that the above-mentioned system architecture could be transformed to be stochastic, with no absolute governance. In addition, the data being collected is growing exponentially [41], and thus more metrics are going to become available for processing. A non-deterministic system operating in such a way would neither be in the state of maximum entropy, nor would it be completely stable. Such a state is referred to as *Dynamic Equilibrium*, where actors are loosely bound to each other while still having plenty of room to improve.

5 Future Research Agenda

To date, research on software-oriented energy efficiency has been focusing almost solely on code-related metrics, such as those presented in Sect. 2. However, no evidence proves the importance of process-related metrics (productivity, turnaround time, throughput, iteration burn-down, error rate, etc.) to the energy efficiency. Thus, our research agenda includes primary research to investigate the correlation of above-described metrics to the energy consumption and saving levels.

In addition, we aim to extend the list of energy consumption code metrics considered by the dashboard. For example by knowing the Number of Classes (NoC) in the source code we can easily calculate other metrics like: Number of Immediate sub-classes of a Class, Response for a Class, Weighted methods per Class as well as the Number of Children. This may lead to performance benefits and ultimately savings in computing power. Performance is one of the key aspects that is also a part of our research agenda.

Finally, we would like to supplement metrics with a reliable prediction system [42–45].

---

[2] Crossover is combination of parents' genetic information, and mutation is a change in agent's genetic information.

6   Conclusions

Energy efficiency, the minimization of the amount of energy required to provide products and services, has become a growing issue. Mobile phones, smart watches and other portable devices operate in a very power-constrained environment. Research in the area of energy efficiency would facilitate the efforts to cut energy costs, and ultimately reduce greenhouse gas emissions [46].

Advent of software solutions, on the other hand, have profoundly impacted almost all spheres of human existence. To date, more attention has been given to the study of energy efficiency in hardware, rather than in software [47]. This paper considered code, as well as process and project-related metrics as indicators of potential energy savings. Additionally, we presented a dashboard that tracks such metrics and only displays the ones that are most relevant. It manages to do so by combining the notions from Complexity Theory (Non-linear dynamics, Dynamic Equilibrium) with Evolutionary Algorithms (natural selection) to synthesize an adaptable stochastic tool.

Acknowledgments. The work presented in this paper was supported by the grant of Russian Science Foundation #19-19-00623.

References

1. Pinto, G., Castor, F., Liu, Y.D.: Mining questions about software energy consumption. In: Proceedings of the 11th Working Conference on Mining Software Repositories, pp. 22–31. ACM (2014)
2. Pinto, G., Castor, F.: Energy efficiency: a new concern for application software developers. Commun. ACM **60**(12), 68–75 (2017)
3. Liu, K., Pinto, G., Liu, Y.D.: Data-oriented characterization of application-level energy optimization. In: Egyed, A., Schaefer, I. (eds.) FASE 2015. LNCS, vol. 9033, pp. 316–331. Springer, Heidelberg (2015). https://doi.org/10.1007/978-3-662-46675-9_21
4. Few, S.: Information dashboard design (2006)
5. Few, S., Perceptual Edge: Dashboard confusion revisited. Perceptual Edge, pp. 1–6 (2007)
6. Malik, S.: Enterprise Dashboards: Design and Best Practices for IT. Wiley, New York (2005)
7. Danovaro, E., Remencius, T., Sillitti, A., Succi, G.: PKM: knowledge management tool for environments centered on the concept of the experience factory. In: Companion of the 30th International Conference on Software Engineering, ICSE Companion 2008, pp. 937–938. ACM (2008)
8. Janes, A., Sillitti, A., Succi, G.: Effective dashboard design. Cut. IT J. **26**(1), 17–24 (2013)
9. Ivanov, V., Rogers, A., Succi, G., Yi, J., Zorin, V.: Precooked developer dashboards: what to show and how to use - poster. In: Proceedings of the 40th International Conference on Software Engineering Companion, ICSE 2018, Gothenburg, Sweden, May-June 2018. ACM (2018)

10. Ivanov, V., Pischulin, V., Rogers, A., Succi, G., Yi, J., Zorin, V.: Design and validation of precooked developer dashboards. In: Proceedings of the 2018 ACM Joint Meeting on European Software Engineering Conference and Symposium on the Foundations of Software Engineering, ESEC/SIGSOFT FSE 2018, Lake Buena Vista, FL, USA, 04–09 November 2018, pp. 821–826 (2018)
11. Coman, I.D., Robillard, P.N., Sillitti, A., Succi, G.: Cooperation, collaboration and pair-programming: field studies on backup behavior. J. Syst. Softw. **91**, 124–134 (2014)
12. Janes, A., Succi, G.: Lean Software Development in Action. Springer, Heidelberg (2014). https://doi.org/10.1007/978-3-642-00503-9
13. Pedrycz, W., Russo, B., Succi, G.: A model of job satisfaction for collaborative development processes. J. Syst. Softw. **84**(5), 739–752 (2011)
14. Pedrycz, W., Russo, B., Succi, G.: Knowledge transfer in system modeling and its realization through an optimal allocation of information granularity. Appl. Soft Comput. **12**(8), 1985–1995 (2012)
15. Maurer, F., Succi, G., Holz, H., Kötting, B., Goldmann, S., Dellen, B.: Software process support over the Internet. In: Proceedings of the 21st International Conference on Software Engineering, ICSE 1999, pp. 642–645. ACM, May 1999
16. Sillitti, A., Vernazza, T., Succi, G.: Service oriented programming: a new paradigm of software reuse. In: Gacek, C. (ed.) ICSR 2002. LNCS, vol. 2319, pp. 269–280. Springer, Heidelberg (2002). https://doi.org/10.1007/3-540-46020-9_19
17. Corral, L., Sillitti, A., Succi, G.: Software assurance practices for mobile applications. Computing **97**(10), 1001–1022 (2014). https://doi.org/10.1007/s00607-014-0395-8
18. Lee, Y.C., Zomaya, A.Y.: Energy efficient utilization of resources in cloud computing systems. J. Supercomput. **60**(2), 268–280 (2012). https://doi.org/10.1007/s11227-010-0421-3
19. Kovács, G.L., Drozdik, S., Zuliani, P., Succi, G.: Open source software for the public administration. In: Proceedings of the 6th International Workshop on Computer Science and Information Technologies, October 2004
20. Fitzgerald, B., Kesan, J.P., Russo, B., Shaikh, M., Succi, G.: Adopting Open Source Software: A Practical Guide. The MIT Press, Cambridge (2011)
21. Di Bella, E., Sillitti, A., Succi, G.: A multivariate classification of open source developers. Inf. Sci. **221**, 72–83 (2013)
22. Li, D., Halfond, W.G.J.: An investigation into energy-saving programming practices for android smartphone app development. In: Proceedings of the 3rd International Workshop on Green and Sustainable Software - GREENS 2014. ACM Press (2014)
23. Chatzigeorgiou, A., Stephanides, G.: Software Qual. J. **10**(4), 355–371 (2002)
24. Vasile, C.V., Pattinson, C., Kor, A.-L.: Mobile phones and energy consumption. In: Kharchenko, V., Kondratenko, Y., Kacprzyk, J. (eds.) Green IT Engineering: Social, Business and Industrial Applications. SSDC, vol. 171, pp. 243–271. Springer, Cham (2019). https://doi.org/10.1007/978-3-030-00253-4_11
25. Keong, C.K., Wei, K.T., Ghani, A.A.A., Sharif, K.Y.: Toward using software metrics as indicator to measure power consumption of mobile application: a case study. In: 2015 9th Malaysian Software Engineering Conference (MySEC). IEEE, December 2015
26. Cruz, L., Abreu, R.: Performance-based guidelines for energy efficient mobile applications. In: 2017 IEEE/ACM 4th International Conference on Mobile Software Engineering and Systems (MOBILESoft). IEEE, May 2017

27. Vernazza, T., Granatella, G., Succi, G., Benedicenti, L., Mintchev, M.: Defining metrics for software components. In: Proceedings of the World Multiconference on Systemics, Cybernetics and Informatics, vol. XI, pp. 16–23, July 2000
28. Sillitti, A., Janes, A., Succi, G., Vernazza, T.: Measures for mobile users: an architecture. J. Syst. Architect. **50**(7), 393–405 (2004)
29. Scotto, M., Sillitti, A., Succi, G., Vernazza, T.: A relational approach to software metrics. In: Proceedings of the 2004 ACM Symposium on Applied Computing, SAC 2004, pp. 1536–1540. ACM (2004)
30. Few, S.: Dashboard design: taking a metaphor too far. Inf. Manag. **15**(3), 18 (2005)
31. Few, S., Perceptual Edge: Data visualization: past, present, and future. IBM Cognos Innovation Center (2007)
32. Louch, J.O., Peyton, E.S., Hynes, C., Forstall, S., Christie, G.N.: Synchronization of widgets and dashboards, 22 October 2013. US Patent 8,566,732
33. Patterson, M.G.: What is energy efficiency?: Concepts, indicators and methodological issues. Energy Policy **24**(5), 377–390 (1996)
34. Corrado, A.J.: Dynamics of Complex Systems. CRC Press, Boca Raton (2019)
35. Thompson, J.M.T., Thompson, M., Stewart, H.B.: Nonlinear Dynamics and Chaos. Wiley, New York (2002)
36. Sivanandam, S.N., Deepa, S.N.: Genetic algorithms. In: Introduction to Genetic Algorithms, pp. 15–37. Springer, Heidelberg (2008). https://doi.org/10.1007/978-3-540-73190-0_2
37. Forrest, S.: Genetic algorithms: principles of natural selection applied to computation. Science **261**(5123), 872–878 (1993)
38. Bäck, T., Fogel, D.B., Michalewicz, Z.: Evolutionary Computation 1: Basic Algorithms and Operators. CRC Press, Boca Raton (2018)
39. Blickle, T., Thiele, L.: A mathematical analysis of tournament selection. In: ICGA, vol. 95, pp. 9–15. Citeseer (1995)
40. Greewood, G.W., Fogel, G.B., Ciobanu, M.: Emphasizing extinction in evolutionary programming. In: Proceedings of the 1999 Congress on Evolutionary Computation-CEC99 (Cat. No. 99TH8406), vol. 1, pp. 666–671. IEEE (1999)
41. Anagnostopoulos, I., Zeadally, S., Exposito, E.: Handling big data: research challenges and future directions. J. Supercomput. **72**(4), 1494–1516 (2016). https://doi.org/10.1007/s11227-016-1677-z
42. Musílek, P., Pedrycz, W., Sun, N., Succi, G.: On the sensitivity of COCOMO II software cost estimation model. In: Proceedings of the 8th International Symposium on Software Metrics, METRICS 2002, pp. 13–20. IEEE Computer Society, June 2002
43. Ronchetti, M., Succi, G., Pedrycz, W., Russo, B.: Early estimation of software size in object-oriented environments a case study in a CMM level 3 software firm. Inf. Sci. **176**(5), 475–489 (2006)
44. Rossi, B., Russo, B., Succi, G.: Modelling failures occurrences of open source software with reliability growth. In: Ågerfalk, P., Boldyreff, C., González-Barahona, J.M., Madey, G.R., Noll, J. (eds.) OSS 2010. IAICT, vol. 319, pp. 268–280. Springer, Heidelberg (2010). https://doi.org/10.1007/978-3-642-13244-5_21
45. Sillitti, A., Succi, G., Vlasenko, J.: Understanding the impact of pair programming on developers attention: a case study on a large industrial experimentation. In: Proceedings of the 34th International Conference on Software Engineering, ICSE 2012, pp. 1094–1101. IEEE Press, Piscataway, June 2012

46. Brookes, L.: The greenhouse effect: the fallacies in the energy efficiency solution. Energy Policy **18**(2), 199–201 (1990)
47. Capra, E., Francalanci, C., Slaughter, S.A.: Measuring application software energy efficiency. IT Prof. **14**(2), 54–61 (2012)

Using FLOSS for Storing, Processing and Linking Corpus Data

Damir Mukhamedshin⬤, Olga Nevzorova(✉)⬤, and Alexander Kirillovich⬤

Kazan Federal University, Kazan, Russia
damirmuh@gmail.com, onevzoro@gmail.com,
alik.kirillovich@gmail.com

Abstract. Corpus data is widely used to solve different linguistic, educational and applied problems. The Tatar corpus management system (http://tugantel.tatar) is specifically developed for Turkic languages. The functionality of our corpus management system includes a search of lexical units, morphological and lexical search, a search of syntactic units, a search of N-grams and others. The search is performed using open source tools (database management system MariaDB, Redis data store). This article describes the process of choosing FLOSS for the main components of our system and also processing a search query and building a linked open dataset based on corpus data.

Keywords: Corpus linguistics · Corpus manager · Linked open data

1 Introduction

In this paper, we discuss the development of the corpus management system for the Tatar National Corpus "Tugan Tel" [1]. The corpus is organized as a collection of texts covering different genres, such as fiction, news, science, official, etc. A text consists in sentences (called contexts). The words from a sentence are provided with morphological annotation. The annotation of a word includes the lemma, POS and the sequence of grammatical features expressed by the affixes.

Access to the corpus is provided by the corpus management system. The system allows users to search for word tokens with a specified full form or lemma and grammatical features. The search results are represented as a list of the sentences containing the found word tokens. Figure 1 shows the search result for the word *kuman* 'book' in the plural number and the genitive or the directive case. The tooltip under one of the found tokens contains its morphological annotation.

The general architecture of the corpus management system is represented at Fig. 2. This model includes three main components: a web interface, a search engine, and a database. The system imports the annotated texts from the corpus annotation tool, and exports them to a triplestore of the LLOD publishing platform.

Development of the corpus management system cannot begin without a clear understanding of which tools will be used to store and process corpus data. Therefore, one of the important factors when choosing and using tools for data storing and processing is

© IFIP International Federation for Information Processing 2020
Published by Springer Nature Switzerland AG 2020
V. Ivanov et al. (Eds.): OSS 2020, IFIP AICT 582, pp. 177–182, 2020.
https://doi.org/10.1007/978-3-030-47240-5_17

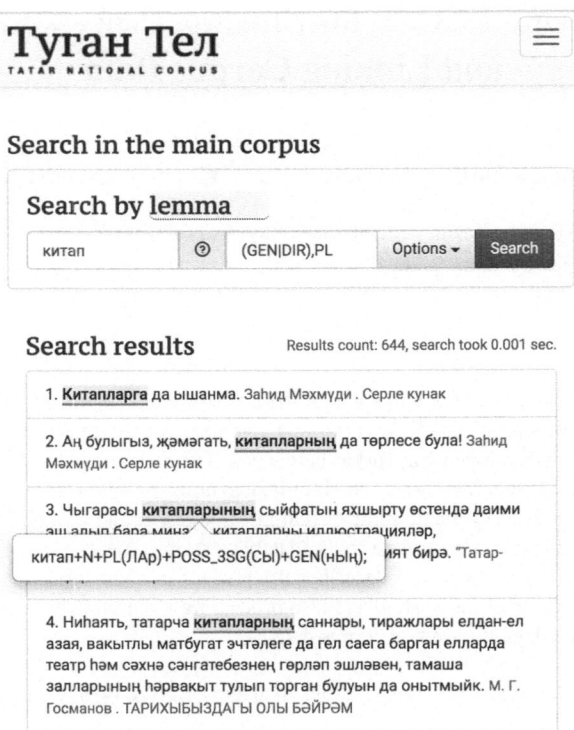

Fig. 1. The corpus manager GUI

for us their open source code, which is fundamental to ensure transparency and flexibility of the tool.

When choosing tools for processing and storing corpus data, we were faced the task of finding a set of FLOSS to ensure high speed of performing search queries (no more than 0.1 seconds for direct search queries, no more than 1 second for reverse search queries), wide search capabilities (at least direct and reverse search, search in parts of word forms and lemmas, mixed search, phrase search), and the possibility of further growth of system performance and functionality.

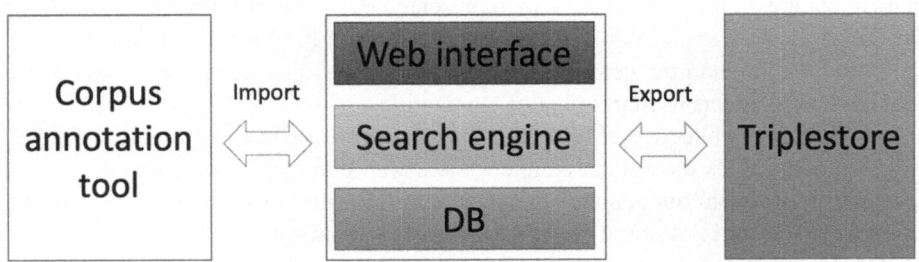

Fig. 2. Abstract structure of the corpus data management system

In Sect. 2 we describe using of FLOSS in the corpus management system, and in Sect. 3 we describe using of FLOSS the LLOD publishing platform.

2   Using FLOSS in Corpus Management System

To choose FLOSS for storing and processing of corpus data, we formed a list of the most important selection criteria:

1. Performance. The solution should produce an average of at least 10 search operations per second.
2. Functionality. The solution should provide a possibility of direct and reverse search by wordforms and lemmas, search by parts of wordforms and lemmas, and phrase search.
3. Compatibility with other software. FLOSS for data storage should work with FLOSS for data processing and vice versa.
4. Completeness of documentation and presence of a large community. Everyone should be able to continue its development, focusing on the documentation and the accumulated experience of the community.
5. Development prospects. The solution should develop and maintain modern technologies.

We analyzed information in public sources [2] and chose FLOSS according to criteria 2–5. The resulting FLOSS set is presented in Table 1.

Table 1. Chosen FLOSS for storing and processing corpus data.

Name	Type and main features
memcached[a]	Storage system of keys and values in memory
memcacheDB[b]	Distributed key-value storage system. It supports transactions and replication
Redis[c]	Non-relational distributed data storage system. It allows storing strings and arrays and making selections from them
FoundationDB[d]	NoSQL database with a shared nothing architecture. It provides an ordered key-value store with transactions
Sphinx[e]	Search system consisting of an indexer and a full-text search module
Elasticsearch[f]	Distributed RESTful search engine. It allows making full-text search for structured data and performing complex search queries
MySQL[g]	Relational DBMS

[a]https://github.com/memcached/memcached
[b]https://github.com/LMDB/memcachedb
[c]https://github.com/antirez/redis
[d]https://github.com/apple/foundationdb
[e]https://github.com/sphinxsearch/sphinx
[f]https://github.com/elastic/elasticsearch
[g]https://github.com/mysql/mysql-server

To verify compliance with the first criterion, we conducted a series of experiments on writing and searching based on the generated data [3]. The best results were shown by the

MySQL + Redis suite, which was chosen by us to store data in the corpus management system.

To build the system based on the selected components, additional elements must be included. So, to bind the PHP interpreter and the Redis data warehouse, we use the PhpRedis extension. In order for the PHP interpreter and MySQL DBMS to work in tandem, we use the php-mysql package, namely the mysqlnd driver, which allows working with the DBMS using its own low-level protocol.

Thus, the scripts executed by the PHP interpreter allow operations with data both from the Redis data storage and from the MySQL DBMS. Performing operations in the order necessary to solve the tasks assigned to the corpus data management system, PHP scripts are the link between indexes and cached data stored in Redis storage, index tables and text data stored in MySQL DBMS.

Let us consider how the processing of a simple direct search query *alma* $_{tat}$/apple $_{en}$ is executed. The process execution of such query is shown in Fig. 3.

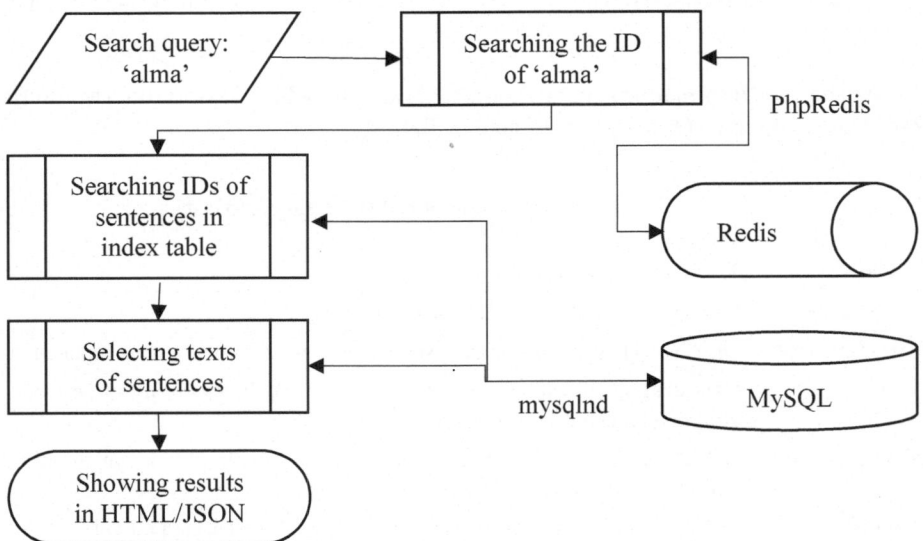

Fig. 3. Process execution of search query *алма*

First of all, the script that performs this task searches the identifier of the word-form *alma* in the Redis database, by making a request using the PhpRedis extension. Already at this point, the script may report an error in the query, if the identifier of the desired wordform is not found in the corpus data.

In the second step, the script makes a request to the MySQL database using mysqlnd. In this case, the script needs to get a list of sentences containing the desired wordform. This data is stored in the index table of corpus data. In response, the script receives a list of context (sentence) identifiers, according to which in the third step the required number of sentence texts is requested. The received data is displayed to an user in the form of an HTML document or a JSON structure.

3 Building a Linked Open Dataset Based on Corpus Data

The corpus has been published on the Linguistic Linked Open Data cloud [4]. The dataset is represented in terms of NIF [5], OntoLex-Lemon [6], LexInfo, OLiA [7] and MMoOn [8] ontologies.

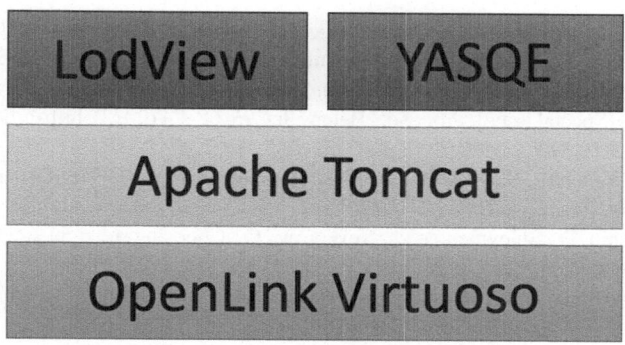

Fig. 4. LLOD publishing platform

LLOD publishing platform consists in the following open-source components (Fig. 4). The RDF is stored in the OpenLink Virtuoso triplestore. The dataset is available via deferrable URI's and SPARQL endpoint. Deferrable URI's are accessible throws the LodView RDF browser, based on the Apache Tomacat webserver. The query interface is powered by YASQE [9].

Publication of the corpus on the LLOD cloud makes possible its interlinking with the external linguistic resources for Tatar, including Russian-Tatar Socio-Political Thesaurus [10], TatWordNet and TatVerbBank.

4 Conclusion

The solutions presented in this article are applied in the developed corpus management system. Using FLOSS significantly reduced the development time and ensured the transparency of processes, flexibility, and possibility of in-depth analysis, as well as opportunities for further development.

The corpus data management system is used to work with Tatar texts. The total volume of the collection of Tatar texts is about 200 million wordforms. The average execution time of the direct search query does not exceed 0.05 s in 98% of cases, and the reverse search is performed by the system within 0.1 s in 82% of cases, which exceeded the expected system performance. In many ways, such performance is provided by FLOSS, used for data storage and processing. Also, thanks to FLOSS, search capabilities were expanded in the system. The search using category lists, the complex search using logical expressions, the search for named entities and other functions were added to the advanced version of the system.

Currently, the corpus management system is in open beta testing and available online at http://tugantel.tatar. After that, we are going to release it under an open license.

Acknowledgements. The work was funded by Russian Science Foundation according to the research project no. 19-71-10056.

References

1. Suleymanov, D., Nevzorova, O., Gatiatullin, A., Gilmullin, R., Khakimov, B.: National corpus of the Tatar language "Tugan Tel": grammatical annotation and implementation. In: Vargas-Sierra, C., (ed.). Selected Papers from the 5th International Conference on Corpus Linguistics, (CILC2013) [Special issue]. Proc. Soc. Behav. Sci. **95**, 68–74 (2013). https://doi.org/10.1016/j.sbspro.2013.10.623
2. Katkar, M., Kutchhii, S., Kutchhii, A.: Performance analysis for NoSQL and SQL. Int. J. Innov. Emerg. Res. Eng. **2**(3), 12–17 (2015)
3. Mukhamedshin, D., Suleymanov, D., Nevzorova, O.: Choosing the right storage solution for the corpus management system (analytical overview and experiments). In: Bouhlel, M.S., Rovetta, S. (eds.) SETIT 2018. SIST, vol. 146, pp. 105–114. Springer, Cham (2020). https://doi.org/10.1007/978-3-030-21005-2_10
4. Cimiano, P., Chiarcos, C., McCrae, J.P., Gracia, J.: Linguistic linked open data cloud. In: Cimiano, P., et al. (eds.) Linguistic Linked Data: Representation, Generation and Applications, pp. 29–41. Springer, Cham (2020). https://doi.org/10.1007/978-3-030-30225-2_3
5. Hellmann, S., Lehmann, J., Auer, S., Brümmer, M.: Integrating NLP using linked data. In: Alani, H., Kagal, L., Fokoue, A., Groth, P., Biemann, C., Parreira, J.X. (eds.) ISWC 2013. LNCS, vol. 8219, pp. 98–113. Springer, Heidelberg (2013). https://doi.org/10.1007/978-3-642-41338-4_7
6. McCrae, J.P., Bosque-Gil, J., Gracia, J., Buitelaar, P., and Cimiano, P.: The OntoLex-lemon model: development and applications. In: Kosem I., et al. (eds.) Proceedings of the 5th biennial conference on Electronic Lexicography (eLex 2017), pp. 587–597. Lexical Computing CZ (2017)
7. Chiarcos, C.: OLiA – ontologies of linguistic annotation. Seman. Web **6**(4), 379–386 (2015). https://doi.org/10.3233/SW-140167
8. Klimek, B., Arndt, N., Krause, S., Arndt, T.: Creating Linked data morphological language resources with MMoOn - the hebrew morpheme inventory. In: Calzolari N., et al. (eds.) Proceedings of the 10th International Conference on Language Resources and Evaluation (LREC 2016), pp. 892–899. ELRA (2016)
9. Rietveld, L., Hoekstra, R.: The YASGUI Family of SPARQL Clients. Seman. Web **8**(3), 373–383 (2017). https://doi.org/10.3233/SW-150197
10. Galieva, A., Kirillovich, A., Khakimov, B., Loukachevitch, N., Nevzorova, O., Suleymanov, D.: Toward domain-specific Russian-Tatar thesaurus construction. In: Proceedings of the International Conference IMS-2017, pp. 120–124. ACM (2017). https://doi.org/10.1145/3143699.3143716

MegaM@Rt2 EU Project: Open Source Tools for Mega-Modelling at Runtime of CPSs

Jesus Gorroñogoitia Cruz[1], Andrey Sadovykh[2(✉)], Dragos Truscan[3],
Hugo Bruneliere[4], Pierluigi Pierini[5], and Lara Lopez Muñiz[1]

[1] ATOS, Madrid, Spain
{jesus.gorronogoitia,lara.lopez}@atos.net
[2] Innopolis University, Innopolis, Russia
a.sadovykh@innopolis.ru
[3] Åbo Akademi University, Turku, Finland
dragos.truscan@abo.fi
[4] IMT Atlantique, LS2N (CNRS) & ARMINES, Nantes, France
hugo.bruneliere@imt-atlantique.fr
[5] Intecs Solutions S.p.A., Rome, Italy
pierluigi.pierini@intecs.it

Abstract. In this paper, we overview our experiences of developing large set of open source tools in ECSEL JU European project called MegaM@Rt2 whose main objective is to propose a scalable model-based framework incorporating methods and tools for the continuous development and runtime support of complex software-intensive Cyber-Physical Systems (CPSs). We briefly present the MegaM@Rt2 concepts, discuss our approach for open source, enumerate tools and give an example of a tools selection for a specific industrial context. Our goal is to introduce the reader with open source tools for the model-based engineering of CPSs suitable for diverse industrial applications.

Keywords: Model-driven engineering · Model-based system engineering · Cyber-Physical Systems · Open source · Tools

1 Introduction

MegaM@Rt2 is a three-years project, which started in April 2017 [1,7] and which is funded by European Components and Systems for European Leadership Joint Undertaking (ECSEL JU) under the H2020 European program. The main goal of MegaM@Rt2 is to create an integrated framework incorporating scalable methods and tools for continuous system engineering and runtime validation and verification (V&V). The framework addresses the needs of the 8 case study providers

This work has received funding from the Electronic Component Systems for European Leadership Joint Undertaking under grant agreement No 737494. This Joint Undertaking receives support from the European Union's Horizon 2020 research and innovation programme and Sweden, France, Spain, Italy, Finland, the Czech Rep.

involved in the project, which come from diverse and heterogeneous industrial domains, ranging from transportation and telecommunications to logistics and manufacturing. The underlying objective is to provide improved productivity, quality, and predictability of large and complex industrial cyber-physical systems (CPSs).

In order to address these needs, 20 technology and research providers contributed with more than 28 tools integrated into the MegaM@Rt2 toolbox. The results enumerated in this paper are a complement to the research achievements discussed in [12]. In this paper, we briefly present the MegaM@Rt2 concept, discuss the choice for the open source in the project, enumerate the open-source tools provided by the project, and finally give an example of an open source tool chain for a telecom application.

2   MegaM@Rt2 Overall Concept

The project addresses the fundamental challenge to support efficient forward and backward traceability between the two main system levels: design-time and runtime. In parallel to these, modern large-scale industrial software engineering processes require thorough configuration and model governance to provide the promised productivity gains. As an answer to the above challenge, MegaM@Rt2 provides a scalable mega-modelling approach to manage all the involved artifacts including the multitude of different types of models, corresponding workflows, and configurations, among others. In this context, an important challenge is to better tackle large diversity of models in terms of nature, number, size, and complexity.

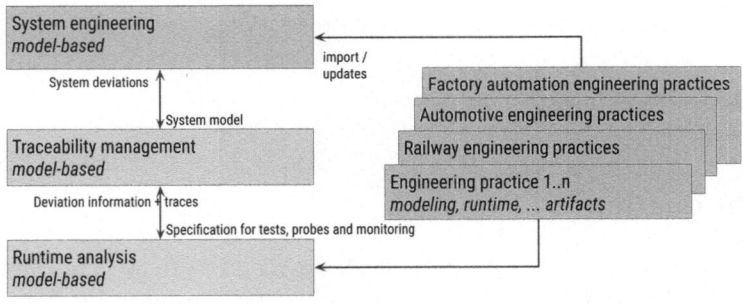

Fig. 1. Conceptual architecture of the MegaM@Rt2 project

Conceptually (Fig. 1), the project proposes to integrate various system modelling artifacts on the System engineering level, while the runtime artifacts such as tests and on-line monitors produce traces that have to be analysed and linked with system artifacts for validation and remediation purposes. Consequently the project provides numerous tools that are categorised in those above-mentioned areas: a) system engineering, b) runtime analysis, and c) traceability management. The end users, industrial case studies, select a subset of the MegaM@Rt2 tools based on their preferred methodologies and technical areas. For example in the railway domain, engineers follow V-life cycle and focus on safety with specific modelling and verification techniques. They benefit from the large variety of the analysis tools that are enabled with the common traceability mechanisms.

Open source is important for the project in many aspects. Releasing tools as open source is important in the project in order to increase the audience and adoption of the tools by the community and industrial partners. Moreover, the project promotes wide adoption of its methods through open source along with other methods. Finally, open source approach is a mechanism to ensure sustainability aiming to create a community of interest around project results and ensure industry for the perennity of their preferred tools.

3   MegaM@Rt2 Contribution to Open Source

In order to put in practice the global approach presented in the previous section, this section introduces the MegaM@Rt2 toolbox. This toolbox is composed of three complementary tool sets covering System Engineering, Runtime Analysis, and Model & Traceability Management, respectively. The toolbox is freely accessible from the MegaM@Rt2 web portal [9] offers detailed information about all the available MegaM@Rt2 tools, including links to their main artifacts such as software downloads, documentation and source code, available in a public repository. In addition, this web portal provides capabilities that facilitate the searching of suitable tools by keyword (i.e., tag cloud) and license type. In this paper, we focus on the tools provided under an open source license scheme and how they have been managed and maintained in the project. The use of open source distribution licenses facilitates a wider adoption of the tools and their support, maintenance and evolution by their own community of users.

Most of the open source MegaM@Rt2 tools are Eclipse-based, which can be installed, as plugins, within an existing Eclipse 2018-09 version. This version has been adopted as the baseline for all tools to be made compatible with, in order to facilitate their integration within a common Eclipse framework. Besides, the MegM@Rt2 toolset packaging and delivery approach is based on common Eclipse packaging and delivery mechanisms: i) a public MegaM@Rt2 Eclipse update site [5] that users can apply to select and install the MegaM@Rt2 tools, and ii) the MegaM@Rt2 IDE (including tools and dependencies) has been published in the Eclipse Marketplace [6], from where users can install it. These mechanisms are well-known among the Eclipse community and they largely simplify the installation of the MegaM@Rt2 toolset. Furthermore, downloadable bundles [5] of the MegaM@Rt2 IDE toolsets with all required dependencies installed have been packaged for Windows, MacOS and Linux.

The tools included in the latest version of the Eclipse bundle can be distributed according to the work packages in the project as follows: a) system engineering - Papyrus and Moka extensions for aspect-oriented modeling and fUML simulation logging, respectively, Collaboro for collaborative language development, EMFToCSP for automatic model verification, S3D for designing the software and hardware of embedded systems, HepsyCode for HW/SW Co-Design of Heterogeneous Parallel Dedicated Systems; b) runtime analysis - PADRE for model refactoring, VeriATL for model transformation verification; and c) traceability and megamodeling - NeoEMF for scalable model loading and handling, EMF Views for building model views and JTL for traceability management.

Additional tools contributing to system engineering are distributed as Eclipse Rich Client Platform applications, e.g. CHESS [2]] - for developing hard real-time, safety-critical and high-integrity embedded systems, or can be downloaded from their developer web site, e.g. Modelio [10] for system modeling in UML, SysML and MARTE; and Refinement Calculus of Reactive Systems - RCSR for model verification and reasoning.

Other MegaM@Rt2 open source tools that are not Eclipse-based are packaged (together with their dependencies and testing examples) and delivered within containerized packages, which can be generated from downloadable images. MegaM@Rt2 offers Docker images [4] and Linux scripts to build tool containers and run the tools right from those images. This approach largely simplifies the burden of installing the tools and their dependencies, and does not require any knowledge of the Docker technology from end-users. For instance, MegaM@Rt2 provides docker images for system engineering, such as PauWARE - for instrumenting Statecharts execution in Java and for run time analysis, such as AIPHS - for on-chip monitoring, and for runtime analysis, such as the LIME tool - for testing and runtime monitoring.

In terms of licensing schemes, the above mentioned tools are released under one of the open source licenses: copyleft or viral licenses, such as GPLv2/3 or LGPLv3, semi-restrictive licenses such as EPLv1/v2, and permissive licenses such as APLv2, and MIT. The choice of licensing scheme for each tool was dictated both by the dependencies of each tool and by the interest of the tool vendors. A detailed description of the capabilities of each tool in the MegaM@Rt2 toolbox, including how it satisfies the requirements of the industrial case studies in the project, can be found in public project deliverables covering the three tool sets previously mentioned D2.5, D3.5 and D4.4, respectively, released in 2019 [8]. Moreover, a second set of public project deliverables provide conceptual aspects, methodologies, and guidelines on how each tool in the toolbox can be used by end users D2.6, D3.6 and D4.5 [8].

4   Open Source Toolchain for a Telecom Case Study

The Teknè case study is a concrete example of how open source tools belonging to the MegaM@Rt framework are applied to solve industrial needs and how MegaM@Rt tool set allows easy and flexible integration with external tools. Actually, the last point is a general issue in the industrial practice where internal processes require formal procedures and consolidated tools. MegaM@Rt addressed the problem by providing a framework that can be easily tailored to user needs, e.g. selecting the subset of needed tools, and integrated in external context exploiting model transformation techniques.

Fig. 2. Tekne wearable mote example

The case study is centered on a wearable mote (see Fig. 2), which is a mobile network node, based on the Ultra-Wideband (UWB) technology, with short range communications, indoor positioning and tracking capabilities. It can be used, for instance, to evaluate collision risks among a set of mobile devices in a construction site.

Among the tools adopted to solve this case study, CHESS, used for design and analysis, and *ρEmbedded* libraries, used to instrument code with monitor probes required to collect runtime traces, are open source tools part of the MegaM@Rt framework, while Yakindu [3] is a commercial tool used for code generation, but a free license is available for non-commercial and academic use.

The CS implementation process shown in Fig. 3 is split in three main steps: i) the requirements analysis and formalisation, the preliminary design and analysis; ii) detailed design and code generation, iii) log collection at runtime and log analysis and back propagation of the results to the design step. In the first step, the CHESS contract-based design approach has been exploited. The system requirements are analysed to derive the system architecture and then they are formalised, deriving the "assumption/guarantee" pairs, using Linear Temporal Logic (LTL), to compose contracts. Contracts are associated with system architectural components. CHESS is seamlessly integrated with the OCRA tool [11] supporting the analysis of the components behavior (expressed as a set of finite state machines) with respect to the associated contracts, to assess the formal correctness of the architecture.

During the second step, the implementation components are derived from the architectural model and MARTE annotations are added to mark the timing constraints to be checked at runtime. The resulting model is exported to Yakindu that allows additional annotation for code generation and instrumentation with monitoring support based on *ρEmbedded* libraries.

The final step provides the collection of the log traces; logs are then given in input to CHESS for the analysis of the non-functional characteristics of the system at runtime and the back propagation of the results to the design environment. In particular the derived properties are traced back to the relevant implementation components of the CHESS model to allow verification with respect

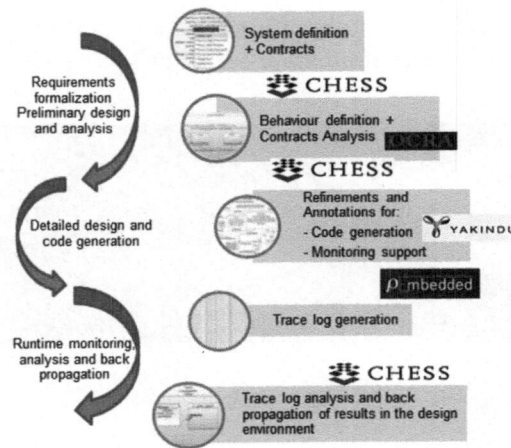

Fig. 3. Tekne case study tool chain and process

to the defined constraints/requirements. Further refinements of the design are then applied if necessary.

The contract based approach supported by CHESS enables the formalization of functional and non functional requirements, and the early validation of the model, while runtime monitoring capabilities provides effective validation tests of the performances that are back annotated in the design model. The approach provides a strong association (i.e. traceability) among requirements, contracts, architectural components and performance values measured at runtime.

The evaluation of the benefits obtained by MegaM@Rt2 focus mainly on design efforts (both in terms of resources costs and development time) and the quality of the final results. The exploitation of the runtime artefacts backtraced to the design models and to original requirements, greatly simplifies the maintenance activities and provides a mechanism to continuously improve design, increasing the level of the obtained benefits.

The use of open source tools foster the experimentation at industrial level of innovative and advanced technologies, highlighting both the positive economic impacts, as mentioned above and the problems related to the complexity of real systems, such as scalability, stability, and ease to use of the open source research solutions. This allowed technology providers to raise the tools proposed in the MegaM@Rt2 framework to an industrial scale.

5   Conclusions

Development of complex CPSs is a challenging activity requiring a combination of many tools. Open source tools for model-based system engineering have gained certain popularity. However, there is still a challenge to combine them into a practical tool chain that would address specific application domain needs. The tool chain should ensure interplay of diverse tools, as well as a transversal traceability for model artifacts. This is especially challenging in the modern context when the runtime analysis of target systems should be analysed with the help of system engineering models for verification and validation. The MegaM@Rt2 project focuses on providing tool sets that deal with model-based system engineering, runtime analysis, and traceability management. MegaM@Rt2 consortium is an active contributor to open source and has extensively applied open source tools within 8 diverse industrial case studies. In this paper, we have presented the overall concept of MegaM@Rt2, we have given indications on open source tools provided for various engineering areas and on the approaches for distribution of a large bundle of open source tools, and, finally, we have illustrated the benefits of our approach with a practical industrial case study example. We believe that this paper is valuable for the community of the CPS developers looking for an operational open source tool set for their purposes.

References

1. Afzal, W., et al.: The MegaM@Rt2 ECSEL project: MegaModelling at runtime - scalable model-based framework for continuous development and runtime validation of complex systems. Microprocessors and Microsystems **61**, 86–95 (2018)
2. Eclipse CHESS, November 2018. https://www.eclipse.org/chess/index.html. Accessed 10 Jan 2020
3. Itemis, A.G.: YAKINDU statechart tools – state machines made easy. https://www.itemis.com/en/yakindu/state-machine/. Accessed 12 Jan 2020
4. MegaM@Rt2 docker images. https://github.com/megamart2/integration/tree/master/docker. Accessed 10 Jan 2020
5. MegaM@Rt2 eclipse update site. https://github.com/megamart2/integration/raw/master/eu.megamart2.platform.site. Accessed 10 Jan 2020
6. MegaM@Rt2 IDE in the eclipse marketplace. https://marketplace.eclipse.org/content/megamart2-ide. Accessed 10 Jan 2020
7. MegaM@Rt2 project website. https://megamart2-ecsel.eu/. Accessed 10 Jan 2020
8. MegaM@Rt2 public deliverables. https://megamart2-ecsel.eu/deliverables/. Accessed 10 Jan 2020
9. MegaM@Rt2 tool box repository. https://toolbox.megamart2-ecsel.eu/. Accessed 10 Jan 2020
10. Modelio open source - UML and BPMN free modeling tool. https://www.modelio.org/. Accessed 6 Jan 2020
11. OCRA, othello contracts refinement analysis. https://es-static.fbk.eu/tools/ocra/
12. Sadovykh, A., et al.: MegaM@Rt^2 project: mega-modelling at runtime - intermediate results and research challenges. In: Mazzara, M., Bruel, J.-M., Meyer, B., Petrenko, A. (eds.) TOOLS 2019. LNCS, vol. 11771, pp. 393–405. Springer, Cham (2019). https://doi.org/10.1007/978-3-030-29852-4_33

.NET Runtime and Tools for Tizen Operating System

Alexander Soldatov(✉), Gleb Balykov(✉), Anton Zhukov(✉),
Elena Shapovalova(✉), and Evgeny Pavlov(✉)

Samsung Research Russia, Moscow, Russia
{soldatov.a,g.balykov,a.zhukov,elena.sh,e.pavlov}@samsung.com
https://research.samsung.com/srr

Abstract. Samsung Electronics and Microsoft Corporation have been developing open source implementation of .NET platform called .NET Core since 2016. This platform is usually used for implementation of server-side and desktop applications, and Samsung has also adopted .NET Core virtual machine and libraries for Tizen OS. This solution was integrated into various ARM CPU based devices e.g. smart watches, TVs and other electronic devices. Tizen has always supported variety of languages and SDKs for developers. .NET has greatly expanded this variety by supporting new tools and new languages. This paper describes major challenges that we have encountered during integration of .NET to Tizen OS as well as optimizations, which were applied to .NET Core to make applications startup and memory consumption better on variety of devices.

Keywords: Managed programming language · Compiler · Language runtime · .NET

1 Introduction

Throughout the long history of Tizen [5], variety of different technologies and languages were available to application developers. Initially developers were provided with native SDK with C/C++ support. This solution has demonstrated good performance and memory consumption of applications, but currently C/C++ languages are not very popular anymore because of difficulty of development. They require long development cycle and provide poor memory safety.

Web applications propose another approach to applications development on Tizen. While JavaScript and HTML5 gained popularity, this approach became very attractive. It allows to create applications very easily and fast. However, this approach is not effective in terms of hardware resources usage, specifically, startup time and memory consumption. Native applications are much better optimized and customized in comparison with web-applications. These metrics

© IFIP International Federation for Information Processing 2020
Published by Springer Nature Switzerland AG 2020
V. Ivanov et al. (Eds.): OSS 2020, IFIP AICT 582, pp. 190–195, 2020.
https://doi.org/10.1007/978-3-030-47240-5_19

are essential for consumer electronics, thus web-applications can not be chosen as the most satisfying development solution.

.NET Core [6] and C# language mitigate problems of the two approaches described above. They provide reach set of features and frameworks for application developers and demonstrate good performance and memory consumption. Table 1 shows comparison for different languages and technologies on the Samsung Galaxy Gear Watch 2 with Tizen 5.0 and Stopwatch application.

Table 1. Comparison of Tizen developer technologies

Technology/Function	Native	Web applications	.NET Core
Memory usage	8.6 MB	65.4 MB	27.3 MB
Application startup time	0.4 s	1.2 s	1.0 s
Memory safety	No	Yes	Yes

Moving an ecosystem to a new operating system and CPU requires a large amount of work and optimization of existing code base. For example, the following parts of virtual machine should be updated or created from scratch: JIT compiler, low level code of virtual machine, which deals with operating system, parts of frameworks interacting with hardware. Furthermore, development tools like debuggers and profilers should also be created for non-supported operating system. All this work has been done for Tizen and ARM CPU, as well as Tizen specific performance optimizations, which allowed to deploy .NET Core on devices with small amount of memory and low- and mid-level CPUs. The details of those optimizations will be described below.

The goal of this paper is to describe Tizen .NET implementation specifics, both of virtual machine and developer tools. Section 2 describes high-level Tizen .NET architecture, with details of .NET Core virtual machine architecture. Section 2.1 includes high-level overview of .NET Core and Tizen optimization details. Section 2.2 describes Tizen-specific development tools.

2   Architecture

Figure 1 shows high level architecture of Tizen .NET platform. All three types of application development technologies used with Tizen rely on native subsystems, giving applications access to different parts of the device. CoreCLR virtual machine [1] and CoreFX basic libraries [2] are the foundation of the .NET ecosystem in Tizen. They interact with operating system directly and allow to execute user's code. TizenFX and Xamarin.Forms are situated on the next level. These are the frameworks which provide additional functionality for developers and allow them to create user interfaces and utilize platform specific functionality from C# code.

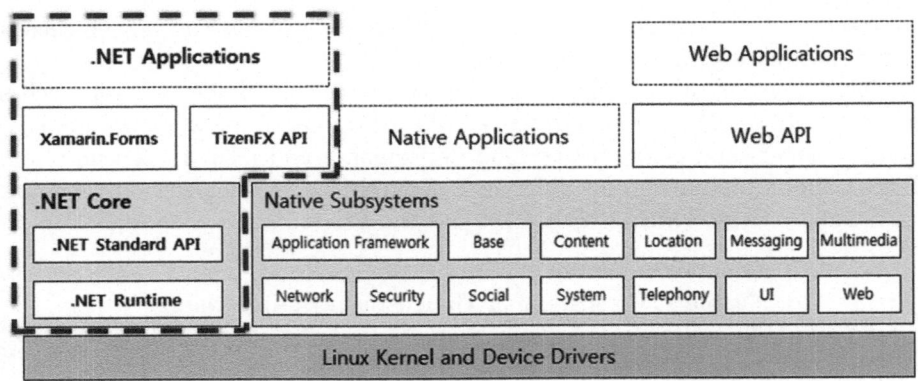

Fig. 1. Tizen .NET architecture

Tizen uses special launchers for different types of applications. .NET specific launcher is called `dotnet-launcher`. It performs initialization of CoreCLR and some additional activities (that will be described below) inside a `candidate process` before the application to be launched is determined. When request to launch application comes, the `candidate process` with prepared runtime already exists.

2.1 .NET Runtime

Main part of work related to enabling of .NET Core on Tizen was performed in runtime, specifically, in JIT compiler. JIT translates stack-based Microsoft Intermediate Language (MSIL) bytecode to the target CPU machine code and applies various optimizations. RyuJIT was chosen as a compiler, but it didn't support ARM. As this support is required for Tizen, it had to be implemented from scratch.

During this work all of the stages of compilation, that precede Code Generation, had to be updated to support ARM. Then some performance and memory consumption optimizations were applied. .NET Core versions differ in performance and memory consumption, thus optimizations applied were not universal.

Removal of Relocations. This optimization reduces memory consumption. It turns out that some applications use the same libraries while being launched. So CoreCLR loads system libraries (DLLs) using `mmap` system call. Then those libraries may be shared between the applications. These DLLs are read-only, but they can be compiled to native images. Native images contain relocations, i.e. data or code, which rely on the actual starting memory address of mmapped file. This data or code should be updated at DLL load time, creating process specific copies of memory pages. The idea of optimization is to reduce number of such relocations making memory pages position independent and read only and, thus, shared between processes. This has been performed for various parts of native images and reduced CoreCLR Private memory consumption of each process by 45% (3 Mb) in average.

Direct Mapping of Assemblies. Previously, plain DLLs with section alignment smaller than a size of a virtual page had to be copied to anonymous memory. This means that each process will contain its own copy of DLL in physical memory. After optimization DLLs without writable sections (this is the case on Tizen) are directly mmaped to the memory. This is the optimization, which made managed DLLs shareable between processes in the first place. After this optimization CoreCLR Private memory consumption of each process was reduced by 9% (645 Kb) in average.

Simplification of Allocators. CoreCLR has many different allocators in different parts, and each allocator serves its purpose. One of the optimized allocators has been simplified to plain `malloc/free` allocator instead of the allocator with default prealloced memory, and this had no effect on performance. The other one (arena allocator) is used by JIT during compilation and never frees its memory by default. This behavior was changed to basically the same `malloc/free` and also had no negative effect on performance. Optimization of the former reduced CoreCLR Private memory of the application process by 11.5% (776 Kb) in average, optimization of the latter reduced Private memory of the whole application process by 8% (1.2 Mb) in average.

Compact Entry Points. CoreCLR uses small thunks of code to perform call indirection, for example, to trigger compilation of method when it is called for the first time. This way a unique entry point is assigned to each method. There are different types of these thunks, e.g. `FixupPrecode`, `StubPrecode` or `Compact` entry points. Compact entry points are designed to occupy as little memory as possible by combining some of the auxiliary data of few methods (see Listing 1). Each compact entry point on ARM occupies 4 bytes and `CentralJump` is 14 bytes. In comparison, each `FixupPrecode` occupies 12 bytes and its equivalent to `CentraJump` is 4 bytes.

Listing 1. Compact entry points

```
entry1:
  mov r12, pc
  b CentralJump
...
entryN:
  mov r12, pc
  b CentralJump
CentraJump:
  ldr pc, pThePreStubCompactARM
  nop
  dw pChunk
  dw pThePreStubCompactARM
```

Previously, `Compact` entry points were not implemented for ARM, and their implementation reduced CoreCLR Private memory of the process by 2.2% (80 kb) in average. Besides, some micro benchmarks showed 15% improvement of performance.

CoreCLR Initialization in Candidate Process. Previously CoreCLR was initialized after the application launch request is sent to `dotnet-launcher` (launcher of C# applications). It consumed startup time observed by users. To improve this point, CoreCLR initialization is now performed before application launch request is received (see Fig. 2). Runtime becomes prepared to launch actual application, mitigating runtime initialization time.

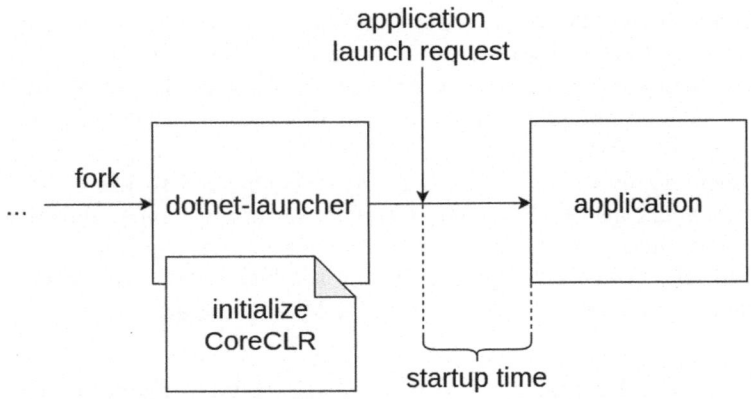

Fig. 2. CoreCLR initialization in candidate process

Class Preloading. Since runtime is now initialized prior to the application launch request and there is some time before this request will actually come in, we can do some additional initialization. The idea of this optimization was to load some common DLLs and C# classes from libraries to memory even before the application launch request. When the class loading for application is performed, some of the classes will already be loaded to memory, thus startup time will be smaller. This optimization reduced startup time of applications by 3.7% in average.

Hydra Launcher. We can go even further with the work we do prior to application launch request. In case the Linux process mmaps native images to memory, then applies relocations and then performs fork, all these dirty memory pages move to the Shared part of memory of all child processes, i.e. only one copy of these memory pages will exist in physical memory, thus reducing memory consumption. By applying the same technique and creating additional parent process called Hydra, which mmaps native images of system DLLs to memory and applies relocations to them, we were able to reduce memory consumption of the whole application process by 14% in average.

2.2 .NET Tools

This section provides a brief review on .NET tools provided by Samsung. Visual Studio Plugin for Tizen [3] is one of major tools for Tizen developers. This plugin includes two components: NetcoreDBG [4] (debugger) and Performance profiler [7]. Both these components were developed from scratch as open source projects.

Samsung NetcoreDBG Debugger. This debugger was developed as an alternative managed debugger for .NET applications. Microsoft provides *proprietary debugger* (VSDBG) for this purpose, but it sets several limitations: it is compatible with VSCode IDE or Microsoft Visual Studio only; it does not support ARM architecture. NetcoreDBG overcomes these limitations: it may be used in several OS-es (MS Windows, Linux, Tizen, Mac OS) and it supports various architectures (x86, ARM, x64).

Samsung C# Profilers. The two major profiling opportunities are performance and memory profiling. The data gathered by profilers is processed and presented in a graphical interface of VS plugin.

The performance profiling mode shows real-time memory usage as well as CPU load. Also it allows to track JIT and GC events depending on the profiling options.

Memory profiler shows amount of dynamically allocated memory by user code and by runtime itself. The allocated memory is classified as Heap Allocated, Heap reserved, unmanaged memory and Span (memory allocated by data type during application lifespan).

3 Conclusion

This paper describes major challenges that we have encountered during integration of .NET on Tizen operating system as well as optimizations, applied to .NET Core to make applications startup and memory consumption better. The next plans are related to the support of new versions of .NET Core and implementation of new ARM-specific optimizations for the newest Tizen releases.

References

1. CoreCLR github. https://github.com/dotnet/coreclr
2. CoreFX github. https://github.com/dotnet/corefx
3. Samsung Visual Studio Tools for Tizen. https://github.com/Samsung/vs-tools-cps
4. Samsung NetcoreDBG last releases. https://github.com/Samsung/netcoredbg/releases
5. Samsung Tizen official. https://www.tizen.org/
6. Microsoft .NET official. https://dotnet.microsoft.com/
7. Samsung .NET Performance Profiler manual. https://github.com/Samsung/vs-tools-cps/blob/master/docs/tools/profiler-user-manual.md

Energy Efficient Software Development Process Evaluation for MacOS Devices

Shokhista Ergasheva[(✉)], Dragos Strugar, Artem Kruglov, and Giancarlo Succi

Innopolis University, Innopolis, Russia
s.ergasheva@innopolis.ru

Abstract. InnoMetrics is the system that aims at collecting software development process metrics in a non-invasive way to access and optimize the development process and its efficiency. This paper demonstrates the development and analysis of energy consumption of MacOS systems based on the software process measurement data. It represents the experience of the development of MacOS system collector and Transfer, in addition to the user interface and early analysis of energy consumption metrics calculations.

Keywords: Energy efficient software · MacOS software development · Software development process metrics

1 Introduction

The importance of energy efficiency of any system and devices becomes sufficient property of the present Information Technology life. Thus, measuring and what is more further analysis of energy efficiency and its prediction can be managed by monitoring the software development process. Before going deep into the software development process metrics let's define what is the measurement itself. The history of measurement can be divided into two generations. The first generation is the Personal Software Process (PSP) - self improvement process that helps developers to control, manage and improve the way they work. This method can be called as invasive as it requires the direct involvement of participants in the data collection process. Users of the-invasive method should create and print forms in which they log their effort, size and defect information. One obvious downside of this invasive approach is the high overhead cost it entails. The developers should often switch between development tasks and metrics collection tasks, which imposes a high cognitive burden to the developers while the second generation of measurements, non-invasive measurements, do not require manual intervention of the participants during metrics collection [4]. The main aim of the successful use of a non-invasive measurement system is to support the

This research project is carried out under the support of the Russian Science Foundation Grant № 19-19-00623.

developers, the development process optimization and maintain the data privacy. Innometrics is one of the promising software development process data collection systems with automatic data collection and transfers to the server for further data analysis. It allows the developers and managers to be aware of the process strength and weaknesses based on the data from the developers performed. The crucial insights are visualized concerning the metrics and analysis. The benefits of such system can be counted as real-time process analysis on a daily basis, the system can be accustomed to different levels of company sizes and audits of the software development process and development itself can be monitored at the same time.

2   Metrics

The first thing in the way to data collection framework was to perform a Systematic Literature Review (SLR) of existing research papers, energy-related metrics and best practices to collect data during the software development process. The Systematic Literature Review surveyed more than 500 studies in the field of software metrics collection and analysis. As a result, at about 170 metrics were derived, and divided into 3 categories as code, product and process metrics. Based on the findings from SLR, we concluded that the mostly unexplored branch of software development metrics is process metrics [8]. Besides, all the tools observed during the research project consider static analysis of the code, nevertheless, the process of developing the software still has no much analysis. The main reason for this insufficient analysis of process measurements is the absence of the tool. Furthermore, the process cost increases, since usually, it requires the developers' participation.

The system of InnoMetrics is developed based on the monitoring of the software development process energy consumption and its efficiency, the developer's productivity. All direct and model-based measurements that involve usage of third-party hardware tools to get energy metrics from various components were considered out of scope of non-invasive software development process analysis approach. The energy consumption of software applications was thoroughly researched and concluded based on the research findings. Battery draining applications result in lower user experience and dissatisfied users [18]. Optimal battery usage (energy usage) is an important aspect that every client must consider.

Application energy consumption is dependent on a wide variety of system resources and conditions. Energy consumption depends on, but is not limited to, the processor, the device uses, memory architecture, the storage technologies used, the display technology used, the size of the display, the network interface that you are connected to, active sensors, and various conditions like the signal strength used for data transfer, user settings like screen brightness levels, and many more user and system settings [18].

For precise energy consumption measurements, one needs specialized hardware [21]. While they provide the best method to accurately measure energy consumption on a particular device, such a methodology is not scalable in practice, especially if such measurements have to be made on multiple devices.

Even then, the measurements by themselves will not provide much insight into how the application contributes to the battery drainage, making it hard to focus on any application optimization efforts.

The InnoMetrics system aims at enabling users to estimate their application's energy consumption without the need for specialized hardware. Such estimation is made possible using a software power model that has been trained on a reference device representative of the low powered devices applications might run on [15,17,19,20,22]. Based on the findings of the research, metrics like following were investigated [10]:

- Software Energy Consumption (SEC) - the total energy consumed by the software;
- Unit Energy Consumption (UEC) - the energy consumed by a specific unit of the software;

Considering our profiling method and the tools available for us, the ability to attribute the energy consumption was possible only at the process level in coarse granularity. However, the hardware resource usage can fill the gap when it comes to accurately relating Energy Consumption (EC) to individual software elements hence enabling the computation of the UEC.

Profiling the performance requires a basic understanding of hardware components that has to be monitored through "performance counters", which is possible in Windows System. While interpreting performance data for further analysis, the context information has to be taken into account (e.g. hardware-specific details).

To evaluate the Unit Energy Consumption (UEC) the following hardware resources should be monitored:

- Hard disk: disk bytes/sec, disk read bytes/sec, disk write bytes/sec;
- Processor: percentage of processor usage;
- Memory: private bytes, working set, private working set;
- Network: bytes total/sec, bytes sent/sec, bytes received/sec;
- IO: IO data (bytes/sec), IO read (bytes/sec), IO write (bytes/sec).

Attributing some weights to elements of the UEC or by some reliable assumption such as considering the power model to be linear in the nature for each individual component, the SEC Metric is computed.

Besides, the energy usage can also be appraised using Performance Counter, Performance Counter Category and related classes that are available with .NET Framework. To be specific, by analyzing the MSDN documentation to attain the goal of collecting energy related metrics, it was concluded that the information about CPU time, Total Processor Time per process, CPU usage, Memory usage, network usage that Performance Counter provides can be reliable.

The bottleneck in this situation is that it is difficult to match up constantly changing application process IDs and names. The energy consumption of the system depends on a variety of factors that are not limited to those which can be collected using the above mentioned performance classes.

2.1 MacOS Energy Metrics

In order to obtain energy-related data in MacOS devices, we explored some of the APIs that MacOS provides. The first and most obvious tool was Activity Monitor, an application that comes built-in every MacOS system. One of its aspects is the Energy consumption, shown in Fig. 1.

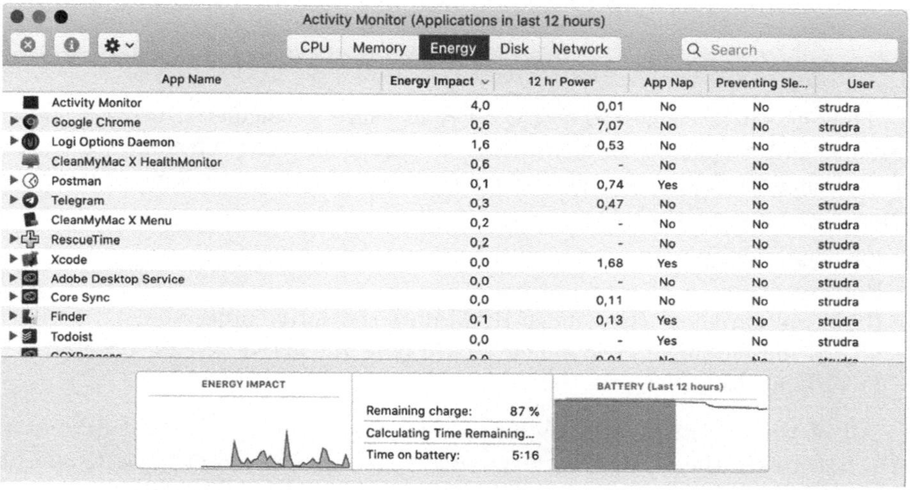

App Name	Energy Impact ∨	12 hr Power	App Nap	Preventing Sle...	User
Activity Monitor	4,0	0,01	No	No	strudra
Google Chrome	0,6	7,07	No	No	strudra
Logi Options Daemon	1,6	0,53	No	No	strudra
CleanMyMac X HealthMonitor	0,6	-	No	No	strudra
Postman	0,1	0,74	Yes	No	strudra
Telegram	0,3	0,47	No	No	strudra
CleanMyMac X Menu	0,2	-	No	No	strudra
RescueTime	0,2	-	No	No	strudra
Xcode	0,0	1,68	Yes	No	strudra
Adobe Desktop Service	0,0	-	No	No	strudra
Core Sync	0,0	0,11	No	No	strudra
Finder	0,1	0,13	Yes	No	strudra
Todoist	0,0	-	Yes	No	strudra
CCXProcess	0,0	0,01	No	No	strudra

Activity Monitor (Applications in last 12 hours)

CPU Memory Energy Disk Network Q Search

ENERGY IMPACT

BATTERY (Last 12 hours)

Remaining charge: 87 %
Calculating Time Remaining...
Time on battery: 5:16

Fig. 1. MacOS energy metrics

The second column, Energy Impact, attracted our attention immediately. We then wanted to figure out what these values (4.0, 0.6, 1.6, etc) represent. It has been then brought to our attention that the definition of Energy Impact is not precisely defined by Apple. According to Activity Monitor's documentation, the definition of Energy Impact says "Energy Impact: A relative measure of the current energy consumption of the app. Lower numbers are better" [3].

As other documentation says "The Energy tab of Activity Monitor displays the Energy Impact of each open app based on a number of factors including CPU usage, network traffic, disk activity and more. The higher the number, the more impact an app has on battery power" [2]. Both of these are vague, and we needed a concrete way of obtaining this metric's values.

One article on the Mozilla blog attempted to figure out a formula for this. They indicated that the result of MacOS's top command line tool which performs periodic measurements of all kinds of metrics; including ones relevant to energy consumption: CPU usage, wakeups and the power measure. The article we mentioned above suggests running the following command to get the above-mentioned information:

Yielding the results (trimmed):

```
top -stats pid, command, cpu, idlew, power -o power -d
```

Table 1. *Top* results

PID	Command	% CPU	IDLEW	Power
50300	Firefox	12.9	278	26.6
76256	Plugin-container	3.4	159	11.3
151	Coreaudiod	0.9	68	4.3
76505	Top	1.5	1	1.6
76354	Activity Monitor	1.0	0	1.0

They go on to suggest that POWER measure is calculated using a simple formula, and a specific configuration file (tuned for every machine's architecture). Using the findings from that article, we decided to use some of the most impacting metrics (Table 1):

- Battery percentage
- Battery status (is charging or not)
- RAM measurement (how much RAM does the active process use)
- vRAM measurement (how much vRAM does the active process occupy)
- % CPU utilized (per process)

All of these metrics were obtained using the macOS command line interface. E.g. to get the current battery percentage we used pmset -g batt, and for other measurements we used the ps -axm -o command with varying parameters (depending on the use case). It was also possible to use the top command, but as we are performing periodic checks anyway, top was not necessary. Incorporating these metrics and collection process to the InnometricsCollector was successful and results are available on GitHub:

https://github.com/InnopolisUniversity/innometrics-agent-os-mac/.

3   Collector Development

InnoMetrics system contains of the following components [14, 23, 26]:

- Data Collectors - the separate for widespread Operating Systems (Windows, MacOS, Linux) data collecting frameworks;
- Server - which includes analytic module of obtained data referring quantitative and qualitative analysis;
- Dashboard - the component that responsible for visual representation of the analyzed development process data.

The scope of the paper do not consider describing the data collectors for all operating systems, nevertheless MacOS collector will be described thoroughly. MacOS collector includes two separate applications using a service oriented approach [25]:

- InnoMetrics Collector
- InnoMetrics Transfer

InnoMetrics Collector is a daemon process, it runs in the background. The only interaction the user has with the application is that the collector sits in the background and collects data. It displays the user information (Fig. 2):

– User Name;
– System version and specifications;
– IP address;
– Mac address of the device;
– as well as the currently open application.

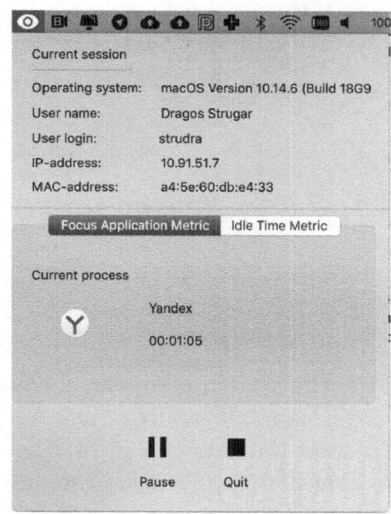

Fig. 2. MacOS Data Collector: Current Process

The Idle Time tab (Fig. 3) shows the total idle time and the top 3 application that have been idle for the longest. In addition, the user can stop the process of collection, as well as they can quit the app.

3.1 Metrics Being Collected

The data being collected on a per-process basis consists the following types:

– Metric type (app focus/idle);
– Application Name;
– Bundle Domain of the app (e.g.com.apple.finder);
– Bundle Path (where the app is installed, e.g. Applications/Yandex)
– Timestamp of the opening of the app/process;
– Timestamp of the quitting of the app/process;
– Duration of the process open (timestamp end-timestamp start);

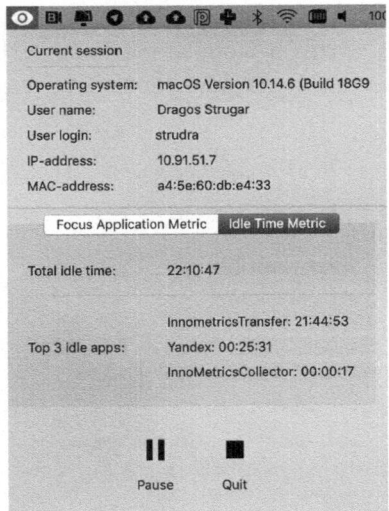

Fig. 3. MacOS Data Collector: Idle Process

- Tab Name (for browser);
- Tab URL (for browser).

After collecting the metrics, the system saves the current session with detailed information (user name, login name, IP address, mac address, etc) only if it has not been changed. Then it saves the data to a local database, allowing the other app (MacOS InnoMetrics Transfer App) to send the data to the server.

Regarding the Innometrics Transfer app, shown in the Fig. 4, it is a separate application. However, it is not a daemon, it is a GUI application which allows users to see all the metrics that have been collected in addition to the functionality of sending such data to the back end.

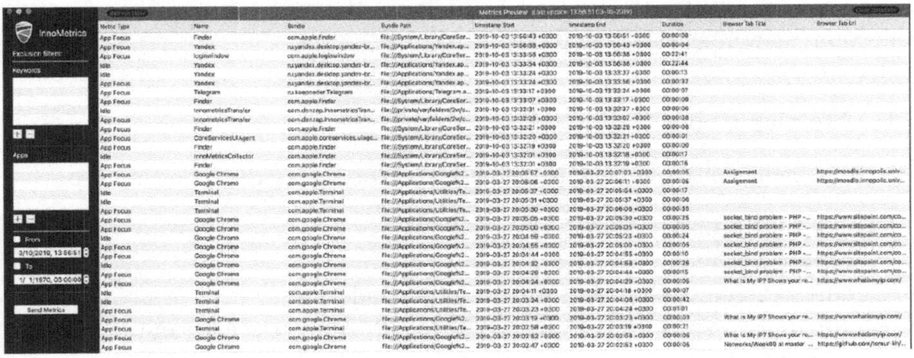

Fig. 4. InnoMetrics Transfer

It consists of two main areas: the left bar and the process metric list on the right. We have the feature to filter the processes based on keywords, applications, by date. Also, the user can select multiple metrics and hit the Backspace key to delete the metrics before sending them to the server (privacy feature). The right panel presents the data obtained from the collector (connects to a local database where collector was sending data). Finally, user can send the metrics to the server. After selecting the metrics user wants to send to the server, and hitting the "Send Metrics" button, user gets presented with a pop up (Fig. 5).

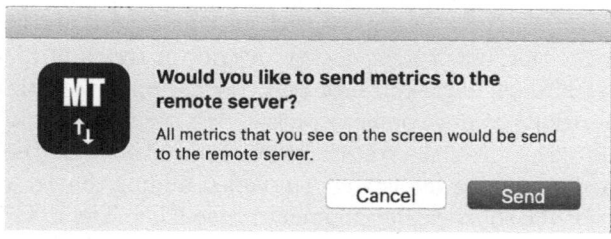

Fig. 5. Popup for sending data to the server

Merging InnoMetrics Collector and InnoMetrics Transfer. As mentioned above, there is a dependency between these two applications. One first needs to collect data using the collector and then transfer the data using transfer. The UX would be better if everything was done in the same application, not requiring users to use both of the apps. That is why it was decided to merge the two applications. As a result of this decision, no longer do the users have to click on the submit button to send the data to the server. The data is automatically and periodically being sent as they are using the computer, without any distractions.

Auto Update Functionality. Desktop applications in general (deployed outside of the Apple App Store) suffer from the inability to update frequently [1]. That is why it was decided to implement the auto update functionality. For this we used the open source framework for auto update of MacOS applications called Sparkle (https://github.com/sparkle-project/Sparkle) [13]. It's a widely known and used framework that allowed to easily update our apps. As the two applications have been merged, there was no need to add the auto update functionality to the Innometrics Transfer. After implementing this functionality, the process of quickly iterating on versions became much quicker and it allows to become more agile when responding to user feedback [5,6,11,16,24]. Let us stress that the use of an open source application appears particularly suited as it enhances the reliability and the adoption of the system, as evidenced in several existing works [7,9,12].

4   Conclusion

To sum up, the system of InnoMetrics was developed for MacOS have been described thoroughly throughout the paper. The energy-related metrics are easily derived from the device with the help of Activity Monitor service in the MacOS. All kinds of metrics were derived and analysed based on the research studies. MacOS framework consists of two basic components: MacOS Collector and Transfer. The details of collecting data and its types, properties and their transfer is integrated in the system. Furthermore, the User Interface developed as a separate system - InnoMetrics Dashboard- for visual representation of the collected data and analysis, was presented. In this report, we have presented: the overall information how to get energy metrics in terms of MacOS systems, a deeper view of how the data collector and transfer operate with the back-end, displayed some results of development phase.

Further improvements of the system will be concentrated on the testing of the system with the functioning industrial companies, adding the external agents for deeper analysis of the software development process like Trello, GitLab, Github, and others. Besides, future work will include exploration of data analysis patterns and best practices for data analysis referring to the data records collected from the Data Collector.

References

1. Mozilla blog: what does the osx energy impact actually measure? https:// blog.mozilla.org/nnethercote/2015/08/26/what-does-the-os-x-activitymonitors-energy-impact-actually-measure/. Accessed 29 Jan 2020
2. About mac notebook batteries (2020). https://support.apple.com/en-au/ HT204054. Accessed 29 Jan 2020
3. How to use activity monitor on your mac (2020). https://support.apple.com/en-au/HT201464. Accessed 21 Feb 2020
4. Bykov, A., et al.: A new architecture and implementation strategy for non-invasive software measurement systems. In: Proceedings of the 33rd Annual ACM Symposium on Applied Computing - SAC 2018. ACM Press (2018). https://doi.org/10.1145/3167132.3167327
5. Coman, I.D., Robillard, P.N., Sillitti, A., Succi, G.: Cooperation, collaboration and pair-programming: field studies on backup behavior. J. Syst. Softw. **91**, 124–134 (2014). https://doi.org/10.1016/j.jss.2013.12.037
6. Corral, L., Sillitti, A., Succi, G.: Software assurance practices for mobile applications. Computing **97**(10), 1001–1022 (2015). https://doi.org/10.1007/s00607-014-0395-8
7. Di Bella, E., Sillitti, A., Succi, G.: A multivariate classification of open source developers. Inf. Sci. **221**, 72–83 (2013)
8. Ergasheva, S., Khomyakov, I., Kruglov, A., Succil, G.: Metrics of energy consumption in software systems: a systematic literature review. IOP Conf. Ser. Earth Environ. Sci. **431**, 012051 (2020). https://doi.org/10.1088/1755-1315/431/1/012051

9. Fitzgerald, B., Kesan, J.P., Russo, B., Shaikh, M., Succi, G.: Adopting Open Source Software: A Practical Guide. The MIT Press, Cambridge (2011)
10. Jagroep, E., Procaccianti, G., van der Werf, J.M., Brinkkemper, S., Blom, L., van Vliet, R.: Energy efficiency on the product roadmap: an empirical study across releases of a software product. J. Softw. Evol. Process **29**(2), e1852 (2017). https://doi.org/10.1002/smr.1852
11. Janes, A., Succi, G.: Lean Software Development in Action. Springer, Heidelberg (2014). https://doi.org/10.1007/978-3-642-00503-9
12. Kovács, G.L., Drozdik, S., Zuliani, P., Succi, G.: Open source software for the public administration. In: Proceedings of the 6th International Workshop on Computer Science and Information Technologies, October 2004
13. Mathur, A.: A human-centered approach to improving the user experience of software updates (2016)
14. Maurer, F., Succi, G., Holz, H., Kötting, B., Goldmann, S., Dellen, B.: Software process support over the internet. In: Proceedings of the 21st International Conference on Software Engineering, ICSE 1999, pp. 642–645. ACM, May 1999. https://doi.org/10.1145/302405.302913. http://doi.acm.org/10.1145/302405.302913
15. Musílek, P., Pedrycz, W., Sun, N., Succi, G.: On the sensitivity of COCOMO II software cost estimation model. In: Proceedings of the 8th International Symposium on Software Metrics, METRICS 2002, pp. 13–20. IEEE Computer Society, June 2002. https://doi.org/10.1109/METRIC.2002.1011321. http://dl.acm.org/citation.cfm?id=823457.824044
16. Pedrycz, W., Russo, B., Succi, G.: A model of job satisfaction for collaborative development processes. J. Syst. Softw. **84**(5), 739–752 (2011). https://doi.org/10.1016/j.jss.2010.12.018
17. Pedrycz, W., Russo, B., Succi, G.: Knowledge transfer in system modeling and its realization through an optimal allocation of information granularity. Appl. Soft Comput. **12**(8), 1985–1995 (2012). https://doi.org/10.1016/j.asoc.2012.02.004
18. Rahmati, A., Qian, A., Zhong, L.: Understanding human-battery interaction on mobile phones. In: Proceedings of the 9th International Conference on Human Computer Interaction with Mobile Devices and Services - MobileHCI 2007. ACM Press (2007). https://doi.org/10.1145/1377999.1378017
19. Ronchetti, M., Succi, G., Pedrycz, W., Russo, B.: Early estimation of software size in object-oriented environments a case study in a CMM level 3 software firm. Inf. Sci. **176**(5), 475–489 (2006). https://doi.org/10.1016/j.ins.2004.08.012
20. Rossi, B., Russo, B., Succi, G.: Modelling failures occurrences of open source software with reliability growth. In: Ågerfalk, P., Boldyreff, C., González-Barahona, J.M., Madey, G.R., Noll, J. (eds.) OSS 2010. IAICT, vol. 319, pp. 268–280. Springer, Heidelberg (2010). https://doi.org/10.1007/978-3-642-13244-5_21
21. Saborido, R., Arnaoudova, V.V., Beltrame, G., Khomh, F., Antoniol, G.: On the impact of sampling frequency on software energy measurements (2015). https://doi.org/10.7287/peerj.preprints.1219v2
22. Scotto, M., Sillitti, A., Succi, G., Vernazza, T.: A relational approach to software metrics. In: Proceedings of the 2004 ACM Symposium on Applied Computing, SAC 2004, pp. 1536–1540. ACM (2004). https://doi.org/10.1145/967900.968207. http://doi.acm.org/10.1145/967900.968207
23. Sillitti, A., Janes, A., Succi, G., Vernazza, T.: Measures for mobile users: an architecture. J. Syst. Archit. **50**(7), 393–405 (2004). https://doi.org/10.1016/j.sysarc.2003.09.005

24. Sillitti, A., Succi, G., Vlasenko, J.: Understanding the impact of pair programming on developers attention: a case study on a large industrial experimentation. In: Proceedings of the 34th International Conference on Software Engineering, ICSE 2012, pp. 1094–1101. IEEE Press, Piscataway, June 2012. https://doi.org/10.1109/ICSE.2012.6227110. http://dl.acm.org/citation.cfm?id=2337223.2337366
25. Sillitti, A., Vernazza, T., Succi, G.: Service oriented programming: a new paradigm of software reuse. In: Gacek, C. (ed.) ICSR 2002. LNCS, vol. 2319, pp. 269–280. Springer, Heidelberg (2002). https://doi.org/10.1007/3-540-46020-9_19
26. Vernazza, T., Granatella, G., Succi, G., Benedicenti, L., Mintchev, M.: Defining metrics for software components. In: Proceedings of the World Multiconference on Systemics, Cybernetics and Informatics, vol. XI, pp. 16–23, July 2000

Author Index